The Zero Carbon Car

Green Technology and the Automotive Industry

The Zero Carbon Car

Green Technology and the Automotive Industry

Brian Long

THE CROWOOD PRESS

First published in 2013 by
The Crowood Press Ltd
Ramsbury, Marlborough
Wiltshire SN8 2HR

www.crowood.com

British Library Cataloguing-in-Publication Data
A catalogue record for this book is available from the British Library.

ISBN 978 1 84797 421 1

Typeset by Jean Cussons Typesetting, Diss, Norfolk

Printed and bound in India by Replika Press Pvt Ltd

CONTENTS

Introduction   6

CHAPTER 1   ZERO CARBON: WHAT EXACTLY DOES IT MEAN?   8

CHAPTER 2   THE DIESEL BOOM   17

CHAPTER 3   PETROL AS A 'CLEAN' OPTION   48

CHAPTER 4   FULL HYBRIDS: THE PETROL-ELECTRIC
             AND DIESEL-ELECTRIC BRIGADE   87

CHAPTER 5   PURE ELECTRIC VEHICLES AND EREVs   113

CHAPTER 6   ALTERNATIVE POWER   146

CHAPTER 7   THE BODY BEAUTIFUL   165

CHAPTER 8   WHAT THE FUTURE HOLDS   187

             Zero Carbon Abbreviations   202

             Index   206

INTRODUCTION

The dreams of men have for centuries posed problems for engineers. Humans had looked skyward for hundreds of years, hoping to soar through the skies like a bird. The dream became a reality first through balloons and gliders, and then, just over a century ago, the world witnessed the beginnings of powered flight. Flying between continents is now something we take for granted, and even space travel is not beyond us.

Closer to the ground, Stephenson's 'Rocket' harnessed the power of steam to become the world's first successful steam train. By the 1920s, steam trains such as 'The Flying Scotsman' were hitting 160km/h (100mph) in Britain, and the elegant streamliners that followed in the next decade would continue to take speeds higher. After the war, the wonders of electricity brought a whole new generation of high-speed trains into being, and now linear motors promise previously unheard-of levels of performance.

As for cars, those early horseless carriages that used to chug along at a snail's pace soon evolved into practical machines that could enter in town-to-town races, with

Ein Auto darf nicht die Welt kosten.

▶ Wer sich in unserem Universum umschaut, merkt schnell, daß es für unsere Erde nirgendwo eine Reparaturwerkstatt oder Ersatzteile gibt. Alles, was wir mit dieser Erde anstellen, müssen wir selbst verantworten, selbst in Ordnung bringen oder selbst ausbaden. Als Erfinder des Autos stehen wir natürlich ganz besonders in der Pflicht. Und wir wissen, daß wir diese Pflicht noch lange nicht erfüllt haben. Auch wenn z. B. unser E 300 DIESEL als erster und einziger die schärfsten Diesel-Abgasnormen der Welt (die von Kalifornien) erfüllt.

▶ Richtiger Umweltschutz wird bei uns bereits da umgesetzt, wo Autos entstehen – z. B. in unserem Werk in Rastatt. Und endet dort, wo sie verschwinden: beim Recycling. Wir wissen, für die Natur kann man nie genug tun. Aber wir arbeiten daran. Schließlich geht es auch um die Existenz des Autos.

Mercedes-Benz
Ihr guter Stern auf allen Straßen.

A fine piece of Mercedes-Benz advertising from 1994, stating that an automobile needn't cost the Earth. A play on words, but the 'Green' message comes through loud and clear. Daimler AG

drivetrain and chassis refinements being introduced on an almost daily basis once motoring had become accepted by the masses. Nowadays, even the average road car is faster than a works rally machine from the early 1970s, and, generally speaking, certainly a whole lot more reliable.

The latest problem facing engineers is not so much about following dreams – creating machines capable of defying the laws of gravity, covering huge distances or possessing stunning levels of performance – but how to develop motor vehicles suitable for everyday use that leave as small a carbon footprint as possible.

Global warming, along with ozone-layer depletion, is something that concerns us all, and not just polar bears. Even if we look the other way now, claiming there's nothing to worry about in the immediate future, there's certainly cause to be worried for the generations to come, including our children. In a number of countries the warning signs are already there, with air pollution creating a very real threat to health and the environment today. Motor vehicles have been singled out as a significant source of the problem, and while cynics such as myself ask why the same level of fuss isn't made over deforestation for logging, or beef production for fast-food chains, the fact is that cars and trucks are simply not 'clean' machines.

Having ignored the risk to the planet's atmosphere – and therefore our own well-being in general – for far too long, we are now rushing to find all manner of ways to clean up the environment. The automobile industry is making a sterling effort to do its part through advanced engineering aimed at reducing emissions and our carbon footprint, all the way from the manufacturing stage to the recycling of a product once it has served its purpose.

In the background, the pace of research on sustainability is being picked up, with alternatives to fossil fuels finally being investigated with an open mind. In fact the second generation bio-fuels could be the answer to a lot of our problems. At the end of the day, engineers can only go so far – they are not capable of miracles, and cleaner, more eco-friendly fuels are therefore an important part of the overall 'Green' picture.

After starting the research for this book, ploughing through a political minefield along the way, even a car-crazy guy like me has to admit that something needs to be done quickly – and it's mildly comforting to record that something is – maybe not as much as could be done, but it's a start.

Putting things in historical perspective – which in itself should bring forth more than a few surprises for the casual observer – this book sets out to outline some of the progress being made in this relatively new field of technology. It also – in order to give balance – sets out to explode some of the myths, to simplify the science into layman's terms to help the reader decide what is and what isn't eco-friendly in the real world, and to break down some of the propaganda in the process.

After all, 'Green' sells in today's marketplace, and with careful wording in the promotional paperwork and snazzy television adverts, some things are made out to be far better for the environment than they are in reality. Car companies, and certain countries as a whole, often push ecology issues for good PR, but mainly for financial reasons and/or political gain, often having little interest in going all the way down the Green or Blue path to tackle problems in a proper fashion. The quandary facing our planet is not new, but it will also be found that some of the solutions have been available to us for decades.

Brian Long
Chiba City, Japan

CHAPTER ONE

ZERO CARBON: WHAT EXACTLY DOES IT MEAN?

Nowadays we hear or see the phrase 'zero carbon' on an almost daily basis, used by government departments and manufacturers in fields as diverse as house building through to the motor industry. But what does it actually mean, both in the literal sense and, just as importantly, in the real world?

Every day we are subjected to 'Greenwashing' – people jumping on the eco bandwagon to further their image or cause. But saving the planet is important. It's also our moral duty, as it's the only place mankind has to live.
NASA-JPL

Basically, zero carbon (sometimes referred to as 'carbon neutrality') describes a nett emissions goal, aimed at significantly reducing, and ultimately eliminating, the release of greenhouse gases (often shortened to the initials 'GHG') that cause damage to the planet's delicate ozone layer. Some of these gases build up and trap the radiation that should bounce off the Earth's surface into space (the greenhouse effect, leading to global warming), while others deplete the ozone layer, leaving us exposed to harmful UVB rays from the sun.

Carbon dioxide (CO_2) is recognized as the main culprit in upsetting the balance of the ozone layer, but worldwide controls are being called for on the discharge of other radiative greenhouse gases, such as methane (CH_4), nitrous oxide (N_2O), chlorofluorocarbons (CFCs), hydrochlorofluorocarbons (HCFCs), hydrofluorocarbons (HFCs), sulphur hexafluoride (SF_6), and perfluorocarbons (PFCs).

After water vapour in the atmosphere, over which we have little control, carbon dioxide is classed as the largest contributor to the greenhouse effect. For clarity, all greenhouse gases are given a 'CO_2 equivalent' (CDE) rating, to bring their damage levels into perspective. Methane is less of a threat by volume, but its global warming potential (GWP) is said to be seventy-two times higher than carbon dioxide over a twenty-year timescale, while nitrous oxide is some 289 times higher. Certain chemicals outlined in the Kyoto Protocol are several thousand times more likely to have a long-term radiative effect, which would ultimately accelerate global warming.

Burning fossil fuels is recognized as being responsible for creating around 21 billion tonnes of carbon dioxide each year, not to mention being a chief cause behind other forms of air pollution. It is the speed with which we are upsetting the balance of nature that frightens scientists, with the eco-system unable to absorb the levels of emissions we are producing.

In the background, the sustainability question also has to

A drawing showing how an increase in GHGs can expedite global warming. NASA-GSFC

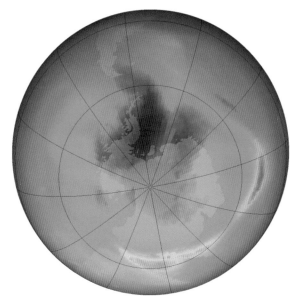

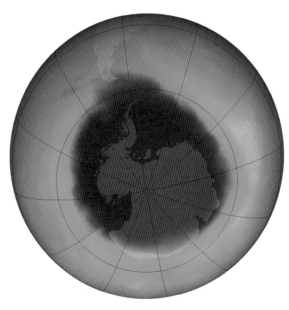

Satellite image of the hole in the ozone layer over the Antarctic. This series of shots was taken in 1979, 1989 and 2006, with dark blue and purple showing the worst affected areas. NASA-GSFC

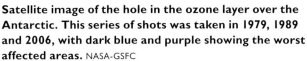

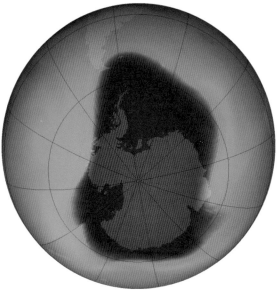

be raised. Even though it is a rather different problem to global warming, our current energy policies mean the two are related. As James Zachos of the University of California recently said: 'With fossil fuels today, we're taking what took millions of years to accumulate and releasing it in a geological instant.'

One should also bear in mind that CFCs and HCFCs, commonly found in refrigerants, aerosols and solvents, have the ability to destroy the ozone layer, as do other gases which are either man-made or occur naturally as part of the mechanism of the eco-system. We talk about the delicacy of the ozone layer, but it's hard to imagine just how flimsy it is. To give the reader some idea of the scale, if it were compressed down to air pressure at 0°C, it is only 3mm (0.12in) thick, yet it absorbs around 98 per cent of the sun's UVB rays, protecting the planet and its inhabitants. Since the 1970s, ozone-layer depletion has been recorded at a rate of about 4 per cent every decade. Due to the unusually cold weather, ozone loss over the Arctic was so severe in 2011 that scientists reported an 'ozone hole' like the one that already exists in the Antarctic.

GLOBAL WARMING

In historical terms, global warming has become a top news item only recently. The greenhouse effect has been recognized for well over a century, but it wasn't until 1974 that ozone depletion was first recognized by scientists. Even then, no one really took any notice, and as a result, the layman had never really considered it to be an issue. Now, of course, in this age of electronic communication, one is bombarded with 'facts' citing gloom and doom, and counter-facts that tell us not to worry.

Certain governments have deliberately employed scientists to challenge established data, saying industry and current lifestyle practices are not the cause of global warming. This is simply a case of politicians pandering to lobbyists who are only interested in protecting their livelihood and short-term profit margins.

Yes, the world may be warming up naturally due to sun-spot activity, and it's easy to point out that Earth has been through phases before, which have taken us through from a world in the tropics to the Ice Age – but to ignore the damage being done by the planet's inhabitants is foolish in

A hole-punch cloud, or a fall-streak hole, photographed by the author in the summer of 2011. This form of cloud seeding is thought to relate to jet aircraft activity, but, being a totally new phenomenon, the exact science behind it, and its impact on local climate, is as yet unknown. B. Long

The British government appointed a 'Royal Commission on Noxious Vapours' in 1876. The smog over Britain today (this picture was taken in April 2011, when the brownish haze hovering over the capital triggered an air quality alert) cannot be blamed on the Industrial Revolution. MODIS Rapid Response Team at NASA-GSFC

the extreme. For instance, the smog that shrouds London, Madrid, Milan and Athens from time to time, as well as Mexico City and highly populated parts of California and Japan, now covers huge chunks of China on a daily basis, and is entirely of our own doing.

We may or may not be able to stop the polar ice caps melting little by little – an unlikely situation in the Antarctic, as it happens, and not really a big problem in the Arctic beyond wildlife concerns, as this is floating ice – though we definitely need to avoid the ice sheets of Greenland melting away, otherwise sea levels could rise by as much as seven metres! However, we can certainly reduce ozone-layer damage, and we can certainly make an effort to keep the air we breathe as clean as possible.

We have the tools to address the problem, but it seems that politicians often feel they have to look after those who funded their rise to power before they think of their children's future. They often appear to be too selective, creating taxes that hurt the 'little man' in a bid to look 'Green' on the surface, whilst happily turning a blind eye towards the real villains in the equation, coming up with wondrous schemes such as 'carbon offsetting', which allows polluting countries to continue gushing out emissions to the same degree as before. It may ease the minds of certain people in government or within a big corporation to know that a tree is being planted somewhere, to show that they have 'done their bit' in saving the environment, but the bottom line is that without further thought regarding the use of commodities and construction materials, waste control and recycling, nothing has changed to any great extent.

Meanwhile the motorist has been an easy target for taxation for decades. People resist less when they are told that the money they are handing over is for the benefit of the planet – but the reality is that cars are only a small part of the problem. Factors such as deforestation, coal-powered electricity generation, cement factories and air travel do far more harm. Even meat production for fast-food chains has a massive impact, accounting for around 20 per cent of the world's CO_2 equivalent emissions – it has been said that to get enough meat for one hamburger produces about the same amount of greenhouse gases as an average car driven for ten miles!

That's not to say finger-pointing is the answer, with certain industries being given an easier ride because they pollute less than others. That is simply sidestepping the issue, something which has been done for far too long already. Something constructive – taking in the big picture – needs to be done on all fronts, from stricter emission controls for all nations (regardless of their 'developed' or 'developing' status) to improving roads and public transport systems.

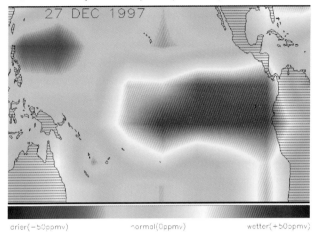

1997 El Nino Development: Humidity Anomaly Measured by UARS-MLS at 10-12 Km

Strange weather patterns are becoming the norm. There are those who are happy to pass this off as a separate issue to global warming, but records show that El Niño and La Niña have been occurring more frequently and with greater intensity since the 1970s.
NASA-JPL

SELLING GREEN

In this day and age there's no doubt that turning attention towards 'Green' issues can be a great selling point, bringing popularity to companies and individuals alike, even if the words they put forward are empty. We only need to reflect on Al Gore's comeback from the political wilderness after taking up the subject of climate change to see how easily public opinion can be swayed.

It wasn't always this way, however, with presentation being as much a part of the problem as the lack of scientific data to back claims up. In reality, the early British 'Green' movement probably did more harm than good, shouting its cause from beaten-up Morris Minors that obviously hadn't been maintained since the day they rolled off the line at Cowley. People more often than not dismissed them as a bunch of scruffy eccentrics – although they did have a point, in that it takes a huge amount of energy to create a new car from scratch (releasing as much as 15 tonnes of CO_2 along the way, according to some estimations), so it's therefore greener to run a vehicle that already exists, assuming that it's still in good all-round condition.

Had the Green brigade said the same thing from a gleaming, in-tune Minor whilst wearing sharp suits, maybe more folks would have listened, and forced British makers to buck up their ideas. Introducing new technology to answer the critics at that time, developing new cars that were attractive, fuel-efficient, eco-friendly and reliable, instead of plodding along with warmed-over running gear from the 1950s, might just have saved the bulk of the UK industry. Who knows?

On saying that, projects with the noble aim of reducing our carbon footprint had of course been tried before, with the Porsche-developed FLA 'Long Life Car' being a perfect example. It featured mechanical components designed to last a minimum of ten years, and corrosion-free body panels made of stainless steel and aluminium (easier to recycle than plastics at the time). Ironically there was so much opposition from within the car industry that the designs were shelved almost four decades ago.

AN IMPOSSIBLE DREAM?

So is the idea of a zero-carbon car an impossible dream? For the time being, at least, it's not easy to achieve, mainly because of our not particularly eco-friendly sources of electrical power, employed not only to create an automobile from scratch (from the manufacture of raw materials to the end of the production line), but to keep what should officially be the cleanest of all cars – the electric vehicle (EV) – charged up and ready to roll.

Solar power gives a close-to-ideal scenario from a 'Green' point of view, assuming the necessary equipment can stay in service for a fairly long period of time (say, twenty-five to thirty years), and panel production techniques are properly monitored, but there are still very few houses equipped with solar panels. Wind energy just isn't practical, so we end up coming back to traditional methods of generating power, which are far from eco-friendly, as is evident from the data table.

CO$_2$ Emissions by Energy Source

Generation	CO$_2$ levels
Coal-fired plant	914g/kWh
Oil-fired plant	653g/kWh
Natural gas-fired plant	410g/kWh
Solar power	47g/kWh
Wave energy	37g/kWh
Nuclear plant	16g/kWh
Wind power	15g/kWh
Hydro-electric plant	11g/kWh

Half of America's electricity comes from coal-fired plants, which may be 80 per cent cleaner than they were in 1970,

Coal-fired electricity plants can bring a question mark over the 'Green' credentials of EVs.
Wknight94/Creative Commons

but the release of CO$_2$ into the atmosphere is still very high, while a third of the UK's electricity is made that way. The zero emissions performance of an EV is therefore wiped out during the battery-charging process, unless the grid is hooked up to a hydro-electric plant (all too rare, often damaging to a local eco-system, and sometimes set up in such a way as to waste as much electricity as it produces!) or a nuclear facility.

Nuclear power is a relatively clean and widespread source of energy in certain countries (possibly even cleaner than wind energy with all things taken into account, and certainly thousands of times more practical), but the recent disaster in Japan has raised many questions, and a wave of public mistrust has swept across Europe, putting plans for further nuclear power stations on hold; it has also provided the US government with an ideal excuse not to invest in its infrastructure while funds are tight, meaning the burning of fossil fuels will continue for many years yet. With coal plentiful and half a million US jobs depending on it, the chance of changing to a cleaner energy is very slim at best.

More chilling, perhaps, is the fact that around 80 per cent of China's electricity is produced using coal-fired plants; moreover, China has no intention of changing its energy policy any time soon (it will probably stay much the same until at least 2020), as coal is still cheap and plentiful in this vast country. It's not so much the recharging of electric vehicles that bothers us here, but the sheer number of components made in China, aptly nicknamed 'the world's factory'. Add this into the equation, along with further damage caused

Engineers may be striving to design more eco-friendly cars and components, but accountants can undo their work in minutes by having parts made thousands of miles from assembly sites – cargo ships are a huge source of pollution, more often than not using low-grade bunker fuel, which has 2,000 times the sulphur content of road transport diesel. The largest ships burn 350 tonnes of fuel a day, creating 300,000 tonnes of CO_2 over a year, and SOx emissions that add up to the equivalent of 50 million cars.

FEMA Photo Library/Robert Kaufmann

The Spread of Energy Generation in Selected Countries

Country	Main energy types
USA	Coal (49%), natural gas (21%), nuclear (19%), others (11%)
China	Coal (79%), hydro-electric (17%), nuclear (2%), others (2%)
Japan	Coal (27%), natural gas (26%), nuclear (24%), others (23%)
France	Nuclear (76%), hydro-electric (12%), coal (5%), others (7%)
Germany	Coal (46%), nuclear (23%), natural gas (14%), others (17%)
UK	Natural gas (45%), coal (33%), nuclear (13%), others (9%)
Russia	Natural gas (47%), coal (19%), hydro-electric (16%), others (18%)
Australia	Coal (77%), natural gas (15%), hydro-electric (5%), others (3%)

KEY
- Coal
- Natural Gas
- Nuclear
- Hydro-electric
- Others

Country	Main energy types
USA	GHG emissions up 7.2% since 1990
China	GHG emissions up 236% since 1990
Japan	GHG emissions down 4.5% since 1990
France	GHG emissions down 8.0% since 1990
Germany	GHG emissions down 26% since 1990
UK	GHG emissions down 27% since 1990
Russia	GHG emissions down 37% since 1990
Australia	GHG emissions up 30% since 1990

0   10   20   30   40   50   60   70   80   90   100

to the environment by long-distance shipping, and unless outsourcing policies within the automotive industry change dramatically, a true zero-carbon car may forever be out of the question.

We also have to consider things such as battery production and disposal, and whether the high costs involved in changing battery packs on ageing vehicles will simply put another serviceable machine off the road prematurely. Yes, the motor industry needs to make and sell new cars, but the energy used in creating and recycling a vehicle is huge. And where does all this energy come from?

ZERO CARBON IN TODAY'S CAR WORLD

In reality, the term 'zero carbon' mainly concerns the energy efficiency of a product after it has been built, but many highly responsible companies with an eye on the future are now making rigorous efforts to reduce their carbon footprint

during the build process as well. It is a question of balancing the release of harmful gases with renewable energy and zero-emission technology.

In the automotive engineering world, reaching zero-carbon goals can be done in many different ways, but by far the most popular approach at the moment is the reduction of exhaust emissions – something actively tackled by countries such as Japan and the US state of California for several decades, albeit with mixed results in the early days, as car manufacturers sought to comply with regulations without reducing performance levels – until very recently, marketing muscle and glamour came before highlighting 'Green' issues.

Still driving men crazy

He bought it for its luxury—but all he talks about is performance. Owners of 1968 Cadillacs are so enthusiastic about the alert response and smooth, quiet operation of the new 472 V-8 engine, that they often fail to mention the other outstanding features. Your authorized Cadillac dealer will point out the brilliant new interiors and innovations such as concealed windshield wipers and improved variable-ratio power steering. Then discover for yourself Cadillac's truly remarkable performance. *Cadillac*
Shown here, the 1968 Cadillac Hardtop Sedan deVille.

Cadillac Motor Car Division   Elegance in action...with the greatest "inside story" in fine car history

You know how it is with Alfas. The way it's always been. A shameless urge to possess one . . . Well, why fight it?

Cars are very much a fashion statement – we've come to expect a little glamour from our steed. And who can blame us? A car is recognized as the second biggest purchase we'll ever make in our lives; for those not interested in housing, it usually becomes number one! At the end of the day, manufacturers make what we demand – very few will have the nerve to try and re-educate us, telling us what we should be buying. Ultimately, the car business is a market-led industry.
GM and Alfa Romeo

THE FUTURE OF OIL RESERVES

Thinking about the environment is something that concerns us all, as outlined in the section 'Global Warming' at the beginning of this chapter. But there's another reason why we have to consider different fuels or alternatives to traditional car engines, and that is the future oil reserve situation.

While Saudi Arabia has for the last couple of decades had around 250 billion barrels of oil reserves in hand, which accounted for almost one-fifth of the world's reserves, recently Venezuela has found a rich heavy crude deposit in the Orinoco Belt. This may or may not be easy to recover, but suddenly Venezuela could be sitting on 300 billion barrels of reserves, as compared to 100 billion four years earlier.

Using the current proven figures (as opposed to estimates and recent finds that may yet yield very little, despite their great potential, due to a combination of extraction costs and technical reasons) – which, by the way, give Venezuela a 7 per cent share of global oil reserves – at the current rate of production and consumption, the world could actually run out of oil in about sixty-five years. This may sound a long way off, but other estimates bring the day of reckoning decades sooner, and can you remember where the last ten years went?

It is also important to consider the rapid growth of motoring in China and developing countries, which would almost certainly bring a faster drain on reserves than any savings that can be made through improved technology. Furthermore, the current wave of global anti-nuclear feeling following the huge M9.0 earthquake off the Japanese coast may also deplete reserves that much more quickly.

Ironically, after all these years of making certain oil-producing

countries rich beyond imagination, talk within the motor industry of moving over to renewable alternative fuels and the more efficient forms of hybrid engineering already has OPEC members calling for compensation for lost earnings! So much for the planet, but it also gives a realistic view of what most corporations, and the countries that house them, really consider to be the most important thing, despite the nice PR handouts. When it comes to a choice between the environment and short-term gain, I'm afraid to say that money wins out every time.

Top Fifteen Countries Ranked by their Oil Reserves

Rank	Country	Global share
1	Saudi Arabia	19.8% share
2	Canada	13.2% share
3	Iran	11.1% share
4	Iraq	10.6% share
5	Kuwait	8.7% share
6	Venezuela	7.4% share
7	United Arab Emirates	7.2% share
8	Russia	4.5% share
9	Libya	3.2% share
10	Nigeria	2.7% share
11	Kazakhstan	2.2% share
12	Qatar	2.1% share
13	United States of America	1.6% share
14	China	1.2% share
15	Algeria	0.9% share

There's a limit to the amount of oil we can drill for, which, in addition to environmental concerns, gives us another reason to use wisely what's available. As well as thinking outside the box with motive power units, we have to start developing alternatives to petroleum products that serve our needs with true long-term benefits, as opposed to short-term visions and hype. No one is saying it will be easy, but time is against us.

Genghiskhanviet

Looking back as a motoring historian, one can conclude with a certain amount of cynicism that the various Middle East crises were responsible for sparking off a dramatic rise in gasoline prices, and that this was often the root cause behind the introduction of more energy-efficient vehicles, rather than concerns for the planet. In addition, stricter safety rules, especially those imposed by America – as well as fashion trends in certain countries (a 2011 survey by Tesco's in the UK, for instance, found that the school run car of dreams was the BMW X5, showing the mindset of ordinary people and the power of image marketing) – brought ever bigger and heavier vehicles into being. As a result, in many cases when one analyses model development, most of the gains that could have been made in creating cleaner, environmentally friendly vehicles were severely compromised.

Returning to the twenty-first century, it's fair to say that combustion technology is being refined all the time on both petrol and diesel engines, as is the development of alternatives to fossil fuels, and electric power, the latter often combined with a petrol powerplant to create a hybrid vehicle. Efforts are also being made to create lighter, more aerodynamic bodies, and across the globe, production techniques and material usage are under constant revision to try and reduce the impact on the planet during the entire manufacturing stage.

Even at the end of a product's useful lifespan, engineers and designers have put in place ways to recycle component parts easily – the role of the traditional scrapyard crusher, used to flatten or sometimes compact a car down to the size of a small cube, is rapidly becoming outdated in the majority of developed countries, with each piece of the vehicle being marked with an international code for separation by material type, which then enables more efficient recycling. Only when a bare steel bodyshell is left does the crusher come into play, with the metal almost certainly being used once again after it has been melted down and re-formed into a useful shape. Recycling steel uses less energy than making steel from iron ore, by the way, so the environment benefits in this way, too.

IN SUMMARY

For numerous reasons, both technically and, most likely, politically, due to certain countries refusing to pull their heads out of the sand, a true zero-carbon industry is probably a long way off. Being totally realistic, it's something that may not be an achievable goal even within our lifetime. But at least problems have been acknowledged, and after decades of ignoring, or skirting around issues at best, the first serious steps – for better or worse – are at last being taken towards making current and future motor vehicles more environmentally friendly. The chapters that follow look into what is being done, with a historical overview to put things into context, before a final section that tries to gaze into the decades ahead.

CHAPTER TWO

THE DIESEL BOOM

In recent years, one can safely say that in any number of major European cities, literally half the new cars on the road are powered by a diesel engine. This is probably as good a time as any to admit that I've never been a fan of diesel, and only a decade ago it would have taken the best salesman in the world to convince me that I should have embraced this technology with the same verve as seemingly every other person in Europe!

In some respects the way diesel has been considered over the years is like tobacco – we all know the health issues, not just for smokers but for innocent bystanders too, but governments continue to support sales due to the huge tax revenues they generate in the short term. Likewise diesel has its problems, but powerful lobby groups, from America to India, somehow kept them off the agenda at times when the damning data should at least have been aired. That said, the author will strive to outline the good and bad points of diesel fairly and objectively (both from today's perspective and historically), pointing out the vast improvements that have been made in emission control, and will try to assess exactly how diesel engines can help reduce our carbon footprint in the future.

Happily it looks as if there is an answer in the pipeline, and one that will silence even the strongest critics. Ironically, in addition to recent leading-edge technology such as the remarkable 'BlueTec' system, part of the equation has been there for almost a century, its benefits left largely untapped thanks to the political wont of certain countries for whom oil is a symbol of wealth and world power.

THE BIRTH OF THE DIESEL ENGINE

Gasoline engines, or at least readily recognizable versions of the breed, had already been around for over a decade before the first diesel powerplant appeared. Interestingly it was Germany that led the way in petrol engine technology, with Gottlieb Daimler refining the four-stroke Otto-cycle principle to make a series of practical units fed fuel through carburettors, while Wilhelm Maybach and Carl Benz provided, respectively, the necessary cooperation and rivalry to keep development moving at a fast pace in these pioneering days of automotive engineering.

The diesel power unit, named after its inventor, Rudolf Diesel, was a completely new concept in internal combustion engines, using the compression stroke to cause ignition of the fuel-air mixture rather than an electrical spark. This meant a reduction in parts, and with ignition components notoriously delicate at the turn of the twentieth century, combined with the promise of better fuel economy, the new motor – often referred to as a CI unit, the initials standing for 'compression ignition' – therefore held great appeal as the first real alternative to the gasoline engine.

Rudolf Diesel was born in Paris in the spring of 1858 to Bavarian parents, but following the outbreak of the Franco-Prussian War in the summer of 1870, he moved to the land

Rudolf Diesel, inventor of the diesel engine. Born in March 1858, he died in mysterious circumstances at sea in September 1913. Some have pointed to a conspiracy theory involving German nationalists, as Diesel had close links with France, Britain and the United States, but an accident or suicide seems a more likely explanation for his death. This German stamp was released to celebrate the 100th anniversary of his birth.
Deutsche Bundespost

of his ancestors to settle with his family in Augsburg. Diesel quickly showed an interest in engineering and then promptly displayed a talent for the subject, both academically and practically: a large number of patents were filed in his name in Germany and France. After working with steam engines, he studied thermodynamics whilst laid up in hospital, and then moved on to develop his own type of powerplant based on the mechanics of the four-stroke cycle – the diesel engine.

Diesel first published a book containing an outline theory and proposal for the construction of what he termed a 'rational heat engine' in 1893. This was the basis for the diesel engine that followed – although it has to be said that without the continued help of MAN AG, the project may never have come to fruition. Notwithstanding, more patents were filed in Europe and America in Diesel's name, and by 1898 his patents had made him a millionaire, as diesel power proved to be far superior to steam in terms of mechanical efficiency – up to seven times higher on paper, although closer to five times higher in reality. Even using the latter figure, it was a significant improvement on the steam engines that had given birth to the Industrial Revolution.

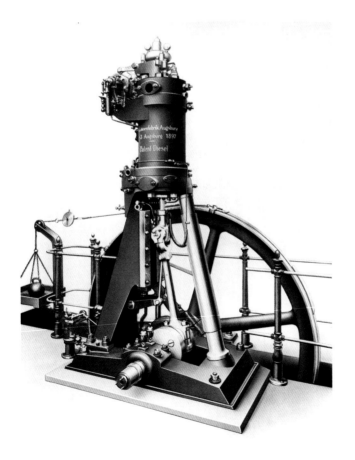

An early diesel stationary engine. MAN Diesel & Turbo

THE OTTO CYCLE

The Otto cycle is another name for the four-stroke system applied to internal combustion engines. The name 'Otto' comes out of respect for Nikolaus August Otto, father of the four-stroke principle, while the four-stroke moniker describes the four piston movements necessary to complete one combustion cycle in conjunction with suitable inlet and exhaust valve operation, a method of igniting a measured fuel-air mixture, and a crankshaft with offset crankpins to keep pistons moving in the desired direction. The four 'strokes' can be summed up as follows:

Intake: As the piston moves down the cylinder, a suitable fuel-air mixture is drawn into the combustion chamber through the open inlet valve. The exhaust valve is closed at this stage.

Compression: Both valves are closed, allowing the fuel-air mixture to be compressed within the combustion chamber as the piston rises in the cylinder.

Power: With both valves closed, the fuel-air mixture is ignited either by a spark or an increase in heat through extreme pressure (via a higher c/r, as in the diesel engine), the resulting controlled explosion pushing the piston back down again.

Exhaust: As the piston starts to rise again, the inlet valve remains shut, but the exhaust valve opens, allowing burnt gases to exit the combustion chamber.

At the start of the next chapter a series of drawings shows the four strokes and the way the engine's internal components move in relation to them.

Slowly but surely replacing stationary steam engines around the world, the diesel engine – in four- and two-stroke guise – became popular in maritime applications after the turn of the century, and then made inroads as the motive power unit for railway locomotives, trucks and buses. It was even being put forward as the powerplant of the future for road cars, with a 1931 article in *Popular Mechanics* of America predicting that by 1940, maintenance-free diesel engines would be the norm.

France was quick to take up diesel engines for production vehicles, with Citroën offering 1750cc Ricardo-developed CI units in family cars from the early 1930s. Peugeot wasn't far behind, although development was delayed due to the outbreak of World War II. Meanwhile Mercedes-Benz had launched this car, the 260D, at the 1936 Berlin Show, seen here in chassis form. It would go down in history as the world's first commercially successful diesel passenger car. Daimler AG

A few prototypes were built on both sides of the Atlantic in the late 1920s, and by the 1930s, 4-cylinder versions were starting to find their way into production passenger cars, such as certain models of the Citroën Rosalie (service trials of the 40bhp engine had started in the summer of 1934), and the Mercedes-Benz 260D, introduced at the 1936 Berlin Motor Show. The Hanomag Rekord was another oil burner announced at the same German event, when diesel was literally half the price of petrol, while Peugeot, who had been working on CI engines behind the scenes since 1921, released a limited number of diesel 402Bs for the 1939 season.

Naturally road car development was interrupted during World War II, but diesel engines powered entire armies and navies, and were also used in a number of aeronautical applications. By this time, fuel delivery systems had long since been perfected via Bosch injection and the later Cummins' common-rail system, and turbochargers had already put in an appearance.

Following the end of hostilities, interest in the diesel engine continued to rise, and any remaining restrictions on private use were gradually withdrawn. Although some countries had been quicker to warm to diesel than others, virtually all ships and railway locomotives used diesel power

within a few years of the war ending; agricultural machinery and heavy-duty generators provided another lucrative market for diesel-engine manufacturers. The road haulage business was yet another huge outlet, of course, with technology being introduced at a rapid rate in this particular field. This, in turn, gave rise to the idea of reviving diesel passenger cars on a more serious, mass-production basis.

POST-WAR DIESEL CARS

The promise of superior fuel consumption (allied to cheaper fuel costs at the pumps in the first place) and power-unit longevity helped give the four-stroke diesel engine a foothold in the passenger car market. Many manufacturers looked at the unit's potential, including the likes of Volkswagen, whose VW Beetle was already known for fuel efficiency – but as the 1950s rolled on, it was still a rare sight in regular automobiles, offered by only a handful of makers around the world: the petrol engine was still king in this sector of the market.

Even so, whilst most technological advances with regard to diesel engines were found in the commercial vehicle field – enhancing power and torque output, improving fuel consumption figures, and eventually reducing emissions – diesel passenger cars were starting to filter through as makers from Britain (Standard, Rover and Austin) and Italy (Fiat) joined the traditional diesel strongholds of Germany and France in offering customers an option to petrol engines.

As the 1960s dawned, in the wake of the Suez Crisis more manufacturers started looking at diesel-engined vehicles as a viable alternative to the bubble cars and microcars of the previous decade, as a means of reducing the cost of motoring. Even Japan joined the diesel game at this stage, with Isuzu listing a diesel Bellel model alongside the petrol-engined derivatives.

The Standard Motor Company was Britain's first car manufacturer to offer a diesel engine option, fitted to the Phase II Vanguards from February 1954 onwards. Standard

The Peugeot 204 was revolutionary in many ways, but it should perhaps be remembered as the car that, more than any other if we use production figures as a gauge, brought diesel power into mainstream motoring. It really paved the way for the small VWs. Peugeot

For a little while, even America caught the diesel bug. The LF9 Oldsmobile V8 diesel engine, introduced in 1978, was used in other GM brands, too, including Cadillac. GM

The Mini had shown that interior space could be combined with compact exterior dimensions if the packaging were right, and Peugeot took the FF concept a stage further in 1968 with the introduction of a diesel version of the 204 model. With a 1.3-litre capacity, the transverse engine was the smallest diesel unit available in a road car, and around 150,000 diesel 204s were built, although a high percentage of them found use as commercial vehicles, being sold as estates or vans – those customers who went for diesel cars usually opted for larger models, such as the Mercedes 200D or 220D, which could be readily pressed into service as a taxi.

Notwithstanding, DAF attempted to bring out a small air-cooled diesel engine in 1973, but the company's financial woes put an end to the project, and all future cars came via Volvo, and all with petrol engines until well into the 1980s. As a result it was left to Volkswagen to make the compact diesel car popular on a global scale, first with the EA111 four in the VW Polo, and more successfully with the EA827 series units in the VW Golf (or Rabbit in the States) from 1976 onwards.

This was an era when America was stunned by the two oil crises of the 1970s, and forced to rethink its car policy – the outcome was the downsizing of domestic vehicles, increased popularity in small import models, and a fresh look at frugal diesel powerplants. This tempted General Motors to join the fray, albeit for a limited period – diesel passenger-car engines were still very much a European speciality.

At the other end of the scale to the Golf there were large saloons such as the ubiquitous Benz W115- and W123-series, and the Peugeot 504 (fitted with an enlarged 2.1-litre engine for the 1977 season, which was also adopted in the contemporary Ford Granada), while the 1979 Model Year 604 was one of the first passenger cars to receive a turbo-diesel (TD) unit – the 2.3-litre XD2S, endowed with a modest 80bhp.

As it happens, the French maker was only a year behind Mercedes-Benz in getting a TD to market. On the Benz (sold only in North America), it was unusual in another respect, having an in-line 5-cylinder configuration – while turbocharging had been common on trucks for some time (even before the war), it was something new on cars, and the straight-five diesel was a world first, although Audi were

The 3-litre turbo-diesel used in the US market Mercedes 300SD model, announced in February 1977, although full-scale production didn't start for over a year. Daimler AG

very close behind, the Ingolstadt firm having already made the first production 5-cylinder petrol engine. Interestingly, sales of diesel Mercedes were so strong in the grip of the oil crisis that there were thoughts of launching a turbo-diesel R107 SL at one time, but falling petrol prices brought back a sense of reality.

Behind the scenes, the Peugeot-Citroën empire (the PSA Group) was readying its legendary XUD power-unit, which would go on to sell in its millions. First used in the face-lifted 'Mk II' Peugeot 305 and the contemporary Talbot Horizon, it was in the Peugeot 205 that it gained real recognition, and later in the 405 and Citroën BX. More than any other engine, it is fair to say that the 4-cylinder XUD indirect-injection (IDI) unit was responsible for making diesel a truly desirable option in Europe. It's ironic to think that the top end was based on technology used by Citroën in the early 1930s, when the famous British consulting engineer, Sir Harry Ricardo, designed the Comet cylinder head (with high charge turbulence to encourage better combustion) for the Paris maker.

Over in Japan, in 1977 Toyota made the country's first domestic diesel power-unit designed specifically for passenger cars – a 2.2-litre four. Meanwhile, Isuzu was exploring the possibilities of using ceramics in diesel engines, joining Kyocera in a technical cooperation agreement. Ultimately, heat is developed whenever an engine is run, but once it becomes excessive, a cooling system of some sort is needed,

to take the heat away. However, heat is energy, and the people at Isuzu knew that an engine could be made more efficient if the heat was allowed to build up to higher temperatures.

The use of modern ceramics seemed to provide the solution. Traditional ceramics are far too brittle to be of use in automotive applications, despite their excellent resistance to heat, friction, chemicals, corrosion and wear, but

The Peugeot 405 was one of several cars to make good use of the legendary XUD engine. Peugeot

Bosch's EDC system, first used by BMW.
Bosch

BELOW: **The first car to carry the TDI badge was the Audi 100 of 1989 vintage. This is the estate (or Avant) version.** Audi

the 1970s saw a new generation of ceramics, such as silicon nitride and silicon carbide, and with a suitable type of mixing or fibre reinforcement, these can actually be made stronger than iron and just as tough. Other ceramics, such as alumina and zirconia, allowed more specialized components to be made.

Ceramic glowplugs were introduced by Isuzu in 1981 (sparkplugs had used ceramics for decades, after all), although there were far more ambitious plans afoot, finally taking shape in the form of the P306Y engine – a turbocharged diesel unit with no radiator or cooling fins that delivered 30 per cent more power and fuel economy thanks to the adiabatic properties of the ceramic valves, piston surfaces and rings, and combustion chamber walls, allowing the engine to operate at a highly efficient 800°C.

Announced in 1985, during testing the P306Y engine showed that it was capable of lasting five times longer than a cast-iron lump, and it was naturally a substantial amount lighter than its metal counterpart, too. Sadly, technical difficulties, including machining time and cost, put an end to the dream of the ceramic engine, but today, many small components are produced in ceramic materials, with Kyocera still at the forefront of this technology.

Coming back to more conventional engineering, Bosch introduced the EDC (electronic diesel control) module in 1986, an engine management 'black box' that we take for granted now, but which at the time was cutting-edge technology, the control unit gathering data from a number of sensors to ensure smoother engine running, as well as lower emissions and fuel consumption. First seen on the BMW 524TD – the diesel powerplant was a new venture for the Munich concern, starting in 1983, although the unit also found its way into the Lincoln Continental Mk VII – EDCs would quickly find use throughout the industry, being updated on a regular basis in an age of staggering progress in the electronics field.

Bosch was also responsible for the injection system on the first Fiat Croma, released in the mid-1980s. This was the world's first passenger car with a direct-injection (DI) turbo-diesel engine, although it's fair to say that the VW-Audi Group (with its signature TDI moniker) brought this

ABOVE: **The TDI trademark is synonymous with the Volkswagen brand. This is one of the first Mk IV Golfs, introduced for the 1998 season.** Volkswagen

BELOW LEFT: **The first generation CRD system from Bosch.** Bosch

BELOW RIGHT: **A Mercedes-Benz common-rail diesel set-up from 1997.** Daimler AG

technology into the mainstream, increasing the efficiency of diesel powerplants a huge amount by injecting the fuel directly into the cylinder rather than into a prechamber.

A major difference between the Fiat and Volkswagen/Audi engines was the use of electronically controlled injection on the German models, giving superior performance and tighter emission control. According to Peugeot's figures for their latest HDI (high-pressure direct-injection) engines, the benefits of DI add up to a 20 per cent reduction in the release of carbon dioxide, a 40 per cent drop in carbon monoxide, hydrocarbon emissions halved, and a 60 per cent reduction in particulate matter compared to the old XUD unit.

A common-rail diesel (CRD) system – which basically uses the 'rail' that runs the length of the engine as a high-pressure fuel reservoir – had been patented by Clessie Cummins during World War II, although CRD-type arrangements had appeared on marine engines as early as 1916. The Swiss took the idea a stage further in the 1960s, but it was left to the Japanese to bring CRD to the marketplace – Nippondenso (now known as Denso) making the injection system for the 1995 Hino Ranger truck series. Not long after, in 1997, the first common-rail diesel passenger car appeared – the Alfa

DIESEL FUEL REFINING AND GRADES

A recognized 'barrel' holds 159ltr (35 Imperial/42 US gallons) of crude oil, although it generally ends up providing about 5 per cent more product by volume due to the modern refining process. Nowadays, once the crude oil has been refined into various types of petroleum-based fuels and other by-products, petrol accounts for almost half of the barrel's volume, diesel a quarter, and aviation fuel about 10 per cent.

The refining process is basically the distillation of crude oil into its component elements (or fractions) by the application of extreme heat, as the different hydrocarbons that make up crude oil each have different boiling points, and later, further refining can take place through the so-called 'reforming' and 'cracking' processes, which use a combination of heat, catalysts and pressure to manufacture more profitable products from less useful liquids such as naphtha. Impurities are taken out along the way, with the removal of sulphur being a key part of the diesel fuel production process.

Whilst fuel with a low sulphur content is kinder to catalytic converters (sulphur poisons cats and NAC – NOx Absorber Catalyst – units) and the environment in general (PM – diesel soot, or particulate matter, often shortened to the initials PM – is dramatically reduced), sulphur removal has been blamed for the escalation in the price of diesel, which now costs more than petrol in Britain, and North America, too. This wasn't always the case – quite the opposite was true for decades, until diesel cars started to become popular in the UK and threatened to become popular in the States, as if by an amazing coincidence. One can also make allowances for the fact that, compared with gasoline, less diesel is produced per litre of crude, and, to a lesser extent, acknowledge that more is spent on marketing diesel fuel than petrol.

As it happens, the manufacture of LPG is by far the most efficient use of crude oil if one takes as the gauge the amount of product that can be made from a set volume. More realistic, though, is to compare petrol and diesel, and here we can see that for every 100ltr (22gal) of diesel produced, 118ltr (26gal) of premium gasoline could be made, or 123ltr (27gal) of regular. Of course, before reaching the pumps, numerous additives find their way into the equation, and modern diesel often has a significant amount of bio-fuel added to reduce emissions and improve lubrication.

But even after taking all these things into consideration, it is

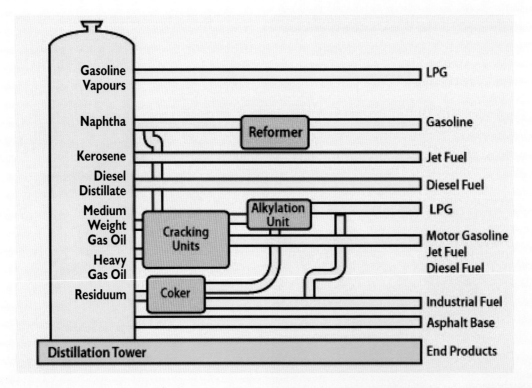

The basic refining process, the crude oil being superheated by steam to about 600°C before entering the distillation column. The heavier products stay lower down in the column, while the lighter ones are separated off as they rise. The temperature is roughly 20°C at the top of the column. US DoE

Making Sense of the Cost of Fuel

Country	Main energy types

In America, according to US Energy Adminstration (EIA) figures, diesel was priced at $1.30 a gallon in 2002, with petrol at $1.39. By 2006 they were much the same price at the pumps, while today, diesel costs $3.80 a gallon, against $3.45 for petrol. These illustrations show how the cost element for each fuel was broken down in America, as of October 2011:

KEY

Crude Oil

Refining

Distribution and Marketing

Others

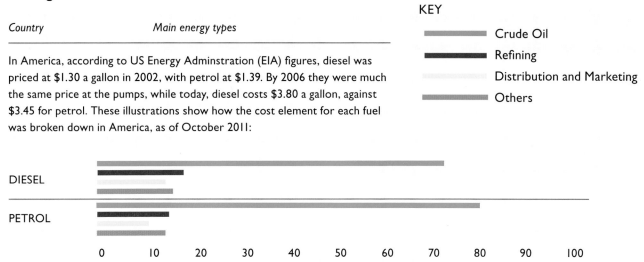

DIESEL

PETROL

0   10   20   30   40   50   60   70   80   90   100

strange that Japan – where diesel isn't at all popular for private passenger vehicles, and steps to reduce the sulphur content were introduced as early as 1994 – can sell it for 117 yen a litre, compared with 139 yen for regular gasoline, and 150 yen for the premium grade. This is the kind of price differential UK customers were used to before diesel car sales started booming.

Interestingly, a House of Commons report shows that British taxes (fuel duty) have steadily increased on diesel in line with the diesel engine's popularity as a road car powerplant (a real spike in demand for diesel fuel started in 1982, and continued to rise sharply until 1998), and are now the same as for petrol, whereas they used to be fractionally lower. On the Continent, meanwhile, diesel is still far cheaper than petrol in virtually all the mainland European countries due to the significantly lower taxes applied to the former.

In fact most countries didn't call for reduced sulphur content until the turn of the century, with Bill Clinton making the first steps in America in a May 2000 speech, for instance. It took several years for proposals to filter through, however, and the EU ended up being slightly ahead of the game, but still a fair way behind the likes of Japan.

The basic, pre-low-sulphur diesel is still sold today, though it is officially reserved for off-road, farm and construction vehicles. Known as 'red diesel' in Britain, due to the dye used to identify it (as opposed to 'DERV', or 'white' diesel), it is included in a significantly lower tax level, which also tends

to attract shady dealing. A police clampdown found as many as one in five private cars using red diesel in certain areas of the UK, thus completely negating the original idea of improving the air we breathe.

Further reductions in the amount of sulphur contained in diesel fuel led to 'ultra-low sulphur diesel' (ULSD) becoming the norm in most parts of the world from about 2006 onwards. Lowering the sulphur content in diesel helps PM filters work more efficiently, and also reduces certain exhaust emissions that contribute towards the build-up of acid rain. However, sulphur helps lubricate engine components, so bio-fuels are generally added to replace the sulphur's properties. It therefore seems ironic that so few countries are willing to take the leap and make pure bio-fuels available on the service station forecourt.

Other additives include succinimide-based detergents to reduce deposits on injectors; olefin copolymers to stop diesel freezing so easily; cetane enhancers, which can improve the self-ignition properties of poor quality fuel, being of particular help in terms of reducing noise and improving cold-start efficiency; and certain organo-metallic compounds to reduce smoke, although the latter have been found to promote emissions of ultra-fine PM and their use is therefore under review. Incidentally, Swedish diesel is specially blended to be kinder to the environment, with a lower aromatic hydrocarbon content, and carries a slight price premium as a result.

Alfa Romeo brought a sporting twist to the diesel saga with the 156 JTD. Only a decade earlier, the words 'sporting' and 'diesel' used in the same breath would have been unthinkable. Bosch

The lightweight Ford Prodigy was another mild hybrid, with an electric motor providing an idle-stop facility and assisting the 1.2-litre turbo-diesel engine under hard acceleration. Based on the P2000 LSR (with LSR standing for low storage requirement), the car made its debut at the 2000 Detroit Show, which opened on 29 December 1999. Ford

The ESX-III was the second Chrysler PNGV concept to feature a mild hybrid drivetrain – an electric motor assisting the 74bhp diesel engine when necessary. The ESX-II model had been released in 1998, with the ESX-III following in 2000. Cost was one of the main factors in the project not being developed further, with a $7,500 premium hard to justify when prices at US pumps were so cheap. Chrysler

Indeed this popularity, combined with recent calls for more stringent emission controls in the EEC, has led to great leaps in technology. With America also warming to diesel again, to meet more challenging CAFE ('corporate average fuel economy') figures averaged across an entire maker's range, engineers are now busy refining the diesel engine as never before.

JUST HOW 'GREEN' IS DIESEL?

From a greenhouse gas point of view, according to popular beliefs based on the evidence put forward, diesel emissions are considered far cleaner than those of an equivalent petrol engine, as CO_2 levels released from the exhaust are generally accepted as being lower – but in direct comparison (gallon for gallon), they are actually higher. According to figures released by the Irish government in August 2010, burning a litre of petrol generates about 234 grams of CO_2, while burning a litre of diesel produces 270 grams.

However, broadly speaking, diesel gives far better fuel-consumption figures (litre for litre on engine size), which tends to promote and reinforce the point on CO_2 emissions over a vehicle's life. It also helps preserve oil reserves – at least in theory, although it takes more crude oil to produce a gallon of diesel fuel than it does a gallon of gasoline, which wipes out a lot of the latter advantage. And another black mark for diesel from a 'Green' perspective is the huge

Romeo 156 JTD, available in two versions and fitted with a Bosch CRD system that had originally been born as the Magneti Marelli Unijet, designed under Dr Rinaldo Rinolfi of the Fiat Group.

As the twenty-first century dawned, it seemed as if demand for diesel cars had peaked a long time ago in the States as cheap petrol virtually killed off the breed, with only Mercedes-Benz and Volkswagen offering CI models in America, although Europe's unquenched thirst for diesel vehicles made up for the lack of interest across the Atlantic.

escape of methane gas during the oil drilling and refining process, so the more crude needed equals more methane released into the atmosphere.

In addition, the diesel engine's superior thermal efficiency is largely due to the use of higher compression ratios compared to a gasoline unit, although some modern petrol engines boast an extremely high c/r, helping to significantly improve fuel consumption, which again closes the gap.

Perhaps more importantly, a large number of corporations and certain governments have concentrated far too much PR effort on the reduction of CO_2 emissions to create a cleaner planet, thereby making us – and them – fail to see a lot of the big picture. Even the recently proposed EU bill to have car manufacturers allocate a huge amount of space in each advert to Green issues only really calls for fuel consumption and CO_2 emissions to be given any real prominence.

One of the problems is that although we consider nitrous oxide (N_2O) a greenhouse gas, increasing in volume largely through modern farming practices, NOx emissions (a combination of nitric oxide and nitrogen dioxide) seem to escape the spotlight to a great extent, despite occurring every time there is combustion involved, and despite both component parts (NO and NO_2) being recognized air pollutants which can dramatically affect the balance of the ozone layer

Hear no diesel. See no diesel. Smell no diesel.

"Great for economy but bad for ecology."

A common enough complaint with diesels.

Believe it or not, though, they actually emit 25% less carbon dioxide than a petrol engine with a catalyst.

Despite this, we at Volkswagen have not been idle.

The fruits of our labours are there for all to see.

Or rather, not see.

For with the arrival of our 'environ-

ment diesel', of fumes there is scarcely a trace.

How so? By equipping our new 1.6 litre engine with a turbo charger.

Turbo-charging increases the air flow to the combustion chambers, making for (you guessed it) better combustion.

Fire, so to speak, without smoke.

Our new diesel is also equipped with an oxidation catalyst. It snuffles 50% of smelly stuff called polycyclic hydrocarbons.

As for the effect of all this on performance, we're only too happy to come clean.

Compared to our previous diesel (no slouch itself), you get 10% more torque.

And 11% more power.

Wunderbar, you say. But what of the noise element.

Come now, we're talking about a Volkswagen diesel. Which, in its own quiet way, says it all. **Umwelt Diesel** ⓋⓌ

ABOVE: **A wonderful Volkswagen UK advert from 1990.**

Volkswagen

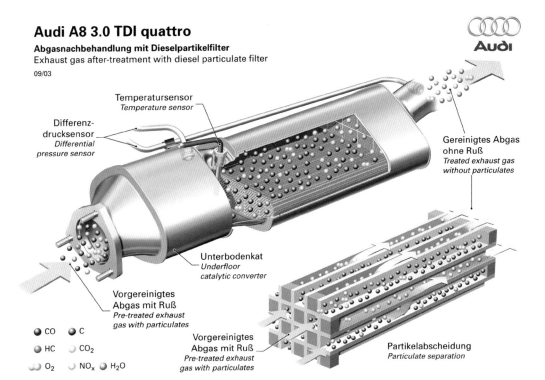

Audi A8 3.0 TDI quattro

Abgasnachbehandlung mit Dieselpartikelfilter
Exhaust gas after-treatment with diesel particulate filter

09/03

Temperatursensor
Temperature sensor

Differenz-
drucksensor
*Differential
pressure sensor*

Gereinigtes Abgas
ohne Ruß
*Treated exhaust gas
without particulates*

Unterbodenkat
*Underfloor
catalytic converter*

Vorgereinigtes
Abgas mit Ruß
*Pre-treated exhaust
gas with particulates*

Vorgereinigtes
Abgas mit Ruß
*Pre-treated exhaust
gas with particulates*

Partikelabscheidung
Particulate separation

● CO   ● C
● HC   ○ CO_2
◗ O_2 ○ NO_x ◐ H_2O

RIGHT: **A modern diesel particulate filter unit, this one fitted to the 2004 MY Audi A8. DPFs were still a real rarity at this time.** Audi

– depleting it in certain conditions, or reacting with it to increase ozone (O_3) levels closer to the Earth's surface to form smog in urban areas; nitric oxide also has the potential to create acid rain. Some of this oversight is due to confusion over which gas is which, and what its effects are, while some of it is a question of 'don't ask, don't tell'. Even when new, compared to their petrol counterparts, NOx emissions are significantly higher on CI engines running on conventional diesel fuel due to the extremely high compression ratios involved (as high as 18.5:1 even today, with over 20:1 being common in the past, before direct injection became popular), and that surely undermines the 'Green' marketing angle to a great extent, especially when we take the GWP (global warming potential) of nitrous oxide into account.

There is also the level of engine tuning and condition to consider. Diesels can be seriously dirty unless they are given the correct fuels and regular servicing. We've all followed trucks and buses belching out clouds of black smoke, and certain dubious operators have been known to continue running vehicles that are pumping out clouds of blue and/or white smoke. The damage to the environment – and people's health – is increased exponentially as the state of engine tune deteriorates.

Certainly petrol engines emit higher levels of noxious carbon monoxide (CO) on paper, but even without the above concerns regarding tuning, diesel soot (particulate matter, or PM) is a problem that's virtually non-existent in petrol power-units. In reality, it is the soot from diesel engines that has always been a major sticking point for the author. It seems odd that we keep pushing diesel as being good for the environment when the particulate matter that CI units release is recognized as an irritant to the respiratory system and a known carcinogenic – not my theory, but conclusions reached in numerous reports filed by, amongst others across the globe, the UK's Health & Safety Executive (the HSE) and America's Environmental Protection Agency (the EPA). It seems to be a choice between global air quality and local air quality, but with more than half of the world's population living in urban areas, a better balance between the two would be prudent.

The Possible Health Issues

Although this is a book on 'Green' technology, and should therefore celebrate advances being made in this direction, some questions need to be raised with regard to the current fashion for adopting diesel – its sudden popularity taking many by surprise, I'm sure. Even Porsche, a company that has never been afraid to stand alone with its unique engineering concepts, has launched a new diesel model in a manner that almost reads: 'If you can't beat them, join them!' And now Mazda has done the same, having announced that it was dropping its signature rotary engine (RE) a few months earlier.

For most of the twentieth century, diesel has powered commercial vehicles of one sort or another, but now passenger car manufacturers are moving over to CI units *en masse*, especially in Europe. Moreover, the trend will probably cross the Atlantic soon, as makers struggle to meet US CAFE (Corporate Average Fuel Economy) fuel consumption targets. But there is something the CAFE figures do not take into account – emissions. And with diesel fumes, warnings have been issued and duly ignored for decades, probably due to the fact that 70 per cent of America's goods are transported by diesel-powered vehicles of one sort or another, and powerful trucking associations are constantly lobbying politicians in order to protect their livelihoods and profit margins.

In 2000, the US State & Territorial Air Pollution Program administrators and the Association of Local Air Pollution Control officials filed a report on health risks associated with diesel exhaust. Its summary read as follows:

> Diesel engines are significant contributors to air pollution. Moreover, the adverse health impacts of diesel pollution are dire, posing a serious threat to public health nationwide, and especially in urban areas. The hazardous mixture that comprises diesel exhaust contains hundreds of different chemical compounds that wreak havoc on our air quality in a variety of ways, playing a role in ozone formation, particulate matter, regional haze, acid rain and global warming. But perhaps the greatest threat posed by diesels comes from their toxic emissions. Diesel exhaust contains over forty chemicals that are listed by the EPA and California as toxic air contaminants, known human carcinogens, probable human carcinogens, reproductive toxicants or endocrine disrupters.

Not long after, the 2001 EPA report read much the same. But both before (as early as 1955, in fact) and after this, numerous independent studies have linked diesel to cancer and other health problems, in places as far afield as America, Britain, Australia and Japan.

Amazingly, a US government report from NIOSH (the National Institute for Occupational Safety and Health) on the subject was held up for fifteen years, and wasn't allowed to be published before a lobby group representing the MARG Diesel Coalition had scanned the publication before it was released. Even now, parts of the report are being held up in congress for one reason or another.

The famous research scientist, Dr Kitty Little, contends that diesel fumes are worse than tobacco as a cause of lung cancer. For her reasoning, she concluded that:

Tobacco smoke contains no carcinogens, while diesel fumes contain four known carcinogens; that lung cancer is rare in rural areas, but common in towns; that cancers are more prevalent along the routes of motorways; and that the incidence of lung cancer has doubled in non-smokers over past decades.

She also observed that there was less lung cancer even though we are generally tending to smoke more.

In Japan, a group of 633 Tokyo residents successfully filed a lawsuit against the city and the auto industry for health issues allegedly caused by long-term exposure to diesel fumes, and in particular the smog and PM relating to them. After eleven years of fighting in court, in 2007 the seven domestic makers associated with diesel trucks and light commercials got together and handed over 1.2 billion yen (about $12 million at the time) in compensation, although they would not admit liability. But the fact that such a huge sum of money was handed over, and not long after Tokyo (as a local government) passed several laws on cleaning up diesel exhaust fumes via a number of measures (notably by retrofitting PM filters on older vehicles entering the capital) shortly after the case was brought to court, in itself speaks volumes.

It's no longer simply good enough to follow trends and happily listen to one side of the story. The 'Green' technology we should be embracing needs to help the planet and preserve the health of mankind, and if it doesn't do that efficiently, it needs to be adjusted to improve it, or be shelved. Thanks to new technology, today's diesel engines may be classed as clean, but diesel per se is not, and older vehicles should not be allowed to ride on the coat-tails of the knights in shining armour. We need to be properly informed before passing any final judgement on what is truly good for the environment.

GIANT LEAPS FORWARD

Within a couple of years of entering the twenty-first century, sales of passenger cars with diesel engines outnumbered those sold with petrol engines in Western Europe. Naturally, with this huge volume of sales, makers were suitably encouraged to find ways to contend with tighter EEC emissions regulations and secure a slice of this highly profitable market. The bonus for manufacturers is the promise of sales in the USA, with diesel being seen as a useful tool in

EXHAUST EMISSIONS STANDARDS

The table below is a review of the tighter emissions standards recently called for in Europe and the USA. Those for petrol engines are also listed for comparison:

Europe – Diesel Engines

	CO	NOx	PM
EURO 1 (1992)	2.72g/km	0.97g/km	0.140g/km
EURO 2 (1996)	1.00g/km	0.70g/km	0.080g/km
EURO 3 (2000)	0.64g/km	0.50g/km	0.050g/km
EURO 4 (2005)	0.50g/km	0.25g/km	0.025g/km
EURO 5 (2009)	0.50g/km	0.18g/km	0.005g/km

Europe – Petrol Engines

	CO	NOx	PM
EURO 1 (1992)	2.72g/km	0.97g/km	-
EURO 2 (1996)	2.20g/km	0.50g/km	-
EURO 3 (2000)	1.30g/km	0.15g/km	-
EURO 4 (2005)	1.00g/km	0.08g/km	-
EURO 5 (2009)	1.00g/km	0.06g/km	0.005g/km

Note: In the EURO 1 and 2 tiers, HC emissions were grouped together with NOx. The EURO 6 proposals for 2014 are not much different to the current EURO 5 regulations. PM limits on petrol engines apply to cars with direct injection only. One should also be aware of ACEA's voluntary limit of 140g/km of CO_2 per car (averaged over a manufacturer's range) by 2008, and plans for 130g/km by 2015.

America – All Engines

	CO	NOx	PM
Tier 1 (1994) (diesel)	3.40g/mile	1.00g/mile	0.08g/mile
Tier 1 (1994) (petrol)	3.40g/mile	0.40g/mile	-
Trans. NLEV (1999)	3.40g/mile	0.40g/mile	-
Tier II Bin 5 (2004)	3.40g/mile	0.05g/mile	0.01g/mile

Note: California had its own LEV 1 and LEV 2 regulations, with LEV 3 due to start in 2014, with preliminary targets being particularly hard on diesel engines. One should also bear in mind the CAFE (Corporate Average Fuel Economy) rules enforced by the USA. After starting off quite low at 13.1ltr/100km (18mpg) in 1978, the figure settled at 8.5ltr/100km (27.5mpg) from 1990 until 2010. Naturally, fuel economy and CO_2 emissions are linked. A new CAFE figure of 6.6ltr/100km (35.5mpg) has been proposed for 2016, with calls for 4.2ltr/100km (56.2mpg) by 2025.

The Ford-PSA 'Lion' V6, otherwise known as the DT17. This was one of the first engines to use CGI technology to reduce the weight of diesel engines. PSA

getting around CAFE (Corporate Average Fuel Economy) requirements. And unlike the old days, when each market had different regulations, with America also calling for significantly tighter emission controls in the so-called Tier II phase, development costs could be spread that much more effectively.

Diesel engines have traditionally been heavy units, and little had been done to remedy the situation, mainly for practical reasons. One of the problems is noise control, and with alloy blocks even being associated with additional noise on petrol engines as a rule of thumb, makers tended to stick with heavy cast-iron cylinder blocks on diesels to contain some of the cacophony of the CI cycle.

In 2001, however, it was announced that the 2.7-litre Ford-PSA 'Lion' V6 would use compacted graphite iron (CGI) for its block material. This technology was made available by the Swedish SinterCast concern, and started to find its way into various production cars from the 2004 season onwards. Ford later approved the use of CGI for other engines, as did Hyundai, and Navistar has recently brought out a new V8, with the CGI block being not only 15 per cent lighter than a traditional cast-iron one, but also stronger and stiffer. Naturally, engineers are delighted with the NVH (noise, vibra-

Making its debut in the spring of 2002, the so-called 'VW 1-litre car' was a lightweight special, with a body made of aluminium, magnesium and carbon-fibre, and a single-cylinder 299cc diesel engine. The '1-litre' actually referred to the fuel consumption – one litre per 100 kilometres! Volkswagen

tion and harshness) qualities and the rigidity of the cylinder block, while the reduced weight translates into fuel savings for the end user.

2001 also witnessed the introduction of Delphi's accelerometer pilot control (APC) system, which was basically a knock-sensor for diesel engines. Attached to the engine block, a piezoelectric accelerometer monitors combustion via vibration levels, and then sends a constant stream of signals to an injector driver module (IDM) working in tandem with the ECU to optimize its calibrations to ensure cleaner, quieter and smoother running. Combined with fast-acting injectors, APC made it possible to improve the pilot-injection event, giving an efficient multiple spray pattern which inevitably leads to enhanced torque output and a reduction in smoke. Launched on the 'Duratorq' 115bhp Ford Focus TDCi engine, APC quickly found service with Renault and the PSA Group before the year was out, with others following soon after.

In a similar vein came Bosch's closed-loop lambda sensor, available for diesel engines for the first time in 2002, despite having been around since 1976 on petrol units. The system basically measures oxygen content in the exhaust gas to inform the engine's ECU of combustion conditions. The ECU can then adjust induction settings to improve fuel consumption and give the lowest possible emissions in relation to engine load.

Bosch was also at the forefront of piezoelectric injector development, giving birth to the third generation of the common-rail diesel injection system. Launched in May 2003,

The third generation of the Bosch common-rail system, with CP4 high-pressure pump, piezoelectric injectors, and ECU board. Bosch

the finer control offered by injector nozzle needles switched by fast- and direct-acting piezo crystals or PZT (lead zirconate titanate) ceramics in an electrical field (as opposed to a traditional magnetic coil) reduced pre-exhaust emissions by as much as 20 per cent. With 75 per cent fewer moving parts and the promise of improved reliability, prompting Denso, Continental (now incorporating Siemens VDO) and Delphi to make their own versions of these injectors.

Further increases in injector pressure on common-rail systems were an obvious route towards obtaining cleaner levels of combustion – but easier said than done, as operating pressures were already extremely high (1800 bar, with 2000 bar at the nozzle in third-generation systems). Bosch was looking into ways of increasing pressure at the nozzle beyond 2000 bar, and variable nozzle geometry seemed to be a way forwards. Developed under Dr Ulrich Dohle, head of Diesel Systems Division at Bosch, a patent was filed in August 2005 – but more work was needed. However, most common-rail systems, whoever manufactures them, now employ piezoelectric technology.

Another huge advance in cleaning up diesel emissions is selective catalytic reduction (SCR). The selective catalytic reduction system has actually been around for quite some time, having been patented by the Englehard Corporation of America in 1957. This used ammonia as a reducing agent, converting NOx emissions into nitrogen and water, but was restricted mainly to industrial use because of logistics. Development continued, and Japan's IHI Corporation had perfected the idea by the late 1970s – a useful component in the country's fight against smog caused by the industrial boom it experienced in the 1960s.

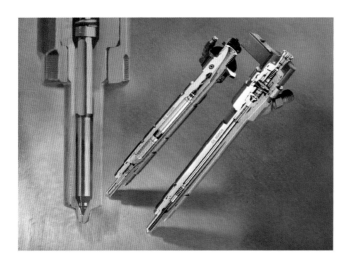

A regular solenoid-activated injector (right) compared with the faster-reacting piezoelectric type. The latter represented a giant leap forward in emission control, prompting all major parts suppliers to harness piezo technology. Bosch

Eventually the SCR system was refined for use on diesel engines, first in maritime and rail applications, and then trucks. Some manufacturers chose metals as catalysts, including precious metals (a different headache to overcome), while others went down the ceramics route in a bid to enhance sustainability and durability. Many, however, chose to stick with ammonia, and the use of urea (also known as carbamide) is now the common alternative, as it is easier and safer to store and handle than ammonia. An interesting bonus is that carbon dioxide is combined with ammonia in the creation of urea, thus making good use of

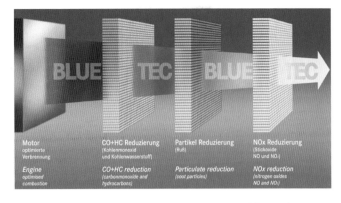

ABOVE: **Mercedes-Benz document showing the basic BlueTec cleaning process in simplified terms.** Daimler AG

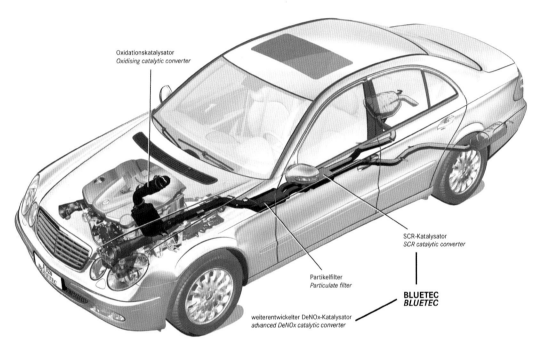

ABOVE & RIGHT: **The BlueTec system on the original W211-series E320, which came without urea injection. The award-winning 3-litre V6 24v turbodiesel was launched as a 2007 model in America, and was sold as the E300 in Europe from the summer of 2007 onwards. To meet ever-stricter regulations, the US version was duly updated with urea injection for 2008.**

Daimler AG

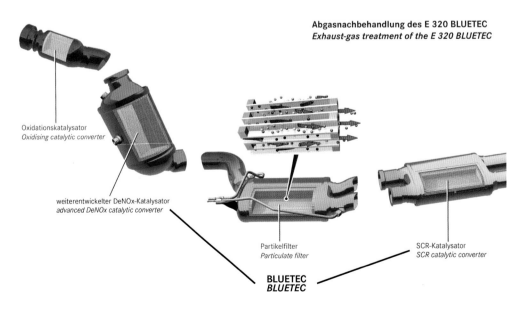

CO_2 emissions, and balancing the CO_2 created when urea is liquefied by adding water to this otherwise solid organic compound.

In 2004, Daimler-Benz announced that it would be introducing a urea-based SCR system for its larger Mercedes-Benz passenger cars – a scaled-down version of that already in use on its commercial vehicles. Depending on the engine size and overall vehicle weight, the modular set-up, market-ed under the BlueTec moniker, could be tailored to reduce costs and best suit packaging restraints.

Combined with the testing of SunDiesel biomass synthetic fuel, this was part of Mercedes' long-term plan to comply with Euro 4 (2005) standards in the EEC and America's 2007 regulations, and was aimed more at the reduction of NOx gases than particulate matter – the German company, along with others in the automotive business, was already fairly

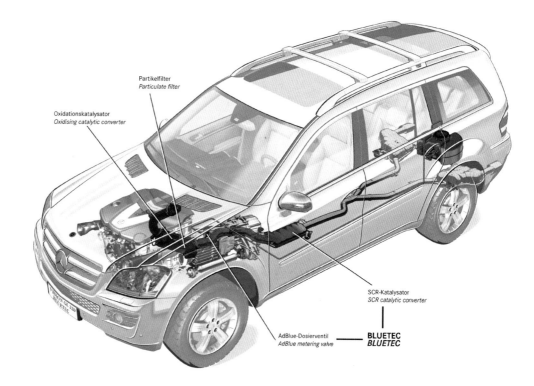

The BlueTec set-up on the larger Mercedes GL-Class, which demanded a urea injection system. Daimler AG

Partikelfilter
Particulate filter

Oxidationskatalysator
Oxidising catalytic converter

SCR-Katalysator
SCR catalytic converter

AdBlue-Dosierventil
AdBlue metering valve

BLUETEC
BLUETEC

Abgasnachbehandlung des Vision GL 320 BLUETEC
Exhaust-gas treatment of the Vision GL 320 BLUETEC

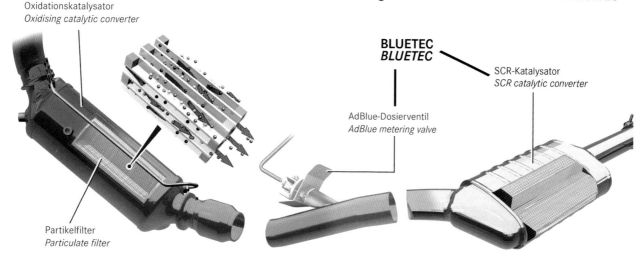

Oxidationskatalysator
Oxidising catalytic converter

Partikelfilter
Particulate filter

BLUETEC
BLUETEC

AdBlue-Dosierventil
AdBlue metering valve

SCR-Katalysator
SCR catalytic converter

confident that PM could be controlled without much effort, mainly thanks to new injectors prompting better combustion, and modifications to the exhaust system, including enhanced filtering.

The key components in the Mercedes SCR system are a diesel oxidation catalyst (often shortened to DOC: a precious metal catalyst that converts carbon monoxide and hydrocarbons into carbon dioxide and water), a NOx absorber catalyst (a NAC, known as a DeNOx-Katalysator in Stuttgart) that firstly traps and then removes oxides of nitrogen as it regenerates with a richer mixture and gives off a measured release of ammonia in the process, a PM filter of some sort, and an SCR cat which treats exhaust gases that have had ammonia (or urea fluid) mixed with them to cause a chemical reaction, converting any remaining NOx gases into harmless nitrogen and water. Generally, depending on the application, the urea fluid (called 'AdBlue' in Mercedes blurb) is stored in a container in the luggage compartment and injected into the exhaust stream just before the SCR unit; in this case, the NAC component is not required.

Launched via the 2007 MY W211-series E320 BlueTec turbo-diesel model in America, and equipped with the more elegantly engineered DeNOx-Katalysator set-up, the Blue-Tec model promised better fuel economy due to its lighter weight (the V6 block was made from aluminium alloy – a world first for a diesel engine), improved burn efficiency thanks to the 4-valve per cylinder combustion chambers and the latest common-rail injection system with piezo injectors, and deletion of any power-draining exhaust gas recirculation (EGR) systems from the engine design. It also delivered a cut in CO and HC emissions, a reduction in PM emissions via

Nissan's M9R engine was used in the X-Trail. Such was the rarity of diesel engines in Japan at the time, Nissan demonstrated the vehicle at the 2008 G8 Summit in Hokkaido, complete with plenty of white cloth on hand to show how clean the exhaust emissions were. Nissan

a particulate trap and higher injection pressures, and NOx levels were reduced by up to 50 per cent via the DeNOx and SCR systems.

With the use of the AdBlue injection system, introduced on the larger GL-, ML- and R-Class SUVs, as well as being employed on the E320 for the 2008 season, NOx levels were cut by up to 80 per cent.

Like many catalysts, however, the efficiency of the SCR system is negligible until the engine has been running for a while to generate enough heat for a chemical reaction to take place. There is also the worry of urea build-up on the catalyst surface, and instances of ammonia slip (when unburnt ammonia escapes through the exhaust pipe), which can actually create a chemical reaction that reverses the good work of the SCR set-up.

Far less technical but just as important, there is also the fear of vehicles running unchecked without a supply of urea (or DEF, standing for diesel exhaust fluid), which then means emissions are up to ten times higher than they should be according to catalogue specifications – unscrupulous owners have the chance to avoid the additional costs and time involved in keeping DEF topped up, because unlike running out of fuel, when an engine will simply stop, running out of DEF makes next to no difference in a vehicle's operation from the driver's point of view.

On the practical side, too, one needs a urea container (or a tank on larger vehicles, as urea consumption is generally speaking 5 per cent that of diesel consumption) and a complicated control system, which takes up space and adds weight, and a suitable infrastructure system for DEF distribution. Also, the relatively high cost of urea has already taken a few by surprise.

For this reason, and the fact that further work was needed to comply with California regulations at the time of the E320 launch, requiring a move up from the DeNOx-Katalysator set-up to the more expensive urea-injection system used by the Mercedes SUVs, not everyone was fully behind the idea. It soon became apparent, however, that this was the way to go, and while Volkswagen had been looking into using a NOx storage catalyst (NSC), the VW-Audi Group ultimately licensed the BlueTec technology, even using the BlueTec name until August 2007, before concentrating on promoting its own TDI brand.

Most of the smaller VW engines didn't need the SCR system, as it happens, since emissions were within limits without it. Nowadays, modern TDI engines use a combination of a DOC converter with an integrated, self-cleaning DPF filter, a low-pressure EGR system, a NAC cat, and a hydrogen sulphide slip catalyst, the latter being introduced to eliminate any toxic H_2S gases (and smell) from the exhaust.

The high-performance, 3-litre six, which **BMW** introduced in August 2006. Endowed with 286bhp, the twin-turbo unit has won several major awards, and eventually found its way to American shores in 2008. BMW

While Toyota continued down the hybrid road in most countries, Honda was looking at the use of diesel engines combined with advanced catalytic converters that eliminated the need for urea injection. Indeed, in September 2006 Honda announced an emissions control system similar in principle to the Mercedes DeNOx-Katalysator one for use on the all-alloy 2.2-litre i-DTEC engine for the 2007 MY Accord for the European market, and was hoping to have a 50-State car ready for America in 2009, although the latter plan never came to fruition.

This type of cat, relying on NOx and ammonia absorption layers in the converter (usually platinum-based) and the ECU adjusting the air-fuel ratio from lean to rich and back again in order to generate the right gases at the right time to first create and then release ammonia, is often called a lean NOx catalyst (LNC) or lean NOx trap (LNT), sometimes giving rise to the LNT-SCR combination.

Nissan also followed this route in its own way, announcing an HC-NOx trap in August 2007, the chemical reactions in the cat in a rich mixture phase converting oxygen and hydrocarbons into hydrogen and carbon monoxide, which in turn react with the gases captured in the NOx-trap layer to produce nitrogen, carbon dioxide and water vapour. The system was made all the more efficient by Nissan's modulated kinetics (MK) technology, reducing NOx and soot emissions in the engine itself via the use of an EGR system (with inte-

grated cooler) that allowed an exhaust-diluted combustion phase combined with a longer ignition delay to encourage a more complete burn under light load conditions.

In the truck world, while most makers on both sides of the Atlantic have followed the BlueTec route, Caterpillar was looking into ways of cleaning up NOx emissions without a catalyst (what would be termed an SNCR system), basing the engine on ACERT technology, introduced in 2003, and which fine-tuned the combustion process, eliminated EGR and treated PM. Things then went quiet until the maker introduced the 2011 CT660 truck for the US market, its engines clearing the tough 'EPA 2010' regulations without urea SCR – but ultimately an Advanced EGR system was required, and engine production was farmed out to Navistar, who developed this exhaust gas recirculation technology.

There is nothing that unusual about V8 diesel engines, but the 6-litre V12 from Audi was certainly an exotic powerplant for a road car. Introduced as a prototype at the 2006 Paris Salon for use in the Q7 SUV, and aping the V12 configuration of the Audi LMP racers, sales officially began in 2008. There were rumours that the reign of the 500bhp TDI unit was to be short-lived, supposedly being phased out in 2011, but sales continued in mainland Europe as this book was being completed in the early part of 2012.

Meanwhile, Subaru announced another novel engine at the 2008 Geneva show: a turbocharged boxer four with an

Although hints had been given in 2007, including motor show displays, it wasn't until the 2008 Geneva Show that the 4-cylinder horizontally opposed Subaru diesel engine made its official debut. Subaru

Only with a man like Ferdinand Piech at the helm can engineering marvels such as this – the 6-litre V12 TDI engine from Audi – be allowed to surface. Audi

DIESEL RACING AND RECORD CARS

For anyone who grew up watching *Grand Prix* or *Le Mans* on the big screen, reading *MotorSport* by torchlight under the blankets, hours after your parents had assumed you'd gone to sleep, the thought of a diesel racing car is about as foreign as an English fish and chip shop serving up nouveau cuisine in yesterday's newspapers. However, it's no longer an unthinkable scenario, and a little research reveals that it's hardly a new idea, either.

Clessie Cummins, who had purchased manufacturing rights to the diesel engine in 1919, led the way in America, setting several diesel speed records in the 1930s; he built the first diesel car to enter the Indianapolis 500. With Dave Evans at the wheel, the Cummins machine (based on a modified Duesenberg chassis) finished the 1931 maiden run in thirteenth place, completing the 500 miles (800km) without the need for a pit stop. Other Indy outings followed thanks to Cummins' enthusiasm, the last coming in 1952, with the beautiful Frank Kurtis-designed open-wheeler playing host to a 6.6-litre turbocharged straight-six that delivered 380bhp. The car was running well until track debris clogged the turbocharger and the engine failed.

In Europe, Peugeot was one of the first to try and enhance the appeal of the CI engine by setting speed records. The French maker had been selling diesel versions of the 403 since 1959, and after its successor (the 404) was launched, a convertible was given a streamlined top and sent to Montlhéry in June 1965. There it set twenty-two international records with a 2-litre engine, and eighteen more in the following month after receiving a slightly larger 2163cc unit.

The Cummins Diesel Special at Indianapolis in 1952.
Cummins

Engine bay of the experimental Mercedes C111-II. Daimler AG

The Germans were the next to use speed as a promotional tool, with the second version of the Mercedes-Benz C111 prototype series being fitted with a 5-cylinder turbocharged diesel engine in 1976. Hitting a top speed of 253km/h (157mph), it set sixteen records at the Nardo track in Italy; however, it was quickly overshadowed by the more aerodynamic C111-III, which achieved a remarkable 327km/h (203mph) at Nardo and set a number of international endurance records along the way in April 1978.

There was still prejudice, however, although BMW and Volkswagen tried to overcome it by entering diesel-powered machines in certain touring car races. A great deal of good publicity was obtained when a BMW 320d led home a gaggle of other 3-series models to win the 1998 Nürburgring 24-hour race.

A key point in the Nürburgring victory was superior fuel efficiency, allowing the Schnitzer Motorsport team to make fewer pit stops during the marathon event. This was the first major race win for a diesel car, but many would follow as we entered the twenty-first century, with wins coming for SEAT in the WTCC and BTCC, Volkswagen in the gruelling Dakar Rally, and for Audi and Peugeot LMP cars at the ultimate motorsport venue, Le Mans.

In the meantime, JCB built the JCB Dieselmax streamliner to challenge the FIA diesel land speed record, set in August 1973 by a US team using the Thermo King streamliner. This American machine had sped across the Bonneville Salt Flats at 380km/h (236mph), but in 2006, the 1500bhp British contender was ultimately clocked at a fraction over 563km/h

(350mph), thus smashing the record by a considerable margin. In some ways it was a mirror image of the rapid progress being made in diesel road cars – the gap between those of the oil shock days and those of today never being more apparent than in the heat of competition.

The Audi R18 TDI that won Le Mans in 2011. Now Audi is working on a mild hybrid version of the car. Audi

alloy block and EGR for emissions control. Endowed with 148bhp and excellent torque characteristics due to a variable-nozzle turbo, the 2-litre unit found service in the Legacy and Outback models, and was eventually sold worldwide, making its way to American shores for the 2010 season.

The variable-nozzle turbo (VNT) – also referred to as a variable-geometry turbo (VGT), a variable-vane turbine (VVT) or a variable-turbine geometry turbocharger (VTG) – has been around in the car world since the late 1980s, but was found to be particularly suitable for the new breed of turbo-diesels, as the lower exhaust temperatures – compared to those found in petrol engines – aided reliability. The basic principle is much the same, however, with movable vanes on the turbine on the intake side, their angles being controlled by the engine management system to optimize turbocharger performance according to engine speed. As well as enhancing fuel economy, the key benefit is that it allows high boost pressures at low rpm, producing a flatter torque curve and reducing turbo-lag.

JAPAN AND 'CLEAN DIESEL'

In Japan the situation is much as it was in Britain in the 1970s and early 1980s: diesel is still largely seen as a fuel almost exclusively for commercial vehicles, despite the fact that in recent years several makers have been given awards for diesel technology, including Isuzu, Mercedes-Benz and Nissan.

About ten years ago, the author saw a flat white rail on a train station platform above a main road in Tokyo peppered with tiny balls of black soot; many current 'clean diesel' machines emit the same type of PM from their exhaust pipes – granted, in far smaller quantities than ever before, thanks to superior combustion technology and particulate filters, but the PM that does make it past the DPF into the atmosphere is significantly smaller, allowing it to enter the respiratory system that much more easily. The filters are also very critical on fuel quality, and to remain efficient they require heat that can rarely be attained on short runs.

Thus in reality, for 'clean' one should be reading 'not so dirty' – but Japanese journalists are taught not to question things even if they can see a problem, and press releases are generally quoted verbatim with little in the way of personal opinion or insight finding its way on to the pages of newspapers and magazines. Ultimately, brave words simply result in raised eyebrows followed by exile, but you only get to know this after having been on the inside.

Diesel is never going to disappear from Japan's roads – the trucking associations linked to prominent politicians and the myriad delivery companies that thrive in the Land of the Rising Sun will see to that. But at least the latter are starting to adopt diesel-electric hybrid vehicles, and the few new cars that are on sale are as clean as modern technology allows – in other words, very clean. Unfortunately, however, there are still too many rogue operators who spoil all the hard work the engineers have put in. The Japanese therefore have two images: diesel is either filthy or clean, with nothing in between.

A little balanced education, stricter regulations on vehicles already in use, and sensible future emission targets rather than those proposed (that simply make new machines more expensive through additional requirements, taking them even further out of reach of the smaller business), would not only allow today's diesel cars to make a breakthrough in the Japanese marketplace, it would also make them worthy in our need to balance environmental concerns with practicality.

'GREEN' FUELS: THE CASE FOR BIO-DIESEL

Bio-fuels have been with us for over a century in one form or another. They were being promoted as the fuel of the future not long after the start of the Great Depression, but just as the idea became practical, failed to make an impact in the marketplace, largely for political reasons.

As a matter of interest, it should be noted that although Rudolf Diesel had always considered mineral oils as the obvious choice for fuel, he was more than happy for his engines to run on bio-fuels, and demonstrated them at the 1900 World's Fair (held that year in Paris) running on peanut oil. Many years later, in 1912, he stated: 'The use of vegetable oils for engine fuels may seem insignificant today, but such oils may become – in the course of time – as important as petroleum and the coal-tar products of the present time.'

The oil barons, protected by those in power who obviously considered it patriotic to keep the wealth of the nation within known entities, had already had a bearing on bio-fuel production, and many diesel engines, especially those used in maritime applications, were set up to run specifically on heavy fuel (often referred to as 'bunker fuel'), which tends to be cheap to buy and easy to store.

Notwithstanding, bio-fuel was all set for a real breakthrough thanks to the fast-growing hemp plant. George Schlichten's decorticator, ultimately patented in America in July 1919 in its final form, made light work of separating the plant's outer fibres from the centre, dramatically saving time and labour in preparing the hemp for its multitude of industrial uses, as well as leading to less wastage of the crop.

The cellulose from hemp could be used for a multitude of things. Henry Ford was investigating the possibilities of using ethanol prepared from hemp as a fuel for automobiles: acre for acre, ultimate yields were almost four times higher than those of typical forestland used by the paper industry, and then there were plastics and more traditional applications, such as rope.

But therein lay the problem: this wonder plant was set to undermine the power of the American establishment, and start cutting into profit margins. Anxious to protect 'Big Oil' interests and those of DuPont (which had come up with a new sulphuric acid process for producing wood-pulp paper, as well as nylon, a synthetic polymer that would find use as a replacement for rayon and much more besides), and backed by the banking magnate and Treasury Secretary, Andrew Mellon, a slur campaign was set in motion. Using William Hearst's publishing empire to spread the word – which in turn protected Hearst's interests in the huge swathes of forest he owned – the campaign was largely managed by the Federal Bureau of Narcotics (FBN), formed via a merger of two older departments on Mellon's instructions in 1930.

With only around 500 tons of hemp being produced per year in the early 1930s, it was fairly easy to quash the fledgling industry without too much backlash, and citing the abuse of marijuana disguised the political blocking on the growth of industrial hemp – two quite different substances, but easy to confuse, given that they come from the same source. Ultimately, the crafty Marijuana Tax Act was passed in 1937, drafted by Harry J. Anslinger, Commissioner of the FBN, who just so happened to be married to Mellon's niece. This put an end to any hopes of ever making full use of hemp's potential.

Interestingly, German submarines used bio-diesel during World War II, not only because of the supply guarantee, but also due to the lower level of noxious fumes – a good idea in an enclosed space, but it also points to technical knowledge that somehow got lost along the way.

Nowadays, bio-fuels (including bio-diesel and the closely related synthetic diesel) are once again being looked at, but with a far more open mind than in the thirties, as the ideal answer when looking for a fuel for the future – a renewable energy source, reducing our dependence on oil, with relatively low overall emission levels.

The best known of the bio-diesels currently on the market is fatty-acid methyl ester (FAME), obtained from a trans-esterification catalytic reaction using vegetable oils (such as rapeseed or soybean oil) or animal fats combined with methanol or ethanol to produce methyl or ethyl esters. The glycerine created by the process – first patented by Charles G. Chavanne of the University of Brussels in 1937 – is sep-

arated and used elsewhere, while remaining traces of the alcohols are recovered and used again.

Many newer engines can use this form of bio-diesel in its pure state (the so-called B100 grade) without any problem, but it is usually blended with petroleum-based diesel – as examples, B30 fuel contains 30 per cent bio-diesel, the popular B20 has 20 per cent, while B5 contains five per cent; B2 is typically the grade with the lowest ratio of bio-diesel content.

Why go for such small percentages when B100 is available? Well, there are still concerns over warranties that need to be addressed when using pure bio-diesel, as older engines (usually built before 1994) revealed unexpected hose, gasket and seal failures, while some makers have pointed to injector corrosion and fuel-line blockage. It's also not a good idea to leave B100 in a fuel tank for an extended length of time, as bacteria growth is common, and dilution of oil in the engine sump has been known to happen on occasion.

The B20 and B30 blends provide significantly better cold-weather performance than B100 (pure bio-diesel can gel quite easily on days when the air temperature drops below freezing), so are necessary in some colder environments, and also have far less particulate matter and NOx in the exhaust – with B100, while the release of some toxic gases is cut dramatically, emissions of nitrous oxides are actually greater than with regular diesel.

However, tests using bio-diesel on vehicles with SCR systems to clean up NOx have shown no ill effects. There are some concerns that unwanted build-up on catalyst surfaces may occur in extreme long-term usage (around 650,000km/400,000 miles) if the fuel contains its maximum allowable traces of magnesium, potassium, sodium and calcium – elements used in certain stages of bio-fuel processing. Generally speaking, though, the traces in fuel supplied to the public are virtually non-existent, failing to register in the 1ppm range. On the subject of cats, Ford's research has also concluded that hydrocarbon poisoning is not an issue, as HC emissions are lower with bio-diesel compared to ULSD fuel.

The lower-content grades are basically there for those with older engines, as the bio-diesel element largely replaces the lubrication qualities previously obtained through sulphur. The cetane number (CN) is also lower on fuels with lower bio-diesel content, encouraging cleaner burning (the lower the cetane number, the faster the fuel will ignite) and therefore reducing carbon build-up on internal engine components, as well as cutting NOx emissions.

The 'tonne of oil equivalent' (toe) unit of measure is very useful in gauging burn efficiency. An actual metric tonne of crude oil releases 42 billion joules (GJ) of energy when burnt, which is therefore considered one toe unit. A tonne of diesel gives a rating of 1.01 toe, against 1.05 for petrol. Unfortunately, the current range of bio-fuels are not able to reach these levels of efficiency, with bio-diesel giving 0.86, and bio-ethanol, touted as an alternative to petrol, a lowly 0.64.

The big difference, of course, is the sustainability element. Rapeseed gives more oil per acre than soybeans, so one can often see fields of yellow nowadays, which is not only pleasing on the eye, but is also a totally renewable source of energy.

In addition, while it's ironic that CO_2 emissions increase by about 5 per cent at the tailpipe on vehicles running with B100 compared to conventional diesel, the absorption of carbon dioxide by the leaves of plants used in bio-diesel production cancels this out several times over – the so-called 'CO_2-negative' situation turning a disadvantage into an advantage. With the B20 blend, CO_2 emissions are only 1 per cent higher than those recorded with regular diesel, so the nett result is even better for the environment.

The only real drawback is that almost two-thirds of rape-seed production goes towards bio-diesel nowadays, and the nitrogen-rich fertilizers used, as well as the preparation of the land itself, can release a lot of nitrous oxide into the atmosphere. Large amounts of N_2O entering the atmos-phere tends to undo some of the good work of bio-diesel – significant reductions in emissions of sulphur oxides and sulphates, carbon monoxide, unburned hydrocarbons and particulate matter; there is also evidence of a reduction in health risks associated with burning diesel fuel.

Bio-diesel made from certain vegetable oils (such as rape-seed and corn) are now known as 'first generation' bio-fuels. There are many other alternative sources of traditional feedstock (the proper word for the base product used in bio-fuel production), such as oil from soybeans (though this is also quite heavy on the release of N_2O), palm oil, coco-nut oil, peanut oil, sunflower oil, and even an old favourite, hemp, although the latter's yields are considered quite low in today's terms.

Newer alternatives use feedstock crops not usually associ-ated with food – ideal candidates include the jatropha plant, the camelina plant, the Chinese tallow tree, the seashore mallow plant and so-called 'energy grasses', which tend to provide higher yields along the way in terms of product per acre, or allow more of the product to be converted – and feedstock from waste (such as woodchips, tallow, or even used ground coffee beans): these are known as 'second gen-eration' bio-fuels, and tend to point the way to the future.

Algae is also being looked at as a 'third generation' bio-fuel, building on technology that first came to light in the late 1970s, as the yield per acre is far superior to crops – up to eighteen times better than rapeseed, twenty-two times higher than sunflower, and a staggering thirty times better than soybean. It also comes with the added benefits that it doesn't clash with food production, CO_2 is absorbed in much the same way as crops, and the fertilizer and field-burning issue is non-existent. While Shell has abandoned the latter, Chevron is still pursuing the idea.

At the same time, Joule Unlimited of Massachusetts is working with a mixture of bacteria, sunlight, wastewater and carbon dioxide emissions from factories and power stations to make diesel fuel. With people trying to get rid of CO_2 via schemes that are often of questionable worth, on the face of it, with only oxygen as a by-product, this sounds like a good way forwards.

From an environmental point of view, however, all these options need following through, because according to a recent EPA study, compared with petroleum-based diesel, bio-diesel produced from soybeans resulted in a 57 per cent overall reduction of lifecycle greenhouse gases, while that made from waste cooking oil (sometimes referred to as yel-low grease) brought about an 86 per cent reduction.

The waste vegetable oil (WVO) option is particularly attractive, because it uses something that would otherwise have to be disposed of. Waste cooking oil is therefore more 'Green' by default, and with America alone dealing with 11 billion litres of the stuff each year, it can supply about 1 per cent of the nation's fuel needs for very little effort, without having to wait for something to grow, as in the case of pure bio-diesel.

In many ways, it's the ultimate form of recycling, although it has to be said that it's impossible to make good quality fuel from all of it, and a suitable filtering system is needed to remove fatty acids, impurities, contaminants and water before the WVO can be processed into fuel – the latter is not required when dealing with straight vegetable oil (SVO) or pure plant oil (PPO), which is prepared for bio-diesel use from the start.

Converting WVO into diesel fuel is not a new idea, having been around since the 1980s, but recently, thanks to a new level of environmental awareness, the concept has taken off. The latest process involves converting the triglycerides found in vegetable oil and animal fats into a bio-gas oil via catalytic hydrogenation, and offers many advantages over transesterification in the by-product stakes. The resulting fuel is also more stable to store, with no oxygen (unlike FAME) and few aromatics.

This type of fuel can be blended with regular diesel in ratios of up to 50 per cent without any worries concerning the need for engine or fuel-delivery system modifications. Running a car with pure WVO requires certain changes, usually relating to ways of reducing viscosity (even keeping the fuel in a liquid state in cold weather), and clearing fuel lines with petroleum-based diesel on starting up and closing down the engine.

Coming back to second and third generation bio-fuels proper, fractional distillation can be used on vegetable oil or certain forms of algae to create so-called 'Green Diesel'. There is also a largely experimental ethanol-based diesel fuel (ED95) on the market, while BP and Martek Biosciences Corporation are working together on a promising sugar-to-diesel process.

Dimethylether (DME) provides another option, offering cleaner CO, PM and NOx values when burnt, but this synthetic diesel fuel is highly flammable, fairly expensive to produce, and requires larger storage tanks if a vehicle's range cannot be compromised. It is therefore finding better use in petrol blending.

Other forms of synthetic fuel are also starting to get a foothold. Paraffinic synthetic diesel has about the same cetane number as B100, and can be produced in several ways, but the basic principle is always the same – the raw material must contain a reasonable amount of carbon, which is then gasified and made into syngas (a mixture of carbon monoxide and hydrogen) before being converted into a liquid via the Fischer-Tropsch system. The process, invented by Franz Fischer and Hans Tropsch in the 1920s, then uses cracking (the application of heat and a catalyst) to separate waste hydrocarbons from usable diesel fuel.

Synthetic diesel can be made from biomass (BTL), making use of waste wood, or new plants with the advantage of being able to use all the material, unlike processes involving transesterification, which generally use only selected parts of the plant. It can also be created from bio-gas or natural gas (GTL), or coal (CTL); the process allowing the latter transformation was perfected by the Germans in the mid-1930s, building on earlier technology developed by Friedrich Bergius, it being ideal for a country with vast coal resources but no oil reserves.

Perfect for blending with petroleum-based diesel, as well as using largely renewable sources of energy (especially in BTL form), paraffinic synthetic diesel has a very low aromatics content, reducing HC, NOx and PM emissions, and is virtually free of sulphur, making it kinder on catalytic converters.

According to Volkswagen's calculations, synthetic diesel made from BTL methods can reduce lifecycle emissions (biomass to tailpipe in this particular case) by very worthwhile amounts when compared to regular petro-diesel – carbon dioxide is reduced by between 60 and 90 per cent, methane by around 90 per cent (thus helping to keep smog in check),

sulphur dioxide by between 3 and 30 per cent (reducing the chances of acid rain), while NOx emissions are down by an average of between 5 and 40 per cent. In addition, it doesn't smell when burnt and gives off less smoke, and it is easy to store and handle, too, all of which prompted the George W. Bush administration to hail it as the fuel of the future.

Bush's government duly provided enormous funding for further research, but this has been scaled back under President Obama, probably due to the upfront costs involved in setting up the facilities to house the complicated refining process. Notwithstanding, the German SunDiesel project and others like it in other countries are showing the way forward, happy to invest in the long-term future of the planet rather than short-term profit.

MORE RECENT INNOVATIONS

The long-term 'Green' answer for diesel seems to lie to a great extent in the promotion of relatively small-capacity diesel engines running on second or third generation bio-fuels (such as that based on algae feedstock, and BTL synthetic diesel, recommended by the French government in a recent 2011 report as the most promising route to take), and making better use of things such as recycled waste cooking oils as another alternative for filling the fuel tank. The sustainability element combined with cleaner emissions has to be the right formula for the future, and quite rightly a lot of effort is currently being directed towards bio-fuel production. In the meantime, while advances in chemistry seem to be making all the headlines, automobile manufacturers have been busy introducing new technology for existing

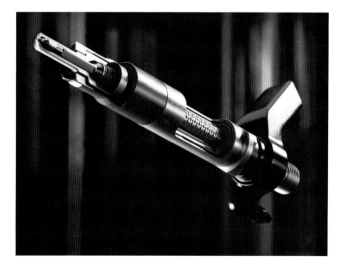

Continental's piezo injector with direct drive and closed-loop needle control, introduced in 2008. Continental

vehicle ranges, coming up with a number of innovative ideas in a bid to clean up diesel emissions once and for all.

A few years after the birth of the first piezoelectric injectors, itself a huge technological leap, we were already starting to see them evolve. Manufactured with tolerances of just one micron, the latest piezo-actuated injectors can react so quickly to the engine management system that it's possible to deliver up to nine lots of fuel spray per compression cycle, promoting a more complete burn that lowers NOx and PM emissions, and smoother operation with reduced levels of noise and vibration.

In the middle of 2008, Continental announced that it had added position sensing to the needle, thus giving the potential to eliminate other sensors, simplifying things and therefore speeding up data processing to give the cleanest possible burn. Figures released by the company noted a 35 per cent reduction in particulate matter and NOx, meaning that it becomes possible – in theory at least – to make more and more diesel engines without the need for costly NOx after-treatment systems.

On the subject of NOx cleaning technology, America's Argonne National Laboratory (attached to the DOE) announced in 2008 that it had developed a new catalyst for diesel engines that could potentially cut NOx emissions by up to 95 per cent in a truly cost-effective manner. A ceramic brick was coated in a special material made up mainly of copper and cerium, using the chemicals found in diesel fuel (in particular, the hydrocarbons contained within) to convert exhaust gases to nitrogen, and the presence of water simply made it more effective. This was a perfect scenario

for OEMs and retrofitting, especially for those dealing with larger passenger vehicles and/or trucks, but manufacturing has been held up for the time being for a number of reasons.

Following hot on the heels of the Argonne catalyst came news that the Eaton Corporation (a name one usually associates with Roots superchargers, but a look at their background reveals an automotive division of far broader scope) had signed a licensing agreement with Clean Diesel Technology to market the latter's Advanced Reagent Injector System (ARIS). This also used diesel fuel to set off a catalytic reaction that lowers NOx emissions, and as such is classed as a Hydrocarbon-SCR (HC-SCR) catalyst.

Tenneco Automotive was also looking into ways of making General Electric's HC-SCR technology work on off-road transport, with a view to marketing it for road vehicles at a later date. Based on an unusual silver catalyst, it was able to work using diesel or E85 ethanol as a reductant, while Hino in Japan announced that successful trials of its own HC-SCR had been completed in 2011, allowing production to go ahead. Furthermore a number of companies around the world are also working on solid urea cats to reduce NOx without the need to deal with fluids.

Smaller engines used in economy cars do not create that much in the way of NOx emissions, so the spring of 2010 saw Delphi take a different route to piezo injectors for the 1.2-litre Volkswagen Polo BlueMotion. For this model, with the cost-performance ratio high on the agenda, Delphi's engineers (led by John Fuerst) upped the pressure on the common-rail system to 2400 bar via a new pump, combined this with improvements in the engine control system and

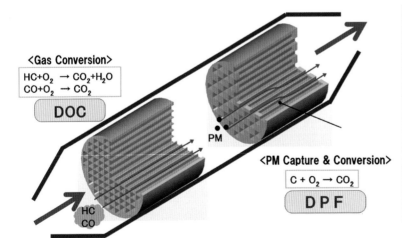

<Gas Conversion>

$$HC + O_2 \rightarrow CO_2 + H_2O$$
$$CO + O_2 \rightarrow CO_2$$

DOC

PM

<PM Capture & Conversion>

$$C + O_2 \rightarrow CO_2$$

DPF

HC
CO

Diesel Exhaust Gas

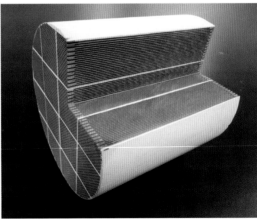

A combined DOC-DPF unit from Panasonic, the graphic showing the way exhaust emissions are cleaned, while the other shot shows a diesel particulate filter coated in a special alkali metal-based catalyst developed by Panasonic Ecology Systems. This reduces the need to rely on precious metals such as platinum. Panasonic

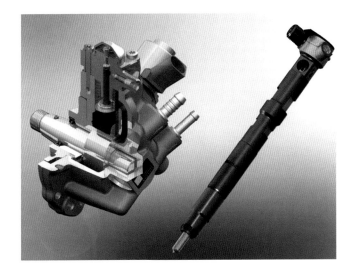

The Delphi injectors and pump used on the 1.2-litre Volkswagen Polo BlueMotion engine. Delphi

First introduced on petrol engines in the 1980s, idle-stop systems took a long while to take off commercially, but as reaction times were reduced year-on-year, they had become fairly commonplace as we entered the new millennia, creating the so-called 'Micro-Hybrid' vehicle category. The latest Ford 'Auto-Start-Stop' system employed on the 1.6 litre TDCi turbo-diesel unit is said to react in 0.3 seconds, whilst reducing fuel consumption and CO_2 emissions by an average of 5 per cent, rising to as much as 10 per cent during heavy urban usage.

Petrol engine technology is starting to filter through in other areas, too. Mercedes-Benz has an interesting two-stage sequential turbocharger set-up on some of its smaller diesel engines, with one blower being used in low-load conditions, and a larger one kicking in at higher revs when more pick-up is needed. This technology was originally featured on the OM651 engine (a straight four with a cast-iron block), a unit that was first installed in the C250 CDI, launched just in time for the 2009 season.

This elegant twin-turbo engineering solution was also introduced on the contemporary Lancia Delta 1900 MJET Twin-Turbo model, and the BMW 740d, powered by an all-alloy, 3-litre six. This 306bhp machine made its debut in mid-2009 as an early 2010 model. The single-turbo version, the 730d, was offered with a 'BluePerformance' cat set-up

servo-solenoid-activated injectors, and added a fast-acting idle-stop mechanism. The end result was a car that could, given the right conditions, cover 30km (19 miles) on a litre of fuel, whilst releasing just 87g of carbon dioxide for each kilometre travelled.

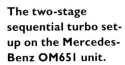

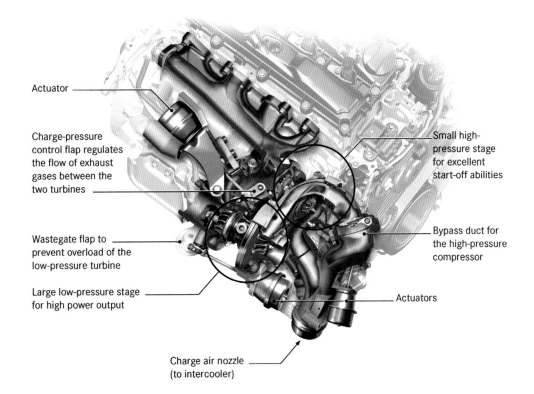

The two-stage sequential turbo set-up on the Mercedes-Benz OM651 unit.

Daimler AG

Actuator

Charge-pressure control flap regulates the flow of exhaust gases between the two turbines

Wastegate flap to prevent overload of the low-pressure turbine

Large low-pressure stage for high power output

Small high-pressure stage for excellent start-off abilities

Bypass duct for the high-pressure compressor

Actuators

Charge air nozzle (to intercooler)

Mitsubishi's 4N13 in motor-show display guise. Mitsubishi

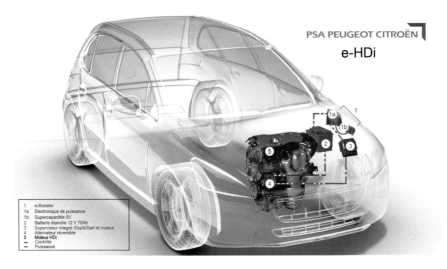

PSA PEUGEOT CITROËN
e-HDi

1	e-Booster
1a	Electronique de puissance
1b	Supercapacités 5V
2	Batterie étanche 12 V 70Ah
3	Superviseur intégré Stop&Start et moteur
4	Alternateur réversible
5	Moteur HDi
—	Contrôle
—	Puissance

at the same time, with a NOx storage catalyst augmenting the existing oxidation one, and the DPF to enable the car to pass the forthcoming EURO 6 emissions regulations.

Hyundai also jumped on the two-stage turbocharger (TST) bandwagon for its new U2 1.7-litre engine, and the latest 2.2-litre R-series unit with low-pressure EGR. Intercoolers are also becoming widely used on turbocharged engines, particularly those found within the VW-Audi Group.

Meanwhile, the Mitsubishi 4N13 became the first diesel engine to feature variable valve timing. This 1798cc four made its debut at the 2010 Geneva Show – an engineering gem, with piezo-injection linked to a common-rail system, a very low 14.9:1 compression ratio to keep NOx emissions in check (the use of a lower c/r is one of the beauties of direct injection, or DI, although particulate matter becomes more of a problem), and a special variable diffuser turbocharger, made by Mitsubishi Heavy Industries. The twin-cam, 16-valve unit was used on the ASX (known as the RVR in Japan) and Lancer, and a 2268cc version was also produced (the 175bhp 4N14) for the larger Outlander model.

As it happens, Mitsubishi have been unusual in offering a domestic range of diesel-powered road cars for some years, on and off, as most Japanese makers have concentrated on petrol engines, and more recently, hybrids, for the home market. The larger one-box minivans and the Pajero sports-utility vehicle have virtually always been offered with a diesel option, although Nissan was one of the few to follow this lead at the start of the new millennium, launching a 'Clean Diesel' version of the X-Trail SUV (powered by the M9R unit, jointly developed with Renault) for Japan at the end of 2008.

Small but meaningful advances are being made all the time, now that diesel cars have found a ready market. It's a well-known fact that EGR coolers can increase efficiency, for

ABOVE: **The PSA Group started adding an idle-stop system to its petrol engines in 2004, but it wasn't until 2010 that the system could be adapted for use with high-compression diesel engines. Soon after, the 1.4-litre e-HDi unit made its debut, with the Valeo stop-start device (a special alternator with the ability to reverse and act as a starter motor on demand, using the alternator drive belt to turn the crankshaft and restart the engine in 0.4sec) which cut fuel consumption by up to 15 per cent in city driving.** Peugeot

BELOW: **The Mercedes E350 BlueTec engine on display at the last Tokyo Show. Note the oil cooler at the front, and the interesting display behind with giant molecules explaining the BlueTec system.** B. Long

ABOVE: **Renault started production of its 'Energy dCi 130' diesel engine at its Cléon site in April 2011. Coming with a high-swirl combustion chamber and low-pressure EGR, and combined with the latest in idle-stop technology and regenerative braking, the 130bhp 4-cylinder 16v unit cuts fuel consumption and CO$_2$ emissions by around 20 per cent.** Renault

LEFT: **A VW CCS engine, photographed in 2007.** Volkswagen

example. Tokyo Roki of Yokohama are therefore working on an EGR cooler module that simplifies the coolant and lubricant circuits, thereby reducing costs by 30 per cent, as well as cutting weight – both important factors on smaller-engined vehicles. Meanwhile, soot traps have been refined to the point where one can put a white handkerchief over the tailpipe exit and still have something white instead of black or grey a few minutes later.

Delphi recently announced that it was close to perfecting an engine control system that would allow HCCI (homogeneous charge compression ignition), PCCI (pre-mixed charge compression ignition) and LTC (low temperature combustion) power units to become a reality in the near future – the lack of a suitable control system for combustion phasing having been the only thing holding development back.

HCCI engines can run with very lean mixtures, but combustion timing has proved difficult to control, for, unlike in a conventional petrol or diesel engine, when either a spark or fuel are introduced at the right time to cause charge ignition, with an HCCI engine, the fuel-air charge ignites whenever the conditions inside the combustion chamber allow. One is therefore always seemingly reacting to what has happened, rather than instigating an event with precise, pre-set calibrations. Variable valve timing could provide part of the answer, along with direct injection of a pre-mixed charge (PCCI) and/or greater control over induction temperatures, but there is no easy solution as yet.

While Nissan is almost there with its 'Modulated Kinetics' system, the latest electronics may still yet unleash the full potential of HCCI technology, with lean mixtures promising fuel savings as high as 30 per cent, and cooler combustion temperatures reducing NOx emissions. Granted, CO and HC emissions are relatively high, but these can usually be kept in check fairly easily via the use of oxidation catalysts.

Volkswagen has done a lot of work on HCCI engines using diesel fuel, its combined combustion system (CCS) employing a homogeneous intake charge rather than the usual injection of diesel into the combustion chamber. The early success of prototype testing, combining the lower emissions of a petrol engine with the low fuel consumption of a diesel unit (with synthetic diesel, further improvements are noticeable,

The new Honda 1.6-litre diesel engine. Honda

with significant reductions in particulate matter and nitrous oxide emissions), points towards a possible 2015 launch date for this exciting technology.

Considering that heat is very often simply a form of wasted energy, low temperature combustion (LTC) is another area that is being explored, with leaner mixtures (including the options of PCCI and a partially pre-mixed charge, PPCI) lowering the temperature of combustion to reduce NOx emissions. With many current non-urea SCR systems using richer mixtures to form ammonia in catalytic converters, as there is no need for this in an LTC set-up, this cancels out the loss of efficiency (ultimately showing up as higher fuel consumption) caused by dropping the compression ratio. Toyota is known to be looking at LTC in conjunction with enhanced EGR systems.

Ultimately, today's stricter regulations call for balances more than ever, so one cannot simply go all-out for exceptional fuel economy, or at the other end of the scale, super-clean emissions, if the cost to the customer is too high.

CONCLUSION: DIESEL DOES HAVE A FUTURE

As the 2012 season dawned in the showrooms, virtually every car manufacturer in the world offered diesel engines in their line-up. Even if a model was restricted to certain European markets in many cases, the fact is they exist – an unthinkable situation only a couple of decades ago.

It seems ironic, given the level of Europe's current addiction to diesel, that America was quicker to foster the diesel engine than most other countries, yet it has always only ever accounted for a fairly small market share in recent times – only 5 per cent in 2007, for instance. However, the need to comply with CAFE figures has got makers thinking that diesel may be a way forwards, allowing them to retain their more exotic cars in the line-up.

The problem, of course, is that superior fuel economy and emissions are two different things, so only a few years ago, this would have been a very shortsighted plan – using gas mileage as a benchmark instead of exhaust gas content and tight limits on particulate matter. The new technology available for diesel brings sense back to the idea, however, and one only needs to look at the difference in the number of diesel vehicles available in the States during 2010, 2011 and 2012 (and the fact that American makers are already promising new diesel models for the 2013 season) to know that US sales are going to take off in a big way.

In Japan, too, the diesel boom is starting to take hold. At the 2011 Tokyo Show, Honda announced that it was downsizing its 2.2-litre diesel engine to a 1.6-litre unit, reducing internal friction, and optimizing each component to give maximum performance and minimum emissions. Changes to the cooling system alone are said to have realized a 15 per cent drop in CO_2 emissions.

Mazda also used the event to showcase its new diesel engine – the all-alloy, 2.2-litre Skyactiv-D with a two-stage turbocharger set-up. For this engine, Mazda adopted the world's lowest compression ratio for a diesel (just 14.0:1) in a bid to reduce NOx emissions at source, which in turn means that simplified exhaust gas after-treatment equipment can be employed, reducing cost and weight.

Mazda's engineers are basically bringing the benefits of LTC technology closer to reality, the lower c/r bringing about a more uniform burn of the air-fuel mix due to the delayed ignition of the injected fuel. This is the thing that reduces the localized high-temperature areas and oxygen insufficiencies that cause the formation of NOx and PM, and with combustion taking place closer to top-dead centre (TDC), efficiency is increased through a higher expansion ratio – the engine actually does more work for each drop of fuel. Tellingly, Mazda's catchphrase for the show was 'environmental technology, pushing the boundaries of the emotion of motion'.

For decades, other than the typical 'slow, noisy and smelly' preconceptions fired off by so many of us, diesel had escaped the wrath of journalists for one reason or another, when really it was totally undeserving of its 'Green' tag, its more latent bad points successfully managing to duck under the radar. However, thanks to today's current technology – like SCR, along with those due to make headlines in the near future – even the author has to admit that with the correct maintenance, diesel can indeed be kind to the environment, and not just from a CO_2 angle. Typically, in response to the strict EPA 2010 regulations, new trucks sold in America are sixty-five times cleaner than they were in 1988. To me, this shows not only a great advance, for which the manufacturers deserve a pat on the back, but also just how dirty older machines were (older machines that are all too often still in service, by the way!).

Another advance in the bio-fuel arena should make diesel an even better bet for the future, as it enhances the sustainability element, giving traditional engines a chance to compete with EVs on a level playing field. Clean and practical – that's good news for everyone, whatever the 'Green' route one chooses to take.

After diesel, the other boom making waves throughout the car industry is the hybrid vehicle, with the most popular types being based on petrol-electric technology, although a new breed of diesel-electric hybrid car is starting to make an impression as well. Before jumping that far ahead, however, the next chapter takes an in-depth look at the progress of conventional petrol engines.

Mazda's Skyactiv-D engine emits just 119g of carbon dioxide per kilometre – a remarkably low figure! Due to high petrol costs and a 180,000 yen government tax credit for those buying 'Clean Diesel' models, current CX-5 sales in Japan are split 70:30 in favour of diesel – a previously unthinkable scenario in the Land of the Rising Sun. B. Long

Ford's Dagenham Diesel Centre has the capacity to assemble up to a million diesel engines a year, but pulls its entire electricity needs from three wind turbines. Ford is turning to wind power at other plants in other countries, too. Ford

CHAPTER THREE

PETROL AS A 'CLEAN' OPTION

With the phenomenal rise in the popularity of diesel engines, it is easy to write off petrol-powered units as a lost cause. With a head start on top-level emission control that amounts to several decades compared with diesel in mainstream passenger car applications, it's true that the margins for improvement are probably smaller than the giant leaps made in recent CI engine technology – but that doesn't imply that powerplants using gasoline are dirty per se. Indeed, things only start to look bad if one concentrates purely on CO_2 emissions. Granted, we may be approaching the technical limits, but the petrol engine still has a lot to offer, and minor refinements and a few unconventional lines of thought are sure to keep it ticking over for the foreseeable future.

AS OLD AS THE INDUSTRY

While there have been many forms of motive power used in the car itself, it's fair to say that the gasoline engine is the foundation stone of the industry as a whole. Although it's not so easy to pin down the inventor of the petrol engine, as technology tended to build on the further refinement of several existing patents, one can be safe in saying that the modern engine as we know it was a German creation, made possible by the sterling work of legendary figures such as Gottlieb Daimler, Carl Benz and Wilhelm Maybach at the end of the nineteenth century.

After a fairly slow start, the concept took off, and Germany provided the basis for what became the motor industry. The car (or 'horseless carriage', as it was often called) was quickly embraced by France, with the likes of Panhard & Levassor and Peugeot getting in at the start of the boom, and automobile fever then spread rapidly to other parts of Europe. One of the slowest to welcome the car was Britain, its love of the horse being hard to overcome, but eventually rules were changed on the use of highways and byways, and from 1896 motoring became a part of British life. The Emancipation Run, which went from London to Brighton, was organized to celebrate the change in laws, bringing about freedom for motorists. Perhaps with a touch of irony, over a century later the RAC Future Car Challenge runs in

A single-cylinder Daimler engine from 1885. Daimler AG

The first production automobile – the Benz Patent-Motorwagen, seen here in 1888 with Bertha Benz (Carl's wife) buying petrol from a chemist. This was the only way one could buy fuel in the pioneering days of motoring. Daimler AG

 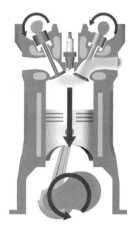

1. 2. First stroke.

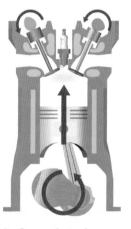 

3. Second stroke. 4.

The four strokes of the Otto cycle, described in the previous chapter, are easier to understand in step-by-step drawings. With more and more hybrids on the road, one often hears of Atkinson-cycle engines. Using the theory of James Atkinson England, the compression stroke and expansion

5. Third stroke. 6. Fourth stroke. 7.

stroke duration can be set independently, improving fuel economy at the cost of power. Atkinson's idea was later refined by America's Ralph H. Miller, with the Miller cycle adjusting the intake valve timing, delaying its closing to reduce 'pumping loss' in the compression stroke and lower combustion temperatures, thus providing better thermal efficiency. However, a supercharger is generally needed to gain full advantage from the concept, boosting low-end torque, or nowadays one can call on the help of an electric motor in a hybrid. Wapcaplet/Creative Commons

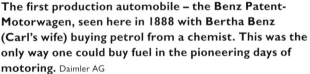

Henry Ford with the Model T – the car that started America's love affair with the automobile. Ford stated that he would have liked his car to run on ethanol, and even had his own hemp farm to produce the fuel. Ford

the opposite direction, with competitors trying to use the lowest amount of energy possible.

In America, the likes of Duryea and Oldsmobile showed the way forwards, joined by a flood of fledgling companies eager to build these new petrol-engined machines. As it happens, the first engines to be built in the States were those produced under Daimler licence by William Steinway, of Steinway piano fame, a deal over manufacturing rights having been struck with the German concern in September 1888. Interestingly, the first diesel engine built in America came via Colonel Adolphus Busch, his Anheuser-Busch firm also being better known for a completely different but equally famous product – Budweiser beer.

The frantic activity of these early years quickly established a basic pattern for the automobile. Multi-cylinder engines in various configurations became the norm, the smaller combustion shocks for each cylinder making for smoother running. Cooling was improved, as was carburetion, and ignition systems changed from 'hot tube' to magnetos, and then to a battery-operated type as self-starters became all the rage. Ignition systems that we can readily recognize today can be traced back to the work of Charles Kettering of Delco, who by 1909 had perfected the coil, points and distributor set-up. Kettering's ignition set was first seen on the 1910 Cadillac line-up.

After World War I, apart from the occasional worthy challenger such as the Knight sleeve-valve engine, most power-units, regardless of their in-line, 'V' or horizontally opposed configuration, employed the same basic principles of operation, working on the four-stroke Otto cycle, with poppet valves somewhere in the equation.

As such it became a battle for which manufacturer could produce the smoothest or most powerful engine, and some magnificent creations were released in the so-called vintage years: twin-cam Alfas, the Hispano-Suiza H6 and Isotta-Fraschini Tipo 8 series, old smoothies such as the Daimler Double-Six, Rolls-Royce New Phantom and Lanchester Straight-Eight, French cuisine from Delage and Talbot, supercharged Bentley and Mercedes models, and American multi-cylinder machines such as the big Cadillacs and the Duesenberg J.

Although the Great Depression had managed to put a damper on things, the 1930s were still responsible for spawning all manner of engineering masterpieces, from straight-eight Daimlers to twin-cam Bugattis, and exotics from the likes of Delahaye, Horch and Cord. At the other end of the spectrum, with an increasing number of people wanting to drive but having rather more modest means than those in the frame for a Derby Bentley, small cars became better and better – the Peugeot 402 and Opel Olympia being perfect examples of vehicles made for the family man.

RIGHT: **A 1937 Bugatti 57S 'Atlantic' on show in Nice in the south of France, with its magnificent straight-eight engine on display to the left.** Bugatti

However, just as automotive engineering had reached new heights of achievement across all sectors of the market, the dark clouds of war fell over Europe, and production lines were reserved for the war effort. The same thing happened in the States a couple of years later, while Japan's fledgling industry was barely out of the starting blocks before the Pacific War put things on hold in the Far East.

EARLY TYPES OF PETROL

The first motorists had to buy gasoline from a chemist's shop, as it was used to treat head lice, although eventually hardware stores began stocking the fuel as cars became more common. The world's first service station was opened in 1905 in St Louis, in the middle of America, but it would be some time before petrol stations became a common sight.

In Britain, petrol started being graded in 1920, with the 60 RON 'No. 1' at the top of the line, sold alongside a cheaper alternative, although 'Pool' petrol (sold between 1939 and 1952) brought reduced quality to all users. Meanwhile, the research of GM's Thomas Midgley in the States, as well as that of Harry Ricardo in Britain, recommended that tetra-ethyl lead, known by the chemical formula $Pb(C_2H_5)_4$ – or 'TEL' for short – be mixed with petrol as an ideal octane booster (or anti-knock additive), replacing alcohol. It also acted as a useful lubricant, helping to prevent valve seat damage.

Sales of leaded fuel began in America in February 1923, albeit with some early controversy in the ensuing months. Notwithstanding sales continued, with leaded fuel becoming the norm worldwide despite several health scares, and public inquiries that mysteriously always seemed to end up inconclusive. Eventually, decades later, the city of Los Angeles announced in the early 1950s that it considered lead to be an air pollutant, but again nothing changed. Only after the World Health Organization (WHO) got involved in 1969, followed by the US EPA in the following year, did the call for taking tetra-ethyl lead (and tetra-methyl lead, or TML, which was also used in some cases) out of petrol start to carry some weight.

By this time, in 1967, 'four star' petrol had replaced the 'premium' grade in the UK, with 'two star' being a lower octane fuel sold alongside it to replace 'standard' petrol. For the record, 'four star' had a 98 RON rating, while the cheaper 'two star' carried a 92 RON rating – the rare 'three star' version sat in between. Very occasionally, back in the days of ignorant bliss, one would see 'five star' fuel, which came with a 101 RON rating thanks to an extra large helping of tetra-ethyl lead. This would have been the equivalent of the earlier 'super' grade.

British petrol advertising from 1956. National Benzole

POST-WAR PETROL-ENGINED CARS

With the end of hostilities, things slowly but surely began to return to normal in the motor industry. Demand far outstripped supply for several years, with vehicle types ranging from utilitarian saloons and estates, all the way through to a huge line of sports and luxury models. If nothing else, the war years had improved metallurgy and reliability levels hugely, and had also helped to refine mass-production techniques.

Gradually, the warmed-over pre-war designs that got the industry active again after its uninvited recess were replaced with more modern vehicles, with cars such as the Standard Vanguard showing the way. Styling made a giant leap forwards in the majority of car-producing countries, as did

First unveiled at the 1967 Frankfurt Show, the Bosch D-Jetronic EFI system was a piece of groundbreaking technology that helped reduce fuel consumption and emissions. In addition to engine revs and temperature, it used intake manifold pressure as one of the key parameters for adjusting the air-fuel mixture, the petrol delivery to the injectors being kept at a constant pressure by newly developed electric fuel pumps. By 1972, no fewer than eighteen car manufacturers had adopted the D-Jetronic system to comply with US regulations. Bosch

The remarkable twin-cam Jaguar XK straight six, in production from 1948 to 1992, picking up all manner of modifications along the way to make it cleaner. Jaguar

The original Mini, launched in 1959. BMC

power-unit technology, with another Coventry company, Jaguar, introducing its dohc XK straight-six, for instance, while side-valve (sv, or flat-head) engines were inevitably replaced by modern overhead-valve (ohv, or pushrod) units such as the Austin A-Series four. Early mechanical fuel-injection systems, developed during the conflict, and the first electronic ignition systems started making their way into high-performance road cars, but with enhanced power delivery being the reason for their adoption at this stage rather than concerns over exhaust emissions.

However, the Suez Crisis of 1956 brought with it a new line of thinking, with petrol shortages in parts of Europe, and Britain in particular, putting fuel economy at the top of the agenda. As well as numerous bubble cars, the Mini was born – the British equivalent to the VW Beetle, Fiat 500 Nuova and Citroën 2CV models already being built in vast numbers on the Continent.

But once the dust had settled in the Middle East, thoughts soon went back to glamour and power, with ecology taking a back seat again. The MGA was replaced by the MGB, but a more telling imprint of the era was the passing of the Jaguar XK150 to make way for the E-type – a 240km/h (150mph) sports car built for the masses.

There were traces of 'Green' thinking with the introduction of positive crankcase ventilation (PCV) at the start of the 1960s – an early form of emissions control consisting of a valve and breather pipe that redirected blow-by gases (those that make their way past the piston rings to gather in the crankcase) back into the intake manifold so as to burn the hydrocarbon-rich mixture more effectively.

On saying that, the tail end of the Swinging Sixties brought with them a supercar boom in Europe, with exotic heavyweights such as the Lamborghini Miura, Ferrari Daytona and Maserati Ghibli joining the likes of the Jaguar E-type and Mercedes-Benz 280SL in the segment of the market occupied by the world's fastest and most desirable sports cars.

It should be noted, however, that regular everyday vehicles had suddenly taken on a more modern image, with cars such as the 1966 Model Year Opel Kadett B and 1968 Ford Escort being perfect examples of the new breed of family saloons in Europe, while Japan's industry was maturing nicely with cars such as the C10 Nissan Skyline and the first Toyota Corolla. America, meanwhile, continued down its own merry path, with typical 4.7-litre V8s producing a measly 200bhp, or 7.0-litre monsters rated at 360bhp, which was probably exaggerated anyway, and most of it needed simply to move the 2,000kg (4,410lb) bodies that were all the rage Stateside. But with gasoline priced at 34 cents a gallon in 1968 (against a Federal minimum wage of $1.60 an hour), wasting petrol hardly crossed people's minds.

Then all of a sudden, the carefree days of the 1960s were behind us, and a new, more responsible era had dawned. Cars were no longer simply regarded as machines that brought personal freedom: they were also considered as a major source of pollution, particularly in the States and Japan.

LEADERS IN EMISSION REGULATIONS

After decades of giving emissions no real thought, the state of California in the USA and the Japanese government in the Far East were the first to start putting pollution from automobiles on the agenda – a combination of dense populations and an abundance of motor vehicles aiding smog formation. In the case of LA, the geography doesn't help the matter,

The Ferrari Daytona featured in a Borg & Beck advert. Although there were shades of 'Green' starting to appear, speed, power and glamour were the key words in sales literature until the first oil crisis of the 1970s started to bite. Borg & Beck

while the booming industry in the Tokyo area in the early post-war years was a more likely source of a major part of the problem. But cleaning up car exhaust emissions couldn't hurt, and a flood of new rules was passed in quick succession aimed at reducing the amount of noxious gases from tailpipes.

As it happens, it was Federal law that started the ball rolling, bringing air pollution from vehicles to the attention of the public at a national level with a 1965 amendment to the Clean Air Act (CAA) passed two years earlier. This legislation, given the Motor Vehicle Air Pollution Control Act moniker, became effective for the 1968 Model Year, and called for the elimination of crankcase hydrocarbon emissions, a 72 per cent reduction in HC released from the exhaust, and a 56 per cent cut in CO emissions.

Government groups that provided the foundation stone for the EPA (Environmental Protection Agency) were behind the US Clean Air Act Extension of 1970 (usually referred to as the 'Muskie Act' in car circles), which was extremely tough – possibly even too tough to be realistic for the technology available at the time. Nonetheless, the Muskie Act called for a 90 per cent reduction in hydrocarbon and carbon monoxide emissions by 1975, and a 90 per cent cut in NOx by the following year.

The Muskie Act also sealed the National Ambient Air Quality Standards (NAAQS) legislation, in which the EPA (operational since December 1970) was given the power to legally control levels of CO, HC, NOx, SOx, PM and photochemical oxidants present in the air. Eventually, however, with the realization that Senator Edmund Muskie and his team was asking for too much, too soon (drivability suffered dramatically, and virtually all manufacturers increased the engine sizes overnight to make up for the drop in performance, so an image of the overall benefits was rather cloudy at best), a new version of the CAA was drafted in 1977, with the hydrocarbon target delayed until 1980, the carbon monoxide standard delayed until 1981, and NOx emissions relaxed from 0.4g/mile to 1.0g/mile, with the revised figure to be enforced from 1981.

While the Federal government had made a sterling effort to get things moving in the right direction, it was the state of California that stood out as the knight in shining armour. Dr Arie Jan Haagen-Smit, a California-based researcher, had linked local air pollution with cars in the early 1950s – not surprising when a typical US vehicle from the time was pumping out an average of 13g of HC, 87g of CO and almost 4g of NOx for every mile travelled.

The California Motor Vehicle Pollution Control Board was established in 1959. It introduced its first batch of emission control rules in 1964 (to become active for the 1966 Model Year), but following the foundation of the California Air Resources Board (CARB) in 1967, things became tighter and tighter for those wishing to sell cars in the Golden State. Historically, however, given the size of the car market in California, makers have had little choice but to swallow hard and comply with CA regulations.

Other than moaning about the difficulty in meeting Federal and Californian law, it's fair to say that the Europeans were doing very little. But at least Japan was serious about cleaning up the atmosphere, its citizens monitoring the air quality on a daily basis via large read-outs outside major train stations for many years. These gauges are no longer deemed necessary, which says a lot for the effectiveness of Japan's clean air programme.

Following the discovery that people living close to main roads in densely populated areas of Tokyo had abnormal levels of lead in their body, and a dramatic rise in smog for-

mation, Japan's regulations were originally based on the US legislation of 1970, with fuels having a reduced lead content being introduced in July 1971, and calls for lower sulphur content coming not long after. The first fairly strict set of rules came into force in April 1973, with minor revisions in 1975, then heavier demands in the summer of 1976, and another round of changes that applied to 1978 Model Year vehicles.

EARLY 'GREEN' THINKING

With the United States having a huge domestic audience and being such an important market for European and Japanese exporters (this was the era in which the Japanese industry really came of age), the various recommendations of the Muskie Act and the California Air Resources Board prompted an unprecedented flurry of activity in the R&D centres of the world.

Evaporative (EVAP) emission controls were first mooted in 1968, becoming law on 1971 Model Year cars to reduce the release of unburned hydrocarbons through fuel evaporation. Charcoal canisters trapped petrol fumes in the fuel tank and intake system, with hoses running from carburettor bowls to reduce evaporation from the 'heat soaking' that occurs after a hot engine has been shut down, for instance, and eventually more and more features were added to the fuel delivery system, such as vented fuel caps. As it happens, the widespread use of fuel injection overcame the heat soaking problem, but refinements continued to be added as electronics evolved, with the OBD-II diagnostic system even monitoring the pressure in the fuel lines to warn a driver of a faulty or missing petrol cap. Changes during refilling at the pumps, such as tighter fuel nozzle-to-tank clearances, have also helped prevent petrol fumes entering the atmosphere.

Overrun fuel shut-off valves, which reduced emissions and fuel consumption at the expense of pops and bangs in the exhaust system, were introduced at around this time. In addition, exhaust gas recirculation (EGR) systems started appearing in 1972, although not all vehicles required them straightaway, and some avoided them altogether. Cars for California were more likely to be fitted with EGR than 49-state models, the system redirecting around 10 per cent of the exhaust gas back into the intake manifold for more thorough burning of the HC and NOx content.

The Bosch K-Jetronic fuel-injection system was introduced in January 1973. This was a simple set-up, being a continuous injection system (CIS) that keeps fuel flowing to the cylinders, using mass airflow into the engine as its main operating parameter, with allowances for throttle position

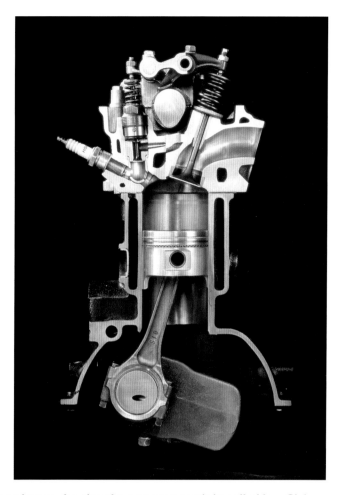

The Honda CVCC engine pictured in December 1973, with one image showing the transverse unit installed in a Civic, the other a cross-section to show the internal workings of the inline-four. Honda

and engine temperature. This was later refined via a closed-loop version (that is, with feedback) for California cars, but K-Jetronic (and the later KE-Jetronic that ran alongside it) was always emissions-orientated, in production for two decades. Other fuel-injection specialists that manufacturers could call on at this time included Bendix, Lucas (CAV), GM and Stanadyne.

Meanwhile, some makers were determined to avoid catalytic converters, employing thermal reactors instead to reduce HC and CO content in the exhaust gases. Thermal reactors required a rich mixture, however, wasting fuel, and an air pump that added yet more weight and cost.

In fact, almost as much as meeting the emissions targets themselves, cost and supply logistics were a major headache for US manufacturers at this time. According to a National Academy of Sciences report published in 1973, the US industry was still largely unprepared to meet the 1975 regulations,

with GM being slightly ahead of Ford and Chrysler at that stage.

Having considered thermal reactors, the 'Big Three' eventually all concluded that the catalytic converter route was the way to go, but with the pellet type (as used in the petroleum industry) versus all-new monolith question and base versus noble metal decision delaying progress. Platinum was the obvious answer, along with other rare metals such as palladium, despite the expense, and then came the need to decide on NOx reduction followed by oxidation, or to produce a single catalyst that would cover both functions, as well as deal with HC and CO emissions. The latter became more attractive with advances in electronic air-fuel mixture controls (including the choke), with Johnson-Matthey, Gulf, ICI and UOP leading the R&D charge.

As for costs, it was thought that a PCV, an EVAP system, EGR, air pumps, electronic ignition and closed-loop

These pictures of the 1974 Porsche flat six provide a rare chance to see European (left) and Federal spec engines side by side, the latter having all manner of additional emissions equipment fitted, which drained power and significantly increased weight and cost. There were concerns about the future of air-cooled engines at this time, with noise and emission control becoming ever stricter. Porsche

emission control systems (including sensors), fuel injection (EFI), a three-way catalyst and improved cooling would add around $395 to the cost of a 1976 vehicle, at a time when the average month's rent was $220. But such is the price of saving the planet.

It is therefore ironic that while all this 'Green' thinking was taking place, other areas in car development were killing the benefits. Vehicles sold in the US needed side-impact bars from the 1973 Model Year, and most cars had heavier bumpers that ultimately became huge over the next couple of years. Whilst done in the name of safety, many of the modifications and resulting weight gains were actually carried out to appease insurance companies. This, combined with emissions equipment sapping power, led most makers to adopt larger engine displacements (usually going for a longer stroke rather than a bigger bore for better emissions) to maintain performance levels, resulting in more fuel being used for very little gain.

There were some innovative ideas that bucked the trend, however, such as the Honda CVCC (compound vortex controlled combustion) unit. Honda's head of R&D at the time, Tasku Date, having been told by Soichiro Honda to stick with the petrol ICE as a base unit for cost reasons (the investment required for all-new manufacturing facilities simply wasn't there), concluded that it was impossible to compete actively with other makers following traditional emission-control routes with the technology available. To promote lean burning was the only way forwards, but this was easier said than done, even though we had men walking on the moon.

Announced in February 1971, way ahead of final testing,

Date and his team came up with a masterstroke, having created a 3-valve per cylinder stratified-charge engine with initial combustion taking place in a pre-chamber before the mixture entered the main combustion chamber. Stratified-charge engines were being developed by a number of makers, notably Ford, but the cost was prohibitive, while fuel consumption suffered and the multi-fuel option was wiped out as soon as all the emissions equipment was added. With CVCC there was no need for fuel injection or a catalytic converter, and a new cylinder head was the only major investment required. Eventually, licensing agreements for this lean-burn technology were duly signed with Toyota, Ford, Chrysler and Isuzu.

Overhead camshaft (ohc) engines were slowly becoming more and more mainstream, and the first of the multi-valve engines were starting to filter through. Sohc units with 2 valves per cylinder were still the norm, however, albeit restricted to upper and sporty grades at this stage due to cost concerns, while dohc engines continued to be a rarity reserved for specialist vehicles. But lightweight alloy cylinder heads were now becoming commonplace, with a few engines sporting aluminium alloy blocks as well; a few exotics had even started using magnesium alloys in places to further reduce weight.

By 1975, fuel supplies in America were being sold with a lower lead content, with unleaded grades a necessity to suit the new wave of catalytic converters. For the 1975 Model Year, all GM cars had cats, three-quarters of the Chrysler range had them, and 70 per cent of Fords. Early catalytic converters loaded with pellets were found to wear prematurely through vibration, as the application was quite different to

1976 advertising for the Lucas electronic ignition (EI) system. Fiat was the first to offer a breakerless EI system as standard (a Magneti Marelli set-up on the Fiat Dino in 1968), but most makers followed suit in the 1970s as a way of improving emissions through better spark performance. Lucas

a petroleum facility, but this was all part of the learning process.

At the end of the day, the results were clear for all to see: a 1965 Chevrolet Malibu produced 8.8g of hydrocarbons, 87g of carbon monoxide, and 3.6g of NOx for each mile travelled. Ten years later, the figures were down to 0.9g of HC, 9.0g of CO, and 2.0g of NOx. Granted, there was still work to do, but the first steps had been taken in the right direction, and the Japanese market followed suit, requiring catalytic converters on all new cars sold in the 1976 season.

As it happens, 1976 brought with it the first lambda sensor from Bosch. This measures oxygen in the exhaust gases to give a signal to the engine's ECU to adjust its running to best suit the catalytic converter, thus making a closed-loop system and maximizing efficiency. Three years later, the same German company launched Motronic – a digital engine management system that, in its original form, used a microprocessor to control the amount of fuel injected and the ignition timing to optimize fuel consumption and emissions, as well as provide smoother running.

The first car to feature Bosch Motronic (which later evolved into the digital DME system) was the BMW 732i, but with three-way catalytic converters becoming increasingly common, it was soon recognized as being the ideal way of adding precision to the combustion process. Naturally, other digital management systems found their way on to the market soon after – the automobile, like the camera world, had entered the electronics age.

Meanwhile, after being passed in 1975, America's CAFE (corporate average fuel economy) legislation kicked in for the 1978 season, but the pitifully low 13.1ltr/100km (18mpg) US target that existed for over a decade simply shows how inefficient most cars sold in the States were. But if nothing else, the timing meant that US makers were already forced to think about fuel consumption before the second major oil crisis of the decade came following trouble in Iran – first a strike by oil workers, and then a toppling of the Shah of Iran's government in the opening weeks of 1979.

Downsizing and research into alternative fuels came as a result, but history has shown that the Americans are quick to forget, and one can lay odds that it would have been business as usual as soon as oil supplies resumed. While the first oil scare already had folks on edge, the high (by US standards) fuel costs and inflation going out of control in the mid-1970s got people thinking a bit harder, and the second big scare came just as the motor industry was reacting to earlier outside influences. It was therefore a situation of continuing down a new path rather than creating a totally new one from 1979 onwards. We would never again see the likes of the tiny runabouts such as the 1981 Suzuki CV-1 and 1983 Yamaha PTX-1 in the States – there were limits! On saying that, import sales made up 22 per cent of the US market in 1979, roughly double compared with ten years earlier.

The majority of 'Green' technology was still something of a knee-jerk reaction to American market demands at this stage, with the Japanese makers falling into line that much more easily due to the strict legislation passed in Japan's own domestic marketplace.

There were times, however, when European makers didn't cave in to the temptation of supplying the world's biggest salesroom. For instance, turbocharging had just become fashionable, with the 'turbo' insignia being a licence to print money in the seventies. Although GM had tried to market turbocharged models in the early sixties, it wasn't until the launch of the German BMW 2002 Turbo and Porsche 930 Turbo models that this type of blower became fashionable, with the Porsche and Saab names quickly becoming synonymous with forced induction. However, faced with modifying their flagship products to satisfy US emissions laws in 1980, the European manufacturers simply stopped selling them in the States – the famous 911 model was kept away from US dealers from January 1980 all the way through to September 1985.

Latent Protectionism Versus Ecology

Despite the author's best efforts, it is all but impossible to steer away from politics, since local markets are driven by the policies of governments, who, because of the power base involved, listen very carefully to lobbyists representing the manufacturing groups, unions, financial institutions and suchlike on their patch. Furthermore, 'latent protectionism' needs explaining, as it's probably a term that doesn't get

BELOW RIGHT: **The Jaguar HE (high efficiency) cylinder head of 1981, inducing a high swirl pattern for cleaner combustion, serves as a perfect example of the steady refinements in conventional engineering that were gradually making cars more economical and less harmful to the environment. The HE head, based on patents filed by the Swiss engineer, Michael May, allowed leaner mixtures and a higher c/r, reducing fuel consumption by as much as 20 per cent at some engine speeds.** Jaguar

BELOW: **The turbocharger was generally thought of as an appendage simply to enhance performance, but a blower can also improve fuel consumption, as it recycles otherwise wasted energy.** BMW

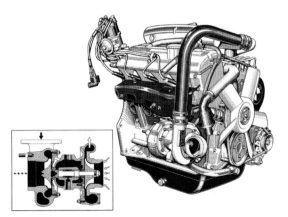

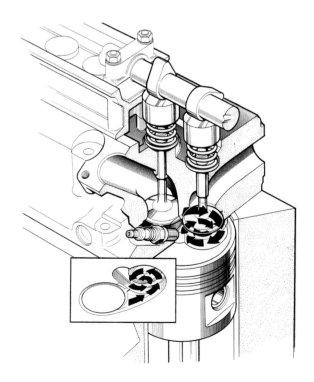

used in the context the author uses it. It's not a question of imposing import quotas, it's the small things aimed at protecting market share by scripting local regulations (for instance, Australia had a policy of only allowing right-hand-drive cars on its roads), or encouraging the popularity of a certain type of vehicle that a specific country specializes in. It's the latter that strikes a chord with the author, especially comparing America with Japan.

For decades, American makers lived by the 'no substitute for cubic inches' code of practice, opting for needlessly large engines with very low levels of thermal efficiency (in 1971 the 5.9-litre Chrysler V8 pumped out just 255bhp, for example), simply because petrol was cheap. These were then placed in bodies that were over-sized, so that most of the power that was available was drained by excess weight. Granted, one could say the same about a V12 Jaguar, but the power-to-weight ratio made it a far more efficient vehicle than it has a right to be with a 5.3-litre engine under the bonnet. And in reality, compared to the US dinosaurs that were extant before the oil crisis years, a Jaguar saloon is in fact a true compact.

But this is where the power of marketing comes in. Ownership of a 'Yank Tank' was part of the American dream – having the latest model on the driveway was a perfect way of advertising to the neighbours that you were doing well, and American cars were seriously cheap: the average price of a car was $3,900 in 1970, while the average wage was close to $10,000. No need to worry about fuel costs either, with petrol at 36 cents a gallon, so even a budget import like the VW Beetle ($1,874 in its cheapest form) or the $1,996 Datsun 510 was hard to justify when you could buy a full-size Chevy Biscayne sedan that would suitably impress the Joneses for $780 more, while the initial cost of prestige brands from Britain and Germany put them in another market altogether.

Other than a few blips that have coincided with severe oil supply problems, American thinking has hardly changed, as petrol has remained cheap. Only as saloons became more compact did the importers stand a chance, but then huge pick-ups and SUVs were touted as the next big status symbol, keeping the wheels of the US industry firmly in motion.

In the months immediately after the Lehman Shock, owners in the States simply abandoned their SUVs at the side of the road, as the trade-in value was worthless. This surely proves the point – a protectionist market of sorts does exist, working perfectly well in the good times, ably supported by gasoline prices that are kept artificially low.

One only needs to look at the sales patterns in America to understand the link – in 1999, with petrol at $1.20 a gallon, no one cared about alternative fuels and EVs, and average prices were even lower two years later. In 2004, the $2.00 gallon arrived, but when it shot up to $3.00 in the following year in the wake of Hurricane Katrina, sales of large SUVs blipped immediately. When petrol hit $4.00 in 2008, political pressure brought it back down to $1.60 before the end of the year. Had the effects of the 'Lehman Shock' not kicked in and petrol prices not gone up again, it is quite easy to imagine what type of cars would be flying out of US showrooms today.

With Japan, it's the other way around, and we have to substitute the words 'too big to be sensible' with 'too small to be sensible', because the 660cc Kei car isn't really that efficient in the real world either.

The idea behind the original Kei was understandable: a lightweight 360cc machine to get Japan mobile in the 1950s. Engine size was upped to 550cc for 1976 in the face of rapidly falling sales, since by now the 'economic miracle' was in full swing and Japan had already joined the ranks of the world's top industrialized nations. What people were saying was that they didn't really need a Kei class – but the engine size was changed again to a 660cc limit in 1990, when the allowable body dimensions were also increased slightly. This, combined with handsome tax breaks, kept the models popular enough to keep the domestic makers busy.

The author's wife had a brand new 660cc NA Daihatsu for a while, and fuel consumption was frankly dreadful, especially in the summer when air conditioning (a necessity in Japan, not a luxury) drained a good proportion of what little power there was. To get it off the line, it would scream away in the lower gears, doing a pitifully small amount of valuable work due to a lack of low-end torque – and tackling hills with all seats occupied was only for the brave. To make the most of the small overall dimensions allowable, the majority of Kei cars are either boxy or tall (sometimes boxy and tall!), which does little for a vehicle's aerodynamic efficiency. This means that more energy is needed to cut through the air, which reduces fuel consumption.

Today, Kei makers are proud to announce 30.2km/ltr in the Japanese JC08 mode, achieved by the Suzuki Alto Eco model, which has an advanced idle-stop feature, stalling the engine before the car comes to a complete halt without affecting steering. Normally, however, something like 24.8km/ltr for the FF Daihatsu Tanto, or 17.6km/ltr for the Honda Life Diva Turbo is more typical of the breed. Compare this with the latest 1.3-litre Mazda Demio, capable of 25km/ltr with an engine twice the size, and it doesn't make sense.

The author was involved in the Shahyo test series, published by Miki Press, bringing together cars compared over exactly the same mix of roads, during the same time of day, and with the same drivers. This not only highlighted a huge gap in published fuel consumption figures versus those recorded in real life situations, it also threw up some big question marks over efficiency. An average fuel consumption figure of 11.7km/ltr was recorded for the turbocharged Honda Vamos, while the Toyota Belta (a 1.3-litre compact sedan) delivered 14.5km/ltr, and was also a fraction cheaper to buy. Even the sporty VW Golf GT TSI gave 11.4km/ltr, proving that optimizing engine sizes and gearing, as well as aerodynamics, is more important than small size on its own. Thus it is clear that protection of market share and the self-interests of car companies, shielded by government policy, is holding back the development of true 'Green' vehicles.

One final note on something vaguely related to the subject of latent protectionism concerns the lack of effective car-sharing policies. Anyone who has driven on a Los Angeles highway during rush hour will know the huge difference in being allowed to drive in the 'Pool' (or HOV) lane – one can either sit, driver only, in the mother of all traffic jams, or have just one passenger and be permitted to travel on what often amounts to almost a private road a few feet to the left of you. It seems crazy that more isn't done to make use of the HOV lane – but of course, if one encourages it too much, vehicle sales are lost, and petroleum companies have to take a hit in profits.

Recently a research group in Japan recommended that car sharing along the lines of one vehicle for five families should be encouraged by means of tax breaks, and so on. This will never happen, as it's not really practical to share to that extent without a full-scale change in lifestyles, but even if people were overwhelmingly in favour of the scheme, there's no way the manufacturers would lie down smiling in the face of an 80 per cent cut in sales.

THE START OF THE MODERN ERA

Following California's lead, albeit rather late, other countries started to introduce stricter emissions regulations. Most of Europe had new emissions regulations that came into force in January 1986. In Germany, for instance, three-way catalytic converters were required, or a heavy pollution tax was charged. Cats became available on most Mercedes-Benz engines in September 1985, and were duly listed as standard within a year. It was a similar story at Porsche, and elsewhere in the German industry.

However, catalytic converters have problems of their own, being useless until they are warmed through, and breaking up and leaving deposits on the roadside (with concentrations in some areas giving rise to the thought of collection

MORE RECENT PETROL TYPES

With the adoption of catalytic converters pretty much across the globe, leaded petrol was no longer an option, as tetra-ethyl lead (TEL) poisoned the unit. In 1970, the US EPA ordered the introduction of unleaded fuel, and called for all new cars to be able to run on lead-free petrol by 1975. On the other side of the Pacific, after reducing lead content in 1971, Japan started selling unleaded fuel in April 1972.

Surprisingly, however, despite repeated concerns that lead oxide particles were a tailpipe emission that was affecting people's health, only America and Japan seemed to make the move at this stage, and the clout of the Ethyl Corporation (the makers of TEL) was obvious when the US courts stated in a 1976 hearing that fuel with a trace of lead (0.13g/litre) could continue to be sold.

However, EPA research on ambient air-lead concentrations, falling in line with usage, and damning

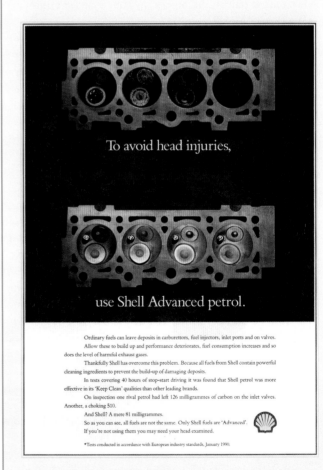

Advertising from Shell. This 1990 piece shows the importance of modern additives. Shell

reports from scientists linking lead in the bloodstream with health disorders, especially in children, meant that the days of leaded fuel were numbered once again. Chicago was the first US city to order a ban on leaded fuel in 1984, and other cities and states would follow, while in 1986, Japan became the first entire country to outlaw sales of leaded petrol.

The Ethyl Corporation stopped making TEL in 1993, but instead imported it from Associated Octel of Britain. This was the last manufacturer of TEL in the world, although an accident at the plant in February 1994 only helped add weight to the UN's call for a global ban on leaded fuel in the spring of that year. At the end of 1995, America joined Japan in becoming a lead-free nation.

Meanwhile in Europe, generally speaking, sales of leaded petrol were banned in the EU in 2000 (Germany made the first move in 1995), although a handful of outlets are sanctioned to supply those with certain classic cars that are deemed to require it to avoid exhaust valve seat damage.

Most of Continental Europe started selling unleaded fuel in the mid-1980s, while Britain joined the fray by marketing 'premium unleaded' from 1990 onwards. It should be noted, however, that lead content in the UK had been reduced before this: from 1986 onwards 'four star' low-lead mix had about one-fifth of the TEL content of the older 'five star' petrol, the latter containing a heady 0.8g of lead per litre. Earlier 'four star' petrol had an average of 0.4g of lead in each litre.

Although there were thoughts of using manganese (MMT) at one stage (like TEL, also made by the Ethyl Corporation), the replacement for lead is usually benzene – which is somewhat ironic, as this is what TEL had replaced worldwide in pre-war days! With lead out of the equation, sulphur was next on the agenda.

The US-based Manufacturers of Emission Controls Association (MECA) published a paper in September 1998 which concluded that sulphur had to be reduced to a level below 80ppm for catalytic converters to have a chance of working properly; the 80ppm figure was proposed as a cap, with 30ppm an ideal scenario.

Following Tier II regulations (passed by Congress at the end of 1999 but not implemented until 2004), the US sulphur content in gasoline went from 300ppm down to 30ppm by the mid-2000s

(gradually phased in to take full effect by 2006) – but now the EPA is currently calling for it to drop further, to just 10ppm. Even before the proposal was published, politicians were asking for things to stay the same, as lowering the content would add around 25 cents to the price of a gallon of petrol. The fact that it would enable catalyst converters to work efficiently and reduce the chances of acid rain seems not to matter, as long as fuel remains the price of water in the States.

As it happens, the Worldwide Fuel Charter states that 10ppm should be the norm, but this is a voluntary international code – Europe and Japan already abide by it, but the whole of North America doesn't see a need to, with Canada sitting on its hands until the USA makes a move.

It seems ironic that senators in the States today are on the one hand pushing for car manufacturers to work harder to make vehicles cleaner, but on the other are not willing to give them the tools to do so, as 6 cents per litre on the price of fuel might lose a few votes. Why not go all the way, and make vehicles cheaper by leaving emissions equipment off completely? Making them slightly cleaner when they are already fitted with components that can make them really clean doesn't seem to make sense, any more than holding up EVs as the immediate eco-friendly course of action without first thinking of the environmental costs of generating electricity via coal.

With the days of leaded fuel numbered, for those worried about valve seat damage, various alternatives were presented in the 1990s, such as this Powerplus device. Other options included lead substitutes from the likes of Red Line, Wynn's and STP. Powerplus

LEFT: **Catalytic converters were required in Germany from January 1986. This is the set-up used on the contemporary Porsche 911.** Porsche

BELOW: **The Bosch KE-Jetronic system was aimed at improving economy and emissions. Introduced in 1983, it found good use during the eighties before other methods were found to curb heavy fuel consumption.** Bosch

for recycling) – and then, of course, there is the question of mining and the use of rare metals. So for every solution that pops into the frame, one is left wondering just how 'Green' is 'Green'?

There was also another problem to confront: a distinct lack of unleaded fuel in many other parts of Europe. As an example, the UK didn't have widespread unleaded petrol availability until 1990, meaning that many makers were unable to fit catalytic converters until this time; most of the Rovers and Jaguars sold on the home market ran without cats until the 1991 Model Year as a result. It wasn't until the beginning of 1993 that all new petrol-engined cars registered in Europe had to be equipped with them by law – by which time Bosch had invented a faster-acting planar lambda sensor.

Amendments to the US Clean Air Act (CAA) in 1990 brought tighter controls on evaporative emissions from the fuel itself, and oil companies were also told to make oxygenated petrol available in areas with high CO levels. Tighter tailpipe emissions and testing procedures were also proposed, to come into effect in 1994 – though amazingly, considering how long the world has been talking about global warming, attention wouldn't turn towards keeping CO_2 emissions in check for another two decades.

One thing that came from this was a rise in the use of onboard diagnostic (OBD) systems. GM was one of the first to promote the use of such systems, as far back as 1980, but it was only when the SAE (the Society of Automotive Engineers) recommended that all vehicles should be fitted with them that their use became widespread. California started blanket use in 1991, but it wasn't until standards were agreed upon that OBD systems were required by Federal law. By the 1996 season, however, all cars in the States had to have OBD-II systems installed, with Europe following in 2001. Basically, onboard diagnostics help with accurate troubleshooting, keeping emission levels spot on, and aid meaningful vehicle testing.

Anyway, with emissions and crash regulations tighter in all the major markets, the 'World Car' era was born, in which makers tried to produce vehicles that were basically suitable for all countries, saving the expense of having to build cars with a totally different specification depending on whether the vehicle was sold in California or another state, or EEC countries for that matter. It was easier to focus on clearing the tougher regulations (see Chapter 2 for a table of emissions standards since 1992) and to spread R&D costs across a wider range sample. Of course, the end result also benefited the environment, as cars were far cleaner in certain areas than they actually needed to be from a purely legal standpoint.

The first all-alloy Alfa Romeo twin-spark engine (later 16v versions went to a cast-iron block to reduce costs). Modern BMW alloy block manufacturing techniques cut emissions by 98 per cent during the production stages, thanks to a new organic binder. Alfa Romeo

With the ICE having had decades to evolve, there was an era when electronics played the biggest part in lowering emissions at this stage – it was a question of honing existing conventional technology, rather than coming up with something totally new. Tiny refinements brought small but worthwhile improvements in efficiency, such as:

- tweaking black boxes and fuel-injection systems (MPFI/MPI being a good example)
- introducing knock sensors (KS) that allowed the engine to run at its leanest limits without risk of damage – by working in conjunction with the ECU, adjusting the ignition timing to keep the engine at maximum efficiency, the latest units can increase torque by 5 per cent and save 9 per cent in fuel costs
- phasing in electronic accelerator pedal modules that convert driver input into an electronic signal sent to the car's ECU

- reducing internal friction on engines and ancillary components
- moving over to electric cooling fans to reduce drag on the crankshaft (now we have electric PAS and air-conditioning pumps for the same reason)
- relocating catalytic converters to make them warm up more quickly – some manufacturers have even resorted to heating them electrically to make them efficient that much sooner.

Turbocharging, too, moved up a notch with the introduction of variable-geometry turbo (VGT) units at the tail end of the eighties, along with the more widespread use of intercoolers.

One should also note the introduction of finer machining tolerances and lighter oils, and saving weight. All-alloy engines were maybe not so quiet as those with a cast-iron block, but they were a great deal lighter – 43kg (95lb) in the case of a Mercedes V8, for instance, which, according to the theories laid out in Chapter 7, means that four horsepower less is required to retain the previous level of performance. By the 1990s, composite intake manifolds were being used more and more – although the author has heard of many cases of these cracking in time, so there is perhaps a sensible limit on how far one can go down the weight reduction route.

As well as this steady stream of improvements on the engine front, another group of engineers was busy refining transmission technology, and in this area of car design there were some truly dramatic leaps forwards.

Jaguar's staggered 'J-Gate' selector on an X-type, with a 'Sport' mode switch for the 5AT. The default setting is biased towards economy. B. Long

Early CVT transmission, as found on DAF Variomatic models. As with today's CVT units, being an automatic transmission, no clutch is needed. DAF

For many years, a manual gearbox (MT) was the only option for an automobile – Emile Levassor summed it up by saying: 'It's brutal, but it works!' There were some early attempts at using a CVT (continuously variable transmission) that came to nothing, at least until DAF tried reviving the idea in 1958. Then we passed through a phase of early automatic transmission provided by linking the fluid flywheel to a pre-selector, but this was a rarity, first offered by Daimler in Britain in 1931.

The first conventional automatic gearbox (AT) was released by General Motors in 1939, with Americans falling in love with two-pedal driving as soon as World War II ended. Based on a short-lived 'Safety' semi-automatic transmission from a couple of seasons earlier, the GM 'Hydra-Matic Drive' was a four-speed gearbox (4AT), initially sold on the 1940 Oldsmobile line. Ironically, GM reported a 10 per cent saving in fuel economy on this first AT unit, but as they became more popular, with three-speeds (3AT) becoming the norm, automatic gearboxes came with a reputation for sapping energy and increasing fuel consumption.

While there was definitely reduced stress on the drive-train, early ATs simply didn't suit smaller engines. In Europe, that meant that while larger luxury models went the AT route, we therefore had contraptions such as the Variomatic CVT and Sportomatic to suit locally built cars and driving conditions – but they were never popular.

Then all of a sudden, as we reached the end of the eighties and moved into the nineties, manufacturers started to embrace the automatic concept, providing features that would allow 'Sport' and 'Eco' modes, specifying more ratios with overdriven top cogs for better fuel economy, and allowing the driver more involvement with the widespread use of staggered selector gates and advanced semi-automatic transmissions such as the Tiptronic and later PDK versions. In addition, having been a minor player for many years, modern technology and the latest manufacturing techniques allowed the CVT to come of age, with European and Japanese makers singing its praises.

LUBRICATING OILS

Although there are lubricating oils for transmissions and axles, this section concerns itself with motor (or engine) oils, as this is an area that is being developed more and more to enhance fuel consumption.

Motor oil comes from crude oil, but with the more volatile elements removed to raise the flashpoint, otherwise the heat from the engine would ignite it. The other important thing about motor oil and its ability to do the job it is intended for, is its viscosity, or weight. This is where the 'eco' angle comes in, because the viscosity determines the level of protective film the oil provides, preventing damage caused by metal-to-metal contact, and the ease with which it flows.

The earliest engine oils are known as straight, or single grade oils. The SAE (Society of Automotive Engineers) viscosity codes put things into perspective, starting at 0 grade, then going up through 5, 10, 15, 20, 25, 30, 40, and occasionally 50 or 60. One often sees a 'W' suffix, which stands for winter (a grade designated after low temperature testing rather than the usual 100°C) – but the main thing that concerns us here is the lower the number, the lower its viscosity.

In other words, the lower the number, the lighter the oil, and therefore the more easily it flows. At the same time, generally speaking, the lighter the oil, the less protection it offers the engine's components, while the heavier it becomes, the more internal drag it creates, and the more strain it puts on the starting system. But one also has to consider that an oil works in a very wide range of operating temperatures, from freezing in winter start-up conditions through to extreme heat after a blast down a motorway in the middle of summer, touching parts at over 300°C. For this reason, in the old days, owners often changed oils according to the season, maybe using an SAE 10 or 20 in winter, and perhaps a 40 in summer.

In 1953, Motul and science came to the rescue. To give an oil a better chance of remaining efficient at both ends of the spectrum, thus giving better all-round power-unit protection, so-called multigrade oils were introduced, which use additives called 'viscosity index improvers' (VIIs). A typical multigrade from not so long ago would be 20W–50 (launched by Castrol in 1968), which means it acts as a fairly lightweight oil when cold, but gives more protection at higher temperatures. The only thing is, VIIs tend to degrade faster than straight oils.

Somewhere along the line, however, car manufacturers realized they could improve fuel efficiency by specifying a lighter oil, and, in turn, use lighter components in the starting circuit. Interestingly, the author queried the 0W–30 listed in the handbook of a new car with the engineer behind it. This was purely to improve the official fuel consumption figure, apparently, and the gentleman uses 10W–40 in his own car! But if nothing else, it does prove that lighter oils enhance fuel economy.

Nowadays oils are far more effective than they were even twenty years ago. They also contain cleaning agents and corrosion inhibitors, and in high performance and air-cooled engines can be made to act as part of the cooling system.

Synthetic lubricants – first developed in the 1930s by the Germans, who were desperate to overcome faltering crude oil supplies and waxing problems in extreme low temperatures – use base oils that contain fewer impurities and are more highly refined, allowing more uniform molecule sizes, thus reducing friction. They contain fewer VIIs, so stay serviceable for longer, and generally flow faster also, meaning less damage when an engine is first started, and speeded up warming-up times, which translates into a reduction in fuel consumption. Such is the advantage of the appliance of science.

Bio-oils, and new technology to create oils using esters, hydrocarbon-esters, polyalkylene glycols, and even plastics, are also coming through, and increasingly there is also the recycling of used oils, duly blended with a certain percentage of fresh oil – this may well add another 'Green' angle in the near future as it becomes a more widespread practice.

The Honda VTEC (variable valve timing and lift electronic control) system shown on a 1991 Prelude engine. Honda

By the start of the nineties, virtually every major manufacturer had moved over to overhead camshaft powerplants in order to get more horsepower without having to resort to a larger displacement – this gave the potential of fuel savings, as well as lower annual car taxes in those countries which class vehicles by the cubic capacity of the engine. Sohc and dohc units were already old news, in reality, and 4-valve per cylinder engines were by now commonplace, but other elements of the valve actuation and intake process were being given the high-tech treatment from makers far and wide.

Camshaft profiles either provided low-down torque, or sporting types could opt for 'high-lift cams' and have plenty of top-end power and very little response at low revs. Ultimately, most camshaft profiles provided a compromise between the two.

The idea of variable valve timing (or VVT), to maximize performance over a wider rev range, had been around since the 1920s, with people mulling over ways to change the valve opening and closing duration, using either mechanical or hydraulic means to alter the timing. However, nothing truly spectacular happened until the Italian engineers, Gio-

vanni Torazza and Giampaolo Garcea, started refining the concept for Fiat and Alfa Romeo production engines in the sixties and seventies. The fleeting reign of VVT was to be short-lived in the Fiat Group camp, however, fading out as soon as Fiat took over the Milan concern, being revived for the VIVAT system of the 1980s.

It was actually the Japanese who brought VVT into widespread use. Nissan was the first to showcase it in the 1987 season, although it wasn't until 1989, with the launch of the Z32 300ZX, that NVCS (the Nissan valve timing control system) went global. This was an electro-hydraulic arrangement operating on the inlet camshaft at low engine speeds to aid drivability whilst reducing fuel consumption and emissions.

To be honest, it was probably Honda's VTEC system – announced in April 1989 – that made a longer-lasting impression, using a computer to control electro-hydraulics that brought a third camshaft lobe and rocker arm into action to create a high-lift profile on each pair of valves at higher revs. The engine could then be tuned for low-end torque, enhanced economy and lower emissions as a default setting, with top-end performance on tap whenever needed. VTEC was updated several times, with VTEC-E biased towards providing better fuel consumption, and i-VTEC, more power.

Not long after Honda introduced VTEC, Toyota announced its VVT system, which became VVT-i after Toyota devised a way to continuously manage the valve timing, selecting the optimum intake and exhaust overlap under all operating conditions. VVT-i was found to be so effective that Toyota was able to eliminate EGR.

Meanwhile Porsche introduced its VarioCam system, and BMW brought out VANOS. These systems were later

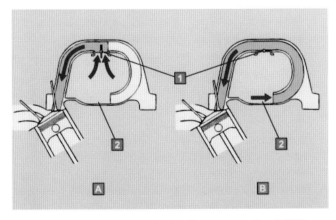

Toyota's acoustic control induction system (or ACIS), with figure 'A' showing the butterfly valve (1) open, and 'B' showing it closed effectively to give a longer intake tract within the suction chamber (2). Toyota

Direct injection as viewed from a Ford EcoBoost perspective. The older Mitsubishi GDI engines used a shaped piston crown to further encourage swirl of the air-fuel mixture. Ford

refined into VarioCam Plus and Valvetronic respectively, while other makers joined the VVT fray one after another – for example, Ford had VCT, which evolved into Ti-VCT, Mitsubishi had MIVEC, Nissan introduced its new VVL and CVTC systems, Subaru had AVCS, and General Motors pushed VVT and DCVCP technology.

Variable length intake tracts were the next big thing, with VLIM and VIM technology being the industry buzzword of the nineties. The idea is much the same as VVT – reducing the level of compromise in operating conditions to improve low-end torque and top-end power (as well as fuel consumption), only this time, using some sort of device (such as a butterfly valve) in the intake manifold to provide a longer tract for low engine speeds and a shorter one for higher revs. Again, virtually every manufacturer of note wheeled out its own variation on the theme, with Toyota announcing T-VIS early on, which evolved into ACIS, Honda having VVIS, Porsche having VarioRam, Mazda having VICS, and so on.

After years of very little happening on the petrol engine front, suddenly techno freaks were being treated to a bumper crop of new and important developments. Next up was direct injection.

Direct injection (sometimes known as 'fuel stratified injection', or FSI) had actually been around since the 1920s, but it wasn't until high-pressure fuel pumps became available at reasonable cost that the idea became feasible on mass-production vehicles. The system, typified by the Mitsubishi GDI (gasoline direct injection) set-up of 1996, injects fuel under extreme pressure directly into the combustion chamber, rather than the intake manifold or port. This allows finer control over the injection settings, ranging from an ultra-lean burn scenario at low revs through to a slightly richer air-fuel mixture at high revs.

The Japanese pioneered the use of DI, quickly followed by the Europeans, and then the Americans. Although carbon dioxide emissions fall by around 20 per cent, lean-burn technology combined with direct fuel injection leads to an increase in NOx, and fuel economy benefits only really come into play at higher speeds – there's no real difference in town running. However, combining a range of technologies can make a worthwhile reduction in fuel economy, hence direct injection's current popularity.

Siemens VDO, Bosch and Delphi all displayed piezoelectric fuel-injection systems at the 2003 Frankfurt Show, with Siemens being the first to bring the petrol version (PDI) to market using lead zirconate titanate ceramics (PZT) for the piezo element. This was a huge step forwards in direct-injection technology, as thanks to the fast-acting injectors a precise amount of fuel could be delivered towards the sparkplug in just 0.0002sec.

Interestingly, however, while most manufacturers were busy struggling to find a percentage point lower here and a percentage point lower there, it seems ironic that the winner of the 'World's Cleanest Car' title in 2000 was the contemporary Porsche 911 Turbo – a 420bhp twin-turbo beast, making the most of VarioCam Plus technology. Ultimately there was little thought of CO_2 emissions at that time, but it does show how blurred the lines are with regard to 'Green' machines.

BIO-FUELS

We looked at the bio-diesel situation in the second chapter, and also related the story of how bio-fuel as an alternative to petrol was very much a victim of political blocking in the States in pre-war days. Now it is being considered with a more open mind (even 'Big Oil' itself is looking into the possibilities, probably to ensure it is not left behind if bio-fuel takes off), while in Europe – notably in EEC powerhouse nations such as Germany and France – it has already gained acceptance as a fuel of the future. In addition, certain poorer countries have been using bio-fuels of one sort or another

Topping up a Ford Taurus flex-fuel vehicle (FFV) at Michigan's first public E85 fuelling facility at the end of the nineties. Ford was planning to begin high-volume production of FFVs in the 1999 Model Year, bringing more FFV products to market each year as the number of E85 service stations increased. Ford

for many years, not particularly for reasons of ecology, but because of a lack of traditional petroleum-based fuels, either due to local supply problems, or cost, putting petrol and diesel out of reach of the common man. In Brazil, for example, ethanol made from sugar cane has been a part of daily life for decades, even becoming a valuable export for the South American nation.

There is the question of sustainability to confront, however, with Brazil giving a perfect example of some of the confusion surrounding farming for bio-fuel production. Some say forests are being cleared, which will upset the balance of nature and bring about soil erosion; others point out that farmers will turn their back on food production in favour of more profitable crops that can be used for fuel.

Scare tactics from certain parties with vested interests in keeping bio-fuels scarce have blurred the results of honest research, but the bottom line is that very little of the Amazon rainforest has been cleared for bio-fuel purposes – over 99 per cent of sugar cane is grown outside this valuable eco-system, while clearing to create cattle pasture is all too common, and illegal logging a far more serious threat. Only 1 per cent of Brazil's arable land has provided half of the country's fuel needs, and the process used to create ethanol is particularly 'Green', with by-products employed to make electricity. In other words, the deforestation and soil erosion argument doesn't really hold up.

Notwithstanding, some will still point out that vegetable oil has become more expensive, hurting the most destitute of families who need it for cooking; but there are plenty of non-edible vegetable oils that can be processed into fuel, and many will grow where regular farming isn't really a feasible option, in poor soil and with very little water. Genetically modified (GM) crops, biomass to liquid (BTL) technology and water desalination plants could help poorer countries make dustbowls into profitable sources of income, reducing the need to buy oil products from outside using currencies out of synch with industrialized nations, which in turn frees up money to buy food and get other infrastructure and agricultural projects off the ground. Rather than create further hardship, it could actually reduce it in places not blessed with oil reserves.

The algae alternative, being looked at by oil giant Exxon-Mobil, as well as the likes of Denso and the IHI Corporation in Japan, should silence all the critics, as it doesn't clash with agricultural land needs, uses seawater that's freely available and doesn't need desalinating, and as well as creating new jobs, is highly space-efficient. But in any case, there are farmers all over Europe being paid not to grow something, so things should ultimately sort themselves out if governments can come up with suitable long-term energy plans.

Gas-friendly to gas-free.

The environment and your commute. Can't we all just get along? Making a difference in our environment is as simple as driving a more fuel-efficient vehicle. That's why Chevy™ currently offers seven models that have an EPA estimated 30 MPG highway or better.¹ Like Cobalt® XFE Coupe with unsurpassed highway fuel economy in its class at an EPA estimated 36 MPG highway.² Other Chevy vehicles that fall into the 30 MPG or higher club include Aveo® Sedan, Aveo5, Malibu® Hybrid,³ and select models of Malibu, HHR,⁴ and HHR Panel. And coming this summer, the newly redesigned 2009 Aveo5 that will have an estimated 34 MPG highway.⁴ But it's not just about cars. Chevy Silverado® offers the best V8 fuel economy of any full-size pickup.⁵ And the full-size Tahoe® SUV delivers best-in-class fuel economy.⁶ And there's more. Every 2008 Chevy car, half-ton truck, and SUV is equipped with a Tire Pressure Monitor that will automatically alert you when your tire pressure is low. Properly inflated tires can improve gas mileage by up to 3%.⁷ A little thing, but if everyone in the U.S. had properly inflated tires, we could save millions of gallons of gas each year. Find out more at chevy.com **AN AMERICAN REVOLUTION**

ABOVE: **Chevrolet advertising from 2008. Flex-fuel vehicles, which have a single fuel tank, as opposed to a bi-fuel model with separate tanks, are currently being pushed by the US 'Big Three' as economically viable 'Green' models.** Chevrolet

RIGHT: **A Peugeot 206 Escapade flex-fuel model in front of a field of sugar. As well as the PSA Group, FFVs are being built by Renault, Ford, GM, Chrysler, Fiat, the VW-Audi Group, Mercedes-Benz, Toyota, Honda, Mitsubishi, Nissan, Kia, Volvo and Saab.** Peugeot

As well as being a renewable and biodegradable source of energy that keeps oil prices in check and has positive 'Green' benefits in terms of the equivalent to a well-to-tailpipe life-cycle, there is also the national security angle, with less reliance on other countries to supply oil. Given America's level of paranoia on this point, and the fact that it turned its back on corn-based ethanol after the public outcry surrounding the 'burning food for fuel' issue, it seems rather odd that an extension of tax credits for small businesses involved in the creation of new bio-fuels was recently rejected by the US Senate!

Despite vast sums of money leaving the country each year to procure crude, not to mention warnings of oil reserves running low, there doesn't seem to be any rush to change the habits of a lifetime. Worldwide, locally created fuels would reduce shipping, which translates into the virtual elimination of spills from ocean-going tankers, as well as a lot of the danger associated with deep-sea oil rigs, and the cost of exploration. Besides which, the basic principle behind the creation of this strain of bio-fuel is simple enough, involving either some sort of chemical reaction to produce an aliphatic alcohol, or the conversion of a feedstock into an alcohol via fermentation.

Ultimately there are four alcohols commonly used as fuels, chemically the same regardless of how they were made: ethanol, methanol, butanol and propanol. The latter is not usually employed in motor vehicle applications, and the use of butanol (something BP is investing heavily in) is a

The highly efficient Ricardo EBDI engine, optimized to run on ethanol. Ricardo

relatively new development – but the other two are widely accepted as an alternative to petrol, having high octane ratings and characteristics that allow them to be used in modern engines with little or no modification, at least when blended with regular gasoline. With a few changes, the latest engines can be run with fuel such as E85, which contains 85 per cent ethanol – cars with these units are usually identified by the 'Flex-Fuel' moniker.

As it happens, ethanol (C_2H_5OH, sometimes simplified to EtOH) is by far the most popular bio-fuel on offer at the moment, with production soaring in the EU countries. In 2000, around one million tonnes of bio-ethanol was produced, but the annual figure had doubled by 2003, and was over six million tonnes just three years later.

Similar increases can be seen in America, too, but ethanol was recognized as an alternative fuel far earlier in the States. For instance, Henry Ford recommended ethanol to power his famous Model T of 1908, and in partnership with John D. Rockefeller's Standard Oil, even had his own hemp farm for producing bio-fuel. A few decades later, the US Army was producing ethanol for blending with regular gasoline during World War II; but then cheap petrol made the Americans turn away from the idea. Until now, that is, in the wake of the 1990 Clean Air Act, with the USA now producing more bio-ethanol than Brazil, and almost ten times what the EEC countries can muster between them.

The traditional way of making ethanol is by fermentation of the glucose and simple sugars found in the likes of sugar cane or corn. Older methods for producing ethanol are largely being abandoned nowadays, as the cost of processing (getting rid of the small amount of water in aqueous ethanol takes a lot of energy, for instance) and the use of only part of a plant (giving a low yield in relation to acreage) makes it difficult to justify commercially without a dire need; a lot of CO_2 results from the process as well, although photosynthesis in the crops absorbs it as part of the bio-fuel lifecycle.

Newer techniques, giving birth to cellulosic ethanol, break down the cellulose in woody fibres to create sugars that can then be fermented. This means that waste products such as wood chips, agricultural by-products, and even paper can be used, as well as full plants, trees and grasses, meaning higher yields per acre and the use of fewer fossil fuels via farming. In a nutshell it means a large reduction in greenhouse gases over a full 'well-to-tailpipe' lifecycle.

General Motors has invested heavily in the development of cellulosic ethanol, signing an agreement with Coskata. Volkswagen signed up with Iogen of Canada in a similar deal, while Toyota recently announced it was using napier grass and a new strain of yeast in its own bio-fuel technology. The Japanese company said it was hoping to commercialize the product by 2020 at the latest, by which time a reduction in the costs involved should make it cheaper at the pumps, and therefore a viable project worthy of financial backing.

In addition, synthetic ethanol can be produced by the catalytic hydration of ethylene, using acids or heated ceramic solids as a catalyst, or by adding water (in the form of steam) to ethene in a suitable industrial facility.

The tonne of oil equivalent (a useful unit which helps gauge energy conversion efficiency) of ethanol is 0.64, against 1.05 for traditional gasoline, so litre for litre, it is less efficient than petrol. Gas mileage is therefore higher as a result, but it is a renewable fuel source with 'Green' credentials, and all alcohols have a higher octane rating than gasoline (113 RON for ethanol, and 116 for methanol, against typical values of 91, 95, 98, or occasionally 102 RON for petrol). The higher the octane number, the less pre-ignition (or knocking) is likely to occur, explaining why E5 or E10, which is petrol blended with a very low ethanol content, has a place on the market. This allows higher compression ratios to be adopted, improving fuel consumption, which goes some way towards closing the gap in ethanol's efficiency when measured by volume in comparison with petrol – at least on cars designed to run exclusively on ethanol-rich fuels, although it has to be said that the higher the c/r, the more NOx emissions are created.

Ethanol blending is commonplace, but Brazil sold cars capable of running on pure ethanol (E100) from 1979 onwards, recalibrating compression ratios and fuel-injection settings, adopting different sparkplugs, changing materials used for seals, hoses and so on to avoid corrosion, and adding a special cold-start system that used petrol from a small auxiliary tank for getting the engine going on colder days. Although Flex-Fuel cars are now the norm, introduced in Brazil in 2003, there are still over two million older vehicles running on E100 – a survival rate of around 40 per cent.

Generally speaking, burning ethanol results in an exhaust gas containing virtually no particulate matter or sulphur, fewer volatile organic compounds (VOC), and compared with gasoline, CO, HC and NOx levels are all reduced at the tailpipe. Indeed, ethanol (and methanol for that matter) is often used as an additive to oxygenate petrol in order to reduce carbon monoxide emissions.

As well as water, carbon dioxide is given off during combustion – less than when burning petrol, but the higher fuel consumption when measured by liquid volume means that CO_2 emissions are actually higher overall. However, in contrast to using fossil fuels, this is then absorbed by plants used as feedstock anyway, while the sustainability angle is also something to be taken into consideration.

Those saying ethanol is bad because of the lower gas mileage are only looking at a small part of the big picture – the bit that can be measured accurately by the fuel bill each month, but with ethanol cheaper than gasoline at the pumps, it doesn't hurt the pocket that much in any case.

On the down side, acetaldehyde is released in much greater volume when compared to burning petrol, along with formaldehyde to a lesser extent (both possible carcinogenics, the latter posing the biggest risk to health), and methane, too, which is a potent greenhouse gas. At least benzine (another carcinogen) emissions are reduced by a significant amount (about 75 per cent), as are those of butadiene, which is really nasty. In reality, the methane release is only troublesome when expressed as a percentage – there's hardly any escaping into the atmosphere in the real world, as we are comparing the amounts to gasoline, which basically releases none or a minute trace at best, and what does escape is largely through fuel system venting rather than combustion.

On the practical front, water absorption is a serious problem, making ethanol difficult to store over any length of time, and it can even take on water whilst in the fuel tank. Vapour lock can occur that much more easily compared with regular unleaded petrol, and ethanol can also damage certain plastics and rubber, even metals. Depending on the grade of fuel, evaporative emissions can come into play to a greater or lesser extent. Notwithstanding, fixes have been incorporated into a lot of today's vehicles (from the use of different materials to the introduction of vapour recovery systems), and with the benefit of modern knock sensors and ECUs that look after and adjust ignition timing automatically, the majority of car manufacturers are happy to recommend the use of E10 fuel at the very least.

Tapping oil wells and the subsequent oil-refining process is one of the largest sources of methane being released into the atmosphere. We've already noted the long-term harmful effect methane has on the environment, yet 'flaring' (the

In 1979, the German government launched the 'Alternative Energies for Road Traffic' programme.
Daimler AG

Mercedes-Benz presented this 300SE flex-fuel model at the 1992 Geneva Show, designed to run on M85 fuel. Mercedes-Benz carried out trials using methanol in W123 and R107 models. Methanol was also chosen for the experimental Nissan TRI-X and Subaru Rioma models of 1991, but it remains a rarity compared to ethanol as a straight fuel. Daimler AG

burning of unwanted gases at a well to release pressure) and venting is still commonplace within the oil and natural gas industry. This is extremely sad, because not only do we have to put up with emissions that speed up global warming, but methane (CH_4) is proving to be an ideal feedstock for alternative fuel, with methanol – derived from methane – taking its place alongside ethanol.

Methanol (also known as MeOH, or more commonly wood alcohol) has the chemical formula CH_3OH, and burns in a similar fashion to ethanol, combustion giving one more part of water in the chemical reaction. While the fuel itself is more corrosive, and the energy content is slightly lower than that of ethanol, it has a major advantage in the cost-effective and sustainable way it can be produced.

In recent years, the methane gas generated by the oil industry is increasingly being collected via new forms of solid catalysts; it can also be tapped from places such as landfill sites, and manure from farming can be converted to methane (or more correctly, bio-gas) by an anaerobic digester. Some countries use coal as a starting point, while biomass is perhaps the ideal 'Green' option, with the feedstock either treated thermally to encourage fast pyrolysis, or subjected to direct gasification. One then uses the Fischer-Tropsch system, employing GTL, CTL or BTL technology (see the section on bio-diesel – 'Green' Fuels: the Case for Bio-Diesel – two-thirds of the way through Chapter 2) to create a syngas that is then heated and passed over metallic catalysts to give methanol. Another noteworthy alternative, developed by the Mitsui Chemical concern in Japan, converts

industrial CO_2 effluent and photocatalyst-produced hydrogen into methanol.

Methanol was used in Indy racing in America for many years, although ethanol is today's choice. For road cars, the European Fuel Quality Directive allows gasoline to contain up to 3 per cent methanol, as long as an equivalent amount of co-solvent is used, along with corrosion inhibitors. Some countries, however, such as China, use far stronger blends with vehicles designed to suit the fuel – M85 is common, in which the methanol content is 85 per cent combined with 15 per cent unleaded petrol, whereas M15 is available for older machines, and the latest engines and fuel systems are being designed to take M100, which is neat methanol.

Interestingly, ExxonMobil patented a way of creating gasoline from methanol (the MTG process), and this has duly been refined by Primus of New Jersey. The system employs dimethylether (DME), the dehydrated derivative of methanol, which is then passed over a series of catalysts to give petrol – although once mixed with LPG, DME itself can be used with gasoline engines, giving another option in the quickly expanding field of alternative fuels.

Butanol is another alcohol-derived fuel, having an 18 per cent higher energy content than ethanol, or 22 per cent higher than that of methanol. Indeed, with an energy density only 14 per cent down on gasoline, its characteristics are very similar to petrol, with an octane rating of 96 RON. It can therefore be used in petrol-engined vehicles largely without modification, although until recently, manufacturing costs have restricted its growth as a bio-fuel. However, BP is convinced it has found a cost-effective way of producing butanol, and confidently predicts that one day, the ethanol-production plant it shares with DuPont will duly be converted into a butanol facility.

During combustion, in addition to heat (the energy needed to run the engine, of course), butanol (C_4H_9OH) burns to give off four parts carbon dioxide and five parts water. Less corrosive than the other alcohols, it can be made from traditional fossil fuels and bio-fuel feedstocks, and – more importantly from a long-term 'Green' perspective – biomass or algae.

On the subject of 'Green' lifecycles, more should be done to encourage the collection of cooking fat, especially in large urban areas. It has proved to be feasible as a source for making bio-diesel, but it can also be made into ethanol. It's certainly an ecological choice, because it recycles waste into something in demand – so why is its greater use being held back? Granted, it would only ever be able to supply a minute amount of the fuel needed annually, but it provides an ideal business scenario for smaller firms.

THE MILD HYBRID BOOM

Whenever we talk about modern petrol-engined cars, we also have to consider so-called 'mild hybrid' models. The easiest way to categorize these vehicles is to say they are fitted with some form of regenerative braking. The first example of a mild hybrid shown at the 1899 Paris Salon – a voiturette built by Pieper of Belgium – was very significant, using an electric motor to assist the petrol engine when the power called for was more than the small air-cooled unit could handle. When not being used as a power booster, such as when the car was cruising or stationary, the electric motor acted as a generator to charge the Tudor lead-acid batteries. Regenerative braking had been born.

The work of Henri Pieper became more widely known through the Auto-Mixte name, with various cars and commercials using the innovative drive system through to the end of World War I. Société Pieper and the Auto-Mixte concern that took over its mantle were very good at selling licences, so we saw the system used by companies such as Mercedes of Germany, Daimler of Britain and Krieger of France, and following the approval of US patent 913846 (applied for in the name of Henri Pieper on 23 November 1905), this 'Mixed Drive for Autovehicles' made headlines across the pond, too.

However, one had to wait a long time before Honda's IMA (integrated motor assist) system brought forth the first of the modern breed of mild hybrid cars – the Insight, announced in September 1999, with technology based on the 1997 J-VX concept.

Henri Pieper's mild hybrid design, which gave birth to the Auto-Mixte system. US Patent Office

The IMA system serves as a perfect example of a contemporary mild hybrid drivetrain, with an electric motor-generator unit (MGU) tacked on to the engine's flywheel. As in the Auto-Mixte system, this MGU not only provided regenerative braking, it worked in parallel with the engine, assisting it whenever the driver's right foot deemed it necessary. This enabled the engineers to specify a powerplant with a smaller displacement, as an electric motor can provide an excellent spread of low-down torque. At the same time, the size – and therefore weight and cost – of the motor and battery pack could be reduced significantly, as they were never called upon to power the car on their own. Another benefit, this time beyond Pieper's wildest dreams, came with idle-stop technology. Whenever a vehicle was left idling, such as when waiting at traffic lights, the engine would cut out, and be restarted again by the MGU.

Honda's IMA system, as seen in 2001. Honda

Mazda's Skyactiv engine fitted with the award-winning 'i-stop' idle-stop facility. The main part of the mechanism can be seen closest to the camera. B. Long

The first idle-stop systems appeared in the 1980s, but it was some time before they became popular, partly due to the high cost, partly due to people's fear of anything new, and partly because reaction times were slow. However, the mild hybrid gave the concept a second wind, and a number of makers started introducing cars with idle-stop features, creating the so-called 'micro-hybrid' vehicle category along the way.

The confusion surrounding what should be classed as a mild hybrid doesn't get any easier when the manufacturers

themselves blur the lines of distinction. As far as the author is concerned, a mild hybrid has a second power source that assists the first only (it cannot provide motive power), while it is safe to say that a micro-hybrid is usually nothing more than a car fitted with idle-stop technology.

Whatever the definitions, literally millions of gallons of fuel are wasted at traffic lights every year, so this was a most welcome piece of technology. Combined with the other benefits of the mild hybrid system, it allowed fuel savings of around 15 per cent in town, and about 9 per cent overall. Indeed, the manual Honda Insight had an original EPA rating of 3.9ltr/100km (61mpg) city and 3.4ltr/100km (70mpg) highway, which is quite remarkable, even though the engine was only a 1-litre, 3-cylinder unit.

The next mild hybrid was from Toyota – the THS-M system being introduced for the Crown in August 2001. This was available in Japan only, however. Four months later, Honda rolled out the Civic Hybrid, which looked just like the regular model but had a 1.3-litre engine assisted by an electric motor in established IMA fashion. It went on sale Stateside in the spring of 2002, being classed as an early 2003 model. More importantly, the folks at the California Air Resources Board gave it an AT-PZEV rating – a pat on the back for the men at Honda, and doubtless one of the main reasons why Honda offers so many mild hybrids nowadays, ranging from the Fit through to the CR-Z.

New York City mayor, Michael Bloomberg (right), pictured with GM's Robert Bothfeld and a Chevy Malibu hybrid, as the mayor's office announced the deployment of 'Greener' vehicles for NYC's vast taxi fleet. Emile Wamsteker/GM

TOP & MIDDLE: **Display model of the BMW ActiveHybrid 7, with detail of the Continental hybrid system and 8AT gearbox at the front, and the Li-ion battery pack at the rear.** BMW

BOTTOM: **Volvo announced it was going to use Flybrid Systems' KERS flywheel, using F1 technology, in 2011. KERS stands for 'kinetic energy recovery system'.** Volvo

There were some short-lived offerings from Mazda (a Demio with an electric motor on the rear wheels aiding the regular FF drivetrain) and also GM. In theory the latter's pick-up trucks were ideally suited to a hybrid system, but sales simply didn't take off, as the potential savings from idle-stop technology versus the option cost made little financial sense for customers. Ultimately, GM moved over to the BAS (belt alternator starter) system, which provided a small amount of drive torque to assist the engine – but the line of Saturns and the Chevy Malibu hybrid didn't last long after the new boss at General Motors declared there was no profit in them. Recently, however, the e-Assist system has revived the BAS idea.

BMW unveiled its X3 Hybrid concept at the 2005 Frankfurt Show – a mild hybrid, using ultra-capacitors in the doors instead of a battery to store electricity. Although Mazda recently used ultra-caps in its Takeri mild hybrid concept, proving that the idea isn't dead, the first production BMW mild hybrid was not nearly so bold, being much the same as the Honda IMA system, albeit with Li-ion batteries rather than a NiMH battery pack. The BMW ActiveHybrid 7 had a CO_2 emissions rating of 219g/km.

The Mercedes-Benz S400 BlueHybrid used a similar Continental set-up to the BMW 7-series model, with a compact 15kW motor between the engine and transmission. The motor, although small, contributed well over a third of the combined maximum torque figure, whilst the recaptured kinetic energy stored in the Li-ion batteries drove several electrical circuits, such as the HVAC system, power windows, and the stereo. This reduced the load on the alternator, lowering parasitic losses.

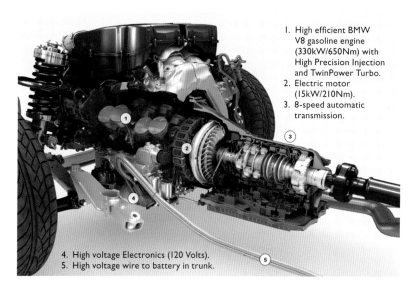

1. High efficient BMW V8 gasoline engine (330kW/650Nm) with High Precision Injection and TwinPower Turbo.
2. Electric motor (15kW/210Nm).
3. 8-speed automatic transmission.
4. High voltage Electronics (120 Volts).
5. High voltage wire to battery in trunk.

1. Lithium-Ion battery (120Volts/800Wh/ 35 cells).
2. Heating/cooling device for battery.
3. High voltage wire to electric motor.

FLYWHEEL KERS
FLYWHEEL MODULE

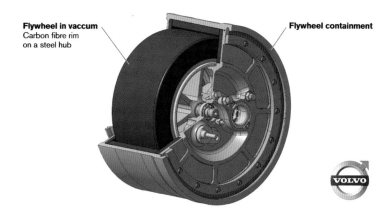

Flywheel in vaccum
Carbon fibre rim on a steel hub

Flywheel containment

EMISSION TARGETS IN EUROPE

As part of the EU's commitment to the Kyoto Protocol, the intention is to cut GHG emissions by 20 per cent by the year 2020, the reduction being based on 1990 figures. In this spirit, Germany proposed a target for motor vehicle emissions of 120g/km at a meeting in October 1994, which was a challenging 35 per cent down on contemporary levels, but the approval was given nonetheless in the following year, with 2005 being the start date for the new legislation to take effect.

As one can imagine, there was a lot of grumbling in boardrooms, and in 1998, the ACEA's voluntary limit was modified to 140g/km of CO_2 per car (averaged over a manufacturer's range) for 2008, with a 120g/km limit being imposed for 2012. Naturally, car firms managed to move the goalposts again, but this time, the word 'voluntary' was changed for 'law' and Europe's mandatory limits on carbon dioxide emissions will come into effect in 2015, set at 130g/km.

The strange thing is there is no real encouragement to make lighter cars, although it's only fair that specialist makers, such as Jaguar and Porsche, with small ranges and low volumes, have certain allowances. But a bonus of some sort for making lighter vehicles, year on year, would surely help push development in the right direction.

The European Federation for Transport and the Environment report that looks back on 2009 makes particularly fascinating reading, given the abundance of scrappage schemes in place all over the EU. An estimated €6 billion was spent, putting an extra 2,000,000 cars on the road, yet tailpipe emissions only went down by 5.1 per cent compared to 2008 – a figure that can be summarized via the effects of lower weight (1.8 per cent), a reduction in power (0.6 per cent), and better technology (2.7 per cent). If we think of manufacturing emissions, the true benefits for the environment are marginal at best, even taking the long-term view on exhaust emissions.

As manufacturers, Fiat topped the league tables in 2008 and 2009, with a fleet average of 131g/km; Toyota was next with a figure of 132g/km. A few makers were as far as 18 per cent off 2015 targets, and, surprisingly, some of those one would least expect to be struggling were often those lagging behind at this stage.

The biggest progress on CO_2 reduction was being made by Toyota, Suzuki and Mazda, but the 2015 limit still looked a long way off, even for this group. Now Europe is already talking about a proposed 95g/km ceiling to be introduced for 2020. Many makers are against such a tight target, saying it would cost too much and be technically difficult to achieve within the allotted timescale. Even Volkswagen, which is one of the more eco-friendly manufacturers, is against the plan, which will need to be finalized in 2013.

ALTERNATIVE ICES

The most popular alternative to traditional four-stroke engines is the two-stroke, with its compact dimensions and lack of valves – thus reducing manufacturing costs and complications – being major advantages. They also deliver a power stroke on every rotation of the crankshaft, giving them a high power-to-weight ratio.

However, the engine lubricant has to be mixed with the fuel, meaning extremely high levels of particulate matter (PM) emissions, and due to the layout of the combustion chamber, a part of the air-fuel charge is wasted, leaking through the exhaust port before it is ignited. HC emissions are therefore very bad, although CO and NOx emissions are actually lower than those of four-stroke engines, generally speaking.

There were a few car manufacturers that used two-stroke engines, with Saab being one of the last notables. But as the environmental damage became more apparent, even motor-

cycle makers started moving towards four-stroke units at the end of the 1970s. Toyota looked at reviving the two-stroke in its 1991 AXV-IV concept, but soon thought better of the idea.

In reality, at least from a pollution point of view, a world-wide ban on two-strokes would be the best thing, unless they can demonstrate a lack of cross-contamination caused by mixing oil with fuel. One such unit that springs to mind is the Grail Engine, with its ingenious valve system devised by Matthew Riley. The inlet valve is contained in the piston head, with the exhaust at the top of the cylinder, surrounded by three sparkplugs and the fuel injector. Combining HCCI (homogeneous charge compression ignition) technology with the Miller cycle, plus the main advantages of a two-stroke unit without a lot of the disadvantages, the concept deserves more than just a passing glance.

On the subject of HCCI technology, a number of makers are currently working on ways to make this a feasible idea, as it promises significant fuel savings. Basically, one compresses

The Mercedes-Benz F700 concept car, first displayed at the 2007 Frankfurt Show. Daimler AG

the air-fuel mix beyond the norm and uses heat to ignite the charge rather than a spark, as in a diesel engine. The difference, of course, is that petrol powerplants do not require the same level of exhaust gas cleaning, so although the fuel saving may not be as high (GM predict around 15 per cent), production costs that need to be passed on to the customer are reduced.

Because heat is necessary to make HCCI work, a spark ignition is provided for cold starting (much like a glowplug in a diesel unit), but this can then be used at certain engine speeds to maintain performance with the latest ECUs coming on to the market. At the same time, the working temperatures are actually a lot lower than they are with spark-ignited fuel, and the burn is a lot faster. With reduced pumping losses and less energy lost through excessive heat generation, efficiency is increased, meaning lower fuel consumption and fewer GHG emissions.

The Mercedes-Benz 'DiesOtto' stands out as a shining example of the promise this unit holds, combining HCCI technology with twin turbos, direct injection and variable valve timing. As shown in the F700 prototype, the 238bhp unit was mated with a 15kW electric motor to smooth the transition from CI to SI mode, giving petrol consumption figures of 5.3ltr/100km, and CO_2 emissions of just 127g/km.

General Motors has allowed journalists to drive a number of vehicles fitted with HCCI engines in recent years, and

both Honda and Volkswagen have also made headway with the HCCI concept. The VW engine (given the gasoline compression ignition, or GCI moniker) has been successfully demonstrated in a Touran, and there are hopes that HCCI power-units will be available in the showroom in 2015.

The rotary engine (or RE), invented by Dr Felix Wankel, has been around for much longer, with the first of its kind

Volkswagen's GCI homogenous charge compression ignition engine, which runs on petrol, but works like a diesel unit. Volkswagen

up and running in 1957. The main advantage is that a rotor can achieve what a regular ICE takes four strokes to do in just one rotation, by which time it has delivered three power pulses. Mazda made the concept practical, and announced its first rotary-engined car in 1964. However, it wasn't until mid-1967 that it was ready for the showroom, such were the technical difficulties in perfecting this compact, lightweight and smooth power-unit.

Having spent so long getting the rotary concept to work properly, the Muskie Act dealt a cruel blow to Mazda's engineers. Although the RE had always struggled with keeping HC emissions in check, NOx weren't so bad. General Motors walked away (there were thoughts that GM might sell as many as 500,000 REs in the seventies, but the $150 million investment ultimately came to nothing), but Mazda persevered, making the unit cleaner and more powerful with each generation, albeit notoriously thirsty.

The RX-8 brought with it the 'Renesis' RE, with fuel consumption reduced by 40 per cent, along with lower emissions. The recent experiments with hydrogen as a fuel

Inside the jewel-like Mazda 'Renesis' rotary engine. Mazda

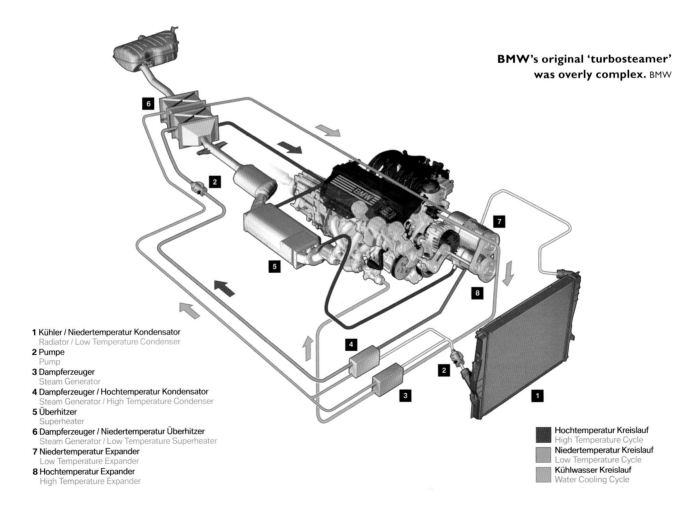

BMW's original 'turbosteamer' was overly complex. BMW

1 Kühler / Niedertemperatur Kondensator
  Radiator / Low Temperature Condenser
2 Pumpe
  Pump
3 Dampferzeuger
  Steam Generator
4 Dampferzeuger / Hochtemperatur Kondensator
  Steam Generator / High Temperature Condenser
5 Überhitzer
  Superheater
6 Dampferzeuger / Niedertemperatur Überhitzer
  Steam Generator / Low Temperature Superheater
7 Niedertemperatur Expander
  Low Temperature Expander
8 Hochtemperatur Expander
  High Temperature Expander

▉ Hochtemperatur Kreislauf
  High Temperature Cycle
▉ Niedertemperatur Kreislauf
  Low Temperature Cycle
▉ Kühlwasser Kreislauf
  Water Cooling Cycle

RIGHT: **The second generation 'turbosteamer' is a far more compact installation, saving weight and cost, and recycling otherwise wasted energy.**
BMW

BELOW: **The Scuderi engine, which separates the intake/ compression and power/ exhaust strokes into two different cylinders, linked by a crossover passage controlled by extra valves. The four strokes can then be accomplished in one revolution of the crankshaft instead of two. It offers the potential of cleaner burning and better fuel economy.**
Scuderi

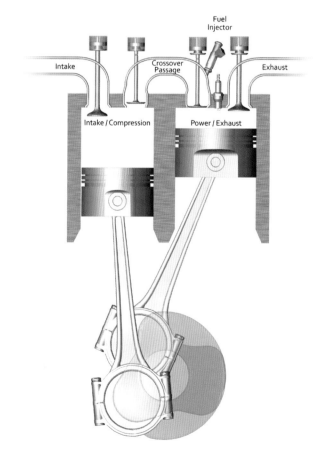

showed promise, but nothing came of the idea. One is now left wondering whether the days of this inspiring engine are numbered.

Traditional normally aspirated ICEs lose up to 42 per cent of their energy through the exhaust (explaining why turbochargers can actually improve fuel consumption, and not just performance) and a further 28 per cent through their cooling system. Heat management is to blame for this, and efficiency gains through new technology are usually fairly marginal in comparison.

The Concept IC engine, invented by Dilip James, uses a sleeve valve for the exhaust instead of a poppet valve, and uses the pressure of the escaping gases to turn a turbine, which can then be used to drive power-sapping ancillaries such as water pumps, oil pumps, alternators, PAS pumps and air-conditioning compressors.

In 2005, BMW came up with a similar observation, and developed a so-called 'turbosteamer' that recycled 80 per cent of the exhaust gases. These gases heat a fluid to create steam, which is then directed into an expansion unit linked to the engine's crankshaft; this assistance increases fuel efficiency by 15 per cent on a typical 1.8-litre power-unit. In 2011, BMW announced a smaller, simplified version, which stands every chance of being production-ready in the next few years.

This leads us to the six-stroke engine, which as yet is still in development, despite various basic principles having been around since the end of the 1980s, with the Swiss Bajulaz concern being the first to release details of its six-stroke cycle.

In the Bajulaz model, a second cylinder gives a stratified charge, so there are two power pulses for every six strokes. Reasonable production costs, aided by fairly minor changes to the engine's overall design, combined with clean burning and a 40 per cent reduction in fuel consumption, should make the concept interesting.

The Velozeta engine, announced in 2006, uses exhaust gases in the combustion chamber to heat air injected into the cylinder at high pressure. The hot air expands, pushing the piston back down, giving an extra power stroke without the use of additional fuel. A 40 per cent reduction in fuel consumption has been reported, along with a 65 per cent drop in carbon monoxide emissions. Several other designs using water injection instead of air have also appeared over the years.

Another variation on the six-stroke theme involves using two horizontally opposed pistons, the second piston replacing the valvetrain of a conventional engine, and allowing higher compression ratios, as well as excellent compatibility with alternative fuels. It may find use one day as an engine linked with hybrid technology.

Meanwhile split-cycle powerplants, at least in principle, have been around since the end of the nineteenth century, but the Backus unit was a stationary engine. It wasn't until 1994 that the renowned thermodynamics engineer Carmelo Scuderi revived the idea for automotive applications, meaning that the whole thing had to be compact, highly efficient (as it had to offer significant benefits over conventional ICEs that had 100 years of development time already put into them), and reasonably easy to make, thereby keeping costs in check.

By July 2001, Scuderi had filed his first of several patents for a new split-cycle engine, and soon after, a link with the Southwest Research Institute was established. Sadly, Carmelo Scuderi died in 2002, but his work was continued, and in the following year, flame speed tests showed incredibly fast combustion rates and low emissions. Prototyping began in 2005, and once the advantage of being able to use existing manufacturing equipment was realized, funding and big name technical assistance were secured for an evolution of the original engine – the Scuderi Air-Hybrid, with a small air tank capturing and reusing wasted energy.

The first working Scuderi engine prototype was fired up in June 2009. Basically, the split-cycle engine separates the four strokes into two cylinders – one handling the intake and compression, the other power and exhaust. This allows better optimization of each cycle, creating a cleaner burn, and the crankshaft only needs one rotation to complete the four strokes instead of two.

The design was then later enhanced by employing a 'v' configuration, providing more engineering flexibility and making turbocharging that much easier. In addition to a worthwhile reduction in NOx and CO_2 emissions, early simulations predicted a 25 to 35 per cent fuel saving over conventional engines, and now that turbocharging has been successfully combined with the Miller cycle, there is the potential for further improvement. Add in compatibility with a wide range of fuels, including ethanol, bio-diesel, CNG and hydrogen, and good torque delivery, and it starts to look like a winner.

The GM split-cycle engine works on a similar principle, but will probably require licensing Scuderi patents to make it work quickly – a little feeling of déjà vu with GM's past experience with the rotary engine, perhaps? The only difference between the two stories is that Mazda deliberately cornered the market on the RE, while Scuderi would prefer to leave others to do the actual manufacturing.

PERFECTING TODAY'S PETROL ENGINES

After the best part of 120 years of evolution, one would have thought the petrol engine had reached its limit of development. However, there were still areas of fine-tuning that were making a significant impact on fuel consumption and emissions. Volkswagen's TSI technology is a perfect example.

Launched in March 2006, the TSI engine brought together fuel stratified direct-injection, a Roots-type supercharger, and an exhaust-driven turbocharger connected in series. The 1.4-litre TSI unit was duly endowed with the power of a typical 2.3-litre engine when the driver called for it, with the supercharger providing low-down torque, and the turbo giving an extra kick at higher revs, taking the place of the supercharger. On a light throttle, though, the combination gave an uncanny combination of drivability and economy, the latter put at 7.2ltr/100km.

Two-stage sequential turbos are nothing new, with the Mazda RX-7 using them for a more linear performance boost, but nowadays the matching of odd sizes is being introduced to give a better fuel-efficiency advantage. The latest BMW and Mercedes-Benz installations are beautifully engineered, with the twin-turbo version of the Mercedes M157 unit having a double-skinned exhaust manifold to reduce heat loss – heat is, after all, energy that can be converted. Meanwhile, Audi adds elegance to forced induction by combining the supercharger with the intercooler on its TFSi V6

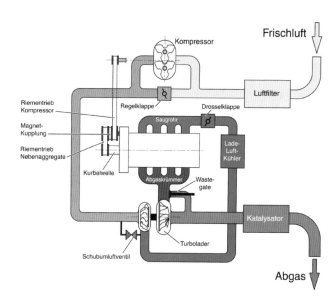

First announced at the 2005 Frankfurt Show, this is the original 1.4-litre VW TSI powerplant, and the TSI system flow chart. Several engine sizes are available nowadays. Volkswagen

engine, thus saving weight through reduced plumbing; it is also a more compact arrangement.

On the subject of compact, it's plain to see that a number of makers are downsizing engines, from Porsche sports cars to Mitsubishi town cars. The new 999cc Volkswagen EA211 3-cylinder engine serves as a good example of the current train of thought. Subaru is also downsizing, and interestingly, dropping its 660cc Kei line at the other end of the scale.

Daihatsu, meanwhile, wouldn't be able to survive without the Kei-car, but the latest 660cc 'Mira e:S' model uses an advanced idle-stop feature that cuts the engine before the car comes to a complete standstill; it also has a higher c/r, new injectors, a revised EGR system, a new CVT with optimized gear ratios, regenerative braking to recharge the battery, and an indicator that guides the driver to coax the best economy from the power-unit. With a weight reduction of 60kg (132lb) and lower rolling resistance as well, the nett result is fuel economy of 30km per litre in the JC08 mode – an improvement of about 13 per cent. According to Daihatsu engineers, a turbocharged 2-cylinder 8v powerplant is next in line – the weight saving being a step in the right direction, and combined with a high-powered ignition system, should promote 35km/ltr fuel consumption without any change in performance.

Suzuki, too, is taking a more rounded approach towards extracting the best possible gas mileage from its machines. For the Alto Eco, the body was lowered, the front panel-

work was made smoother to slip through the air more easily, weight was cut wherever possible, internal friction was reduced in the R06A engine, and the latest idle-stop facility fitted. According to Suzuki, the difference in economy was 30 per cent!

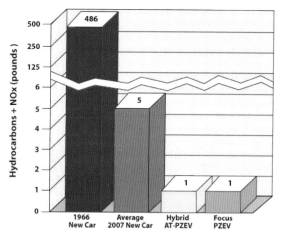

The 2007 Ford Focus used conventional technology, without even the slightest hint of a hybrid system, but still gained a PZEV rating in the States. Ford

Launch of the latest Ford EcoBoost 1-litre engine. Ford

Small petrol engines still hold promise. FEV of Michigan converted a 3-cylinder 698cc Smart Brabus engine into a single-spark turbocharged unit with direct injection, calling it the 'EDE' – the initials standing for 'extremely downsized engine'. Displayed at the 2010 SAE World Congress at nearby Detroit, the EDE provided a specific power output of 135bhp per litre, which is truly remarkable, while low-end torque was improved by as much as 32 per cent. Development work continues.

Moving up the scale, the latest Fords incorporate a range of technologies, including an idle-stop feature, an 'eco-mode' driver-information system combined with a gear-shift indicator to get the best gas mileage possible, and regenerative battery charging, topping up the voltage at the most economical points in a journey. Add in details such as incorporating the exhaust manifold into the cylinder-head design to speed up warming-up times, low friction seals, and low friction coatings on tappets and pistons, and one can see that a lot of effort is going into refining existing technology, as well as introducing new ideas.

Honda goes a similar route, with 'eco-assist' for the driver, and Advanced VTEC under the bonnet. In mid-2011, Honda set itself a goal to reduce CO_2 emissions by up to 30 per cent in its product line compared with 2000 levels, and has overhauled its entire powerplant range as part of the process.

Downsizing aside, it is interesting to note that a 2007 Porsche 911 emits 300 times fewer emissions than its namesake of forty years earlier, despite having a bigger engine displacement, and emits only 266g of carbon dioxide per kilometre. For sure, advances are being made on all fronts.

The latest CVTs, which can keep engines revving at a peak torque sweet spot, are being refined at a fast pace. Nissan's award-winning Extroid CVT and its XTRONIC system show promise, and ZF is developing CVTs for a number of manufacturers, ranging from Ford to BMW. Interestingly, the original automotive CVT maker, Van Doorne, was bought by Bosch in 1995, giving rise to concentrated drive-belt development; CVTs fitted with Bosch's so-called push belt can reduce fuel consumption by up to 7 per cent compared with a manual car. Honda is claiming fuel savings of between 5 and 10 per cent with its newest CVT. As a result, modern CVTs are increasingly being used as a sort of emission control device.

Another alternative is the DSG (direct shift gearbox), which works like the original Porsche PDK unit. Basically,

VITAL STATISTICS

It is fascinating to compare the plus and minus points on opting for petrol or diesel. Taking the Citroën C1 from the 2008 season as an example of a typical modern compact car – a small, front-wheel-drive, five-door hatch – it becomes easy to see why the choice is hardly straightforward:

	Citroën C1 1.0i VTR	Citroën C1 1.4 HDi VTR
Engine type	Petrol	Diesel
Vehicle weight	830kg	890kg
Power	68bhp	55bhp
Torque	69lbft	96lbft
CO2 emissions	109g/km	109g/km
NOx emissions	0.01g/km	0.24g/km
PM emissions	0.00g/km	0.01g/km
CO emissions	0.37g/km	0.18g/km
Fuel economy	62mpg	67mpg
0–60mph time	13.3sec	15.1sec
Price (08MY)	€8,540	€9,890

A view inside the stepless Nissan XTRONIC CVT unit. Nissan

the electro-mechanical dual clutch transmissions (DCTs) allow faster gear changes without interrupting the flow of tractive power. First seen on VW-Audi models, they also allow automatic, semi-automatic or manual shifts, and eliminate the need for a torque converter. Compared to a traditional dry clutch, this can promote a fuel saving of 6 per cent.

Volkswagen's DSG transmission. Note the fast-acting LuK dual clutch unit close to the gear selector. Volkswagen

ZF has recently introduced a 9AT gearbox for FF vehicles – a far cry from the days of 3AT units, which wasn't actually all that long ago. ZF

BMW provides an insight into current manufacturer thinking, with an optimum shift indicator on manual cars, eight-speed automatics, and an 'Eco Pro' mode setting for the ultimate in economy. Likewise, in 2009, Nissan released its 'Eco Mode' setting, which basically smooths out accelerator action to save fuel.

Smaller but no less important steps are being taken in the parts sector. Schaeffler is a good example of a forward-thinking component supplier, offering OAP alternator pulleys that smooth out the crankshaft power pulses to reduce load on the ancillary belt drive. Amazingly, this can save 1 per cent in fuel costs, while roller bearings are used for crankshafts and camshafts to reduce internal friction – racing car technology brought into the mass-production arena.

Schaeffler is also promoting a thermal management module, which acts rather like a precise radiator thermostat for the whole drivetrain, speeding up warm-up times, and keeping certain components within stricter operating limits to optimize their efficiency. It is said that this module can reduce fuel consumption and emissions by up to 4 per cent, which is hardly surprising given how much energy is lost through heat and the engine's cooling system.

Thermal energy recovery is the latest big thing, as it happens. Toyota brought out a system in 2006 that used exhaust heat to warm engine coolant, thereby reducing warm-up times, which in turn saves fuel by allowing the engine to adopt leaner mixtures that much earlier. As another example, part of the BMW Efficient Dynamics programme has brought forth engine encapsulation techniques, a thermoelectric generator, and a waste heat exchanger for oil heating. Hyundai, too, in conjunction with BASF, have developed a thermal engine encapsulation system that retains a minimum of 40°C of heat for almost five times longer than normal, translating into fuel savings of 5 per cent in summer, and 9 per cent in winter.

We are also seeing progress in cylinder deactivation technology. The idea isn't new – indeed, Porsche was looking into closing down half of its V8 for the 928 at

Advances in electronics have helped perfect ECUs. This 2-litre turbocharged Ecotec engine from 2011, used by a number of General Motors' models, employs the GM E39 control module. This is known for being extremely fast in delivering codes that operate the direct fuel injection system, the continuous variable valve timing system for both sets of valves, and the turbocharger. GM

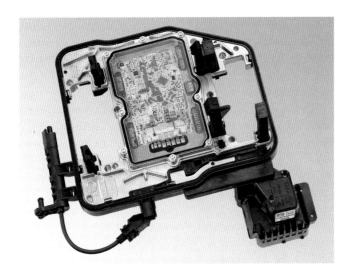

The Continental-developed control unit that looks after the dual clutch. Continental

one stage, and certain American V8s have been fitted with a variable displacement facility since 1981. However, the early systems were flawed, and it only became a vaguely practical concept after Mitsubishi's second attempt in 1993. Even then, the Mitsubishi MD (modulated displacement) feature was to be a short-lived one, as the gains in economy were marginal.

Although Mercedes-Benz used ACC variable displacement on its V12 engine from 2001, and Honda has had VCM (variable cylinder management) since 2003, it was really the Americans that revived the idea in a big way, with the Chrysler Hemi MDS acting as a trailblazer in 2004, along with selected GM V6s and V8s that sported AFM (active fuel management) technology from the same era.

Most recently, Volkswagen has introduced a zero-lift cam to shut down 2 of the 4 cylinders found in the latest range of TSI engines. Likewise, the new AMG M152 engine has the facility to cut off 4 of its 8 cylinders in a staggered formation at low revs, with all cylinders kicking back in above 3,600rpm.

Meanwhile the idle-stop facility has become recognized as a lightweight, cost-effective way to save fuel. Old allies such as the VW-Audi Group and Toyota have been joined by the PSA Group, the Fiat Group, Mazda, BMW, Renault, Volvo, Ford and Hyundai to name but a few, in using this feature. In fact Continental has just won a 'Green' technology award from ADAC for its E-Booster idle-stop system, and is a leader in the field of CVT and dual clutch electronic control units.

In other areas, new oil pumps are being developed by ZF that circulate only the amount of oil required at any given time, thus making a 40 per cent saving in energy; Renault is adopting lightweight DLC carbon tappets borrowed from F1 technology, while Mahle pistons are a fraction the size of earlier versions below the rings, thus reducing weight. Some piston makers even specify narrower skirts to allow smaller pins. One also sees carbon coatings on piston rings to reduce friction, and graphite-coated piston skirts with the same purpose in mind.

All manufacturers, far and wide, are getting the 'Green' bug. Mercedes-Benz has its Blue Efficiency programme, for instance, with VW using the Blue Motion banner. Ford has Econetic, Citroën has Airdream, Opel Ecoflex, Volvo DrivE, and Renault the rather catchy ECO_2 programme name. Yet with all this activity, significant improvements in petrol engines are still coming – the Fiat TwinAir and Mazda Skyactiv-G units being perfect examples.

Fiat's TwinAir unit is an 875cc twin with 4 valves per cylinder. Developed under Paolo Martinelli, it uses a small turbocharger to cut lag and therefore sharpen response, also the familiar MultiAir electro-hydraulic valve system, which improves efficiency by around 10 per cent, idle-stop, and a number of friction reduction measures. With 85bhp on tap,

VW advertising from 2010. Volkswagen

Fiat's turbocharged TwinAir engine. Fiat

hybrids seem worth the hassle. There is also an end-of-life scenario to consider, with petrol engines easier to deal with than a hybrid, which has numerous battery changes, then its final battery pack, hybrid mechanism and a normal engine to dispose of.

But one does wonder if the pace of development can be kept up, what with the US makers having to be bailed out the other day, and Japan seemingly on course to follow Britain as a 'has been' of the motor industry. Will there be the R&D money for the new technology needed to meet new regulations and the expectations of the public?

At least petrol engines are a known quantity – which, granted, makes advances smaller, but probably more cost-effective than something entirely new, as the manufacturing facilities are already in place (in Asia alone, as many as 43 million engines are built each year!). Small cuts in emissions here and there in the manufacturing stage, followed by advances in technology, will doubtless make a difference in our carbon footprint. The petrol engine may just be around for a while yet.

and an excellent 107lbft of torque, it offers a 30 per cent saving in fuel consumption and 95g/km emission levels. A normally aspirated 64bhp version will be available soon, and a 104bhp variant is also on the cards.

In Japan, the author remembers once asking one of the top Mazda engineers how the company was so innovative, given its lack of funds. He replied: 'It's because we have no money that we have no choice but to innovate.' What a refreshing thought.

The 4-cylinder Mazda Skyactiv-G engine was released in 1.3- and 2-litre guise initially, with the smaller 83bhp unit causing quite a bit of excitement, as a 50 per cent increase is fuel efficiency is not to be dismissed lightly. It's worth looking at some of the technology, which includes Denso's new eVCT (electric variable cam timing) system, allowing Miller-cycle timing, a high 14.0:1 compression ratio, i-Stop and a 6AT gearbox – but otherwise nothing that spectacular. Blending lightweight body and chassis components possibly helped boost gas mileage as much as the powerplant, but this improvement in base technologies is a positive step forwards.

With the kind of economy figures the 1.3-litre Mazda engine can deliver (25km/ltr in JC08 mode), it hardly makes

Advertising for Mazda's Skyactiv technology, this piece being released late in 2011. Mazda

CHAPTER FOUR

FULL HYBRIDS: THE PETROL-ELECTRIC AND DIESEL-ELECTRIC BRIGADE

The most popular breed of motor vehicle currently appealing to the 'Green' people among us is the so-called full hybrid car, usually based on petrol-electric technology, but increasingly using a diesel-electric arrangement for motive power and battery charging. Engineers have a lot of freedom in this particular sphere of car design, with new developments – especially in the field of battery technology, covered in detail in the next chapter – making the hybrid a more and more attractive proposition all the time. As far back as 2000, Toyota's chairman at the time, Hiroshi Okuda, stated:

> We believe that hybrid systems epitomize technologies with great future potential, those that are extremely effective in making real contributions towards solving environmental issues. We are convinced that Prius hybrid technology, which controls multiple energy sources, can become the core technology for developing the ultimate practical eco car.

But before going on, we need to clarify exactly what a full hybrid car – also known as the HV, HEV, strong, blended, power-split or series-parallel hybrid – actually is. In simple terms, the full hybrid car is a vehicle that can use two or more sources for motive power. The early Toyota Prius is a perfect example, having an electric motor, but also able to call on a petrol engine to propel the vehicle. Therefore, even though a Chevy Volt has a petrol engine, it is classed as an electric car rather than a hybrid, because the engine is only used to charge the battery packs – motive power is provided by one source, which in this case is an electric drive unit.

BIRTH OF THE HYBRID BOOM

The Toyota Prius will always stand out as being the first full

hybrid, and so it was from a commercial point of view, but historically the HV concept is actually much older, spawned by a new wave of thinking that came in 1966 when the US Congress introduced a bill that recommended electric vehicles be developed to reduce air pollution.

The GM 512 hybrid broke cover in 1969, powered by an electric motor and a 195cc twin-cylinder petrol engine. Using a principle invented before World War I by Woods of Chicago for its Dual Power model, at very low speeds the car used battery power, then a combination of both power

The **GM 512** number was actually allocated to a set of three prototypes built by General Motors, this one having a hybrid petrol-electric power-unit, while the others were propelled by pure electric or pure petrol engine drivetrains. GM

The Briggs & Stratton hybrid of 1979, the bodywork designed by the Brooks Stevens industrial design firm.
Briggs & Stratton

sources as speed increased, before the petrol unit took over completely at about 23km/h (14mph). Although it looked like a golf cart and had a top speed of only 64km/h (40mph), it was nonetheless a very significant development, leading to the building of a more realistic XP-883 PHEV prototype. For some reason, despite there being no technological hurdles, the General Motors hierarchy refused to give the project a green light.

In the meantime, in the background, a team of three scientists (led by Dr George H. Gelb) working for TRW Systems Group of California, developed and patented an electromechanical transmission (EMT) – its arrangement (an outer ring gear, a sun gear in the centre and a set of planet gears in between mounted on a carrier) allowing smaller engines to transmit power more efficiently. It hardly made an impression in 1971, when design work was completed and an SAE paper filed, but it forms an important part of the drivetrain in most of today's hybrids and EREVs.

Another historically significant step towards creating the full hybrid car was made in 1973, with the debut of the Volkswagen 'City Taxi' based on the VW T2 bus. With a rear-mounted gasoline powerplant and a mid-mounted electric motor and battery pack, this was a true hybrid, able to run in either petrol engine or full electric mode, the latter possible for 40km (25 miles). But although tested extensively by the US Department of Energy, the project was allowed to disappear into the woodwork.

The US Congress then passed the Electric and Hybrid Vehicle Research, Development and Demonstration Act of 1976, but there were still few signs of progress until the birth of the Briggs & Stratton hybrid in 1979. This was a futuristic-looking coupé with six wheels (four on the back axle to support the weight of the twelve Globe Union batteries), with a full hybrid drivetrain. One could select the 18bhp air-cooled 694cc twin-cylinder petrol engine or the 8–20bhp electric motor for motive power, or a combination of both. In the same year, Daihatsu released the Charmant petrol-electric

The world's first full hybrid car for public use – the Audi Duo III of April 1997. Only the fancy graphics on the rear flank give an indication that this was a special machine from the outside. Around one hundred were built, the technology being based on Audi's 1989 and 1991 concept cars. Audi

Suzuki exhibited a full (power-split) hybrid with a methanol-powered 660cc engine and electric motor at the 1993 Tokyo Show, the sodium-sulphur batteries being charged by regenerative braking as well as an alternator. Suzuki

Nissan displayed this aluminium-bodied hybrid car – the AL-X – at the 1997 Tokyo Show. Subaru also had a full hybrid for 1997 called the Elten, which was duly updated for 1999. Nissan

hybrid, with a computer determining which power source to use, depending on speed.

The real breakthrough on a global scale, however, came in 1989, when Audi unveiled the first of its 'Duo' hybrid concept cars, based on the 100 Avant model. The car used a 2.3-litre straight-five petrol engine to power the front wheels, and an electric motor for the rear axle.

Looking back, however, we can probably point to the introduction of the 1990 Zero Emission Vehicle Mandate by the California Air Resources Board (CARB) as a turning point in automotive engineering history. More than any other piece of legislation passed before or after, the ZEV Mandate encouraged makers to stop taking small steps, continuously improving existing technology solely to meet required standards, and to take a leap of faith towards the adoption of alternative powertrains, be they electric-based or anything else beyond the conventional.

Forgetting the LA301 petrol-electric hybrid, which, instead of making Los Angeles the first EV-ready city in the world, simply wasted millions of dollars at the start of the 1990s, one of the most successful types of vehicle to spring from the challenge created by the ZEV Mandate is the hybrid car – the HV (standing for hybrid vehicle) or HEV (hybrid electric vehicle) and the more recent plug-in versions (distinguished from the regular hybrids by the PHEV or PHV moniker).

A second version of the Audi Duo was duly displayed at the 1991 Frankfurt Show, with the drivetrain being further refined so that on this prototype the engine was linked to

the rear axle as well as the front one. Eventually Audi introduced the limited-run Duo III diesel-electric PHEV hybrid in April 1997, using an existing A4 Avant body for its platform to help ease production costs. As such, it has the right to claim to be the first of the new breed of hybrids on the road, despite being built in small numbers.

Meanwhile, over in Japan, Suzuki put forward a full hybrid proposal, which ultimately took the form of the EE-10 concept of 1993, and Nissan and Toyota were also keen on the idea. As it happens, Nissan went the pure electric vehicle (EV) route, while Toyota dedicated its efforts to developing high-technology hybrid drivetrains.

In reality, in many ways the hybrid car as it stands is something of a stopgap – a good compromise until other technologies have been honed to a level where they offer a broad range of overwhelming benefits, rather than a series of large plus points on the one hand and equally large minus points on the other.

Basically, the hybrid configuration uses the exceptional mechanical efficiency of an electric motor (see the section on how electric motors work in the next chapter) but overcomes the range problem one encounters with traditional EVs. By using an ICE sparingly, it also allows, at least in ideal circumstances, exceptional fuel consumption figures to be delivered compared to a regular car using a petrol or diesel engine as its only source of motive power. As such, makers can claim excellent economy and very low emissions at a stroke.

PRIUS – TO GO BEFORE

With battery technology – covered in detail in the next chapter – slowly improving to the point where EVs were at last starting to look viable, in January 1992 Toyota released its 'Earth Charter' with the stated goal of developing and marketing cars with the lowest emissions possible. Shortly after, having been snubbed in the US Partnership for a New Generation of Vehicles (PNGV) programme, Eiji Toyoda vowed that his company would lead the world in 'Green' technology, and instigated the formation of the so-called G21 group in September 1993. Four years later, on 10 December 1997

(rather symbolically, a day before the Kyoto Protocol was signed), the result – the Prius, with its Toyota Hybrid System (THS) powertrain – went on sale in Japan.

Having displayed a Prius concept car (project 890T) at the 1995 Tokyo Show, it's fair to say that the pace of development was truly staggering, even for a Japanese firm, as so much of the hardware was all new. But this race was indeed a turning point for the motor industry, with Germany and the rest of Europe taking the lack of interest in the Duo as a sign to concentrate on diesel technology, while Japan's makers saw the niche market open up before them and took to the hybrid road with even greater verve.

BASIC HYBRID SYSTEMS COMPARED

There are advantages and disadvantages to each type of hybrid system, be it series (as in an EREV), parallel (as in a mild hybrid), or full (series-parallel, like the Toyota Prius). According to Toyota's research, a series hybrid has nothing special to offer in the acceleration stakes, but it is improved with a parallel or full hybrid set-up. For continuous high output, only the full hybrid offers a real benefit. As

for enhanced fuel consumption, when compared to a conventional vehicle, the hybrids offered superior economy of varying degrees in the following areas:

	Idle-stop technology	Energy recovery	Overall efficiency
Series hybrid	Good	Excellent	Good
Parallel hybrid	Good	Good	Fair
Full hybrid	Excellent	Excellent	Excellent

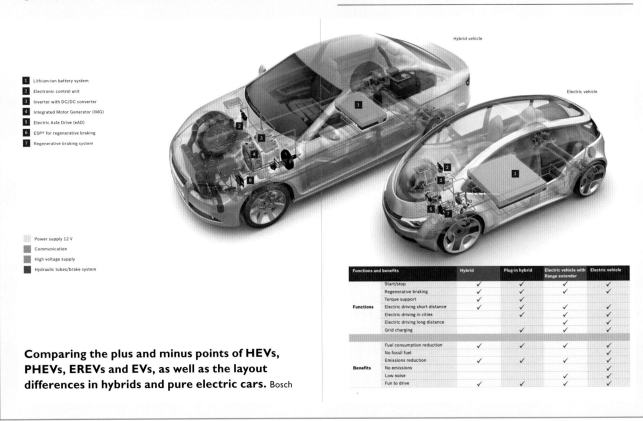

1 Lithium-ion battery system
2 Electronic control unit
3 Inverter with DC/DC converter
4 Integrated Motor Generator (IMG)
5 Electric Axle Drive (eAD)
6 ESP® for regenerative braking
7 Regenerative braking system

▮ Power supply 12 V
▮ Communication
▮ High voltage supply
▮ Hydraulic tubes/brake system

Functions and benefits		Hybrid	Plug-in hybrid	Electric vehicle with Range extender	Electric vehicle
Functions	Start/stop	✓	✓	✓	✓
	Regenerative braking	✓	✓	✓	✓
	Torque support	✓	✓		
	Electric driving short distance	✓	✓	✓	✓
	Electric driving in cities		✓	✓	✓
	Electric driving long distance			✓	✓
	Grid charging		✓	✓	✓
Benefits	Fuel consumption reduction	✓	✓		✓
	No fossil fuel				✓
	Emissions reduction	✓	✓	✓	✓
	No emissions				✓
	Low noise			✓	✓
	Fun to drive	✓	✓	✓	✓

Comparing the plus and minus points of HEVs, PHEVs, EREVs and EVs, as well as the layout differences in hybrids and pure electric cars. Bosch

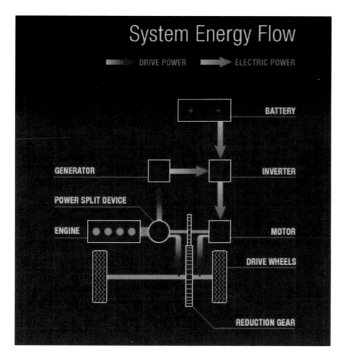

The Toyota full hybrid system, shown here with both engine and motor working in tandem. The flow of electricity through the PCU was dependent on the drive mode, as the batteries were charged via this, too, in low load conditions. Note that all the components shown here, except the battery pack, usually lie in the same plane. Toyota

It's interesting to note that the 1995 prototype used a so-called EMS (Energy Management System) drivetrain, which basically connected an electric motor to a petrol engine via a cone and belt-type CVT. In addition, rather than a battery, an ultra-capacitor was used to store electricity – fast acting, but not able to stash large amounts of energy.

At the next Tokyo Show, which opened on 24 October 1997, the pace of evolution was plain for all to see, and doubtless quite a shock for rival makers. The EMS powertrain had been replaced by the THS version, which involved adding another motor for use as a generator/starter, replacing the CVT with a planetary gear-type transmission, and dropping the ultra-capacitor set-up in favour of a conventional battery pack, albeit using nickel metal hydride (NiMH) technology.

The front-wheel-drive Toyota Hybrid System powertrain consisted of a frugal 1496cc INZ-FXE Atkinson-cycle petrol engine rated at 58bhp, and a main 30kW motor with a converter/inverter called a power control unit (PCU) to bridge the voltage from the battery, and a transmission that enabled smooth transitions between power sources based on the TRW Systems arrangement that Toyota named a power

split device (PSD). The PSD also drove the generator, which could power the electric motor or recharge the batteries. Interestingly, because the generator motor was on the same shaft as the rest of the drivetrain, the battery pack could be charged whenever the car was moving, regardless of whether it was in EV mode or using the engine for propulsion.

As a full hybrid, the system took advantage of the energy-efficient electric motors when the car was running in the low speed range, and called upon the petrol engine (with its Atkinson cycle improving economy, albeit at the cost of a loss in peak power) as necessary in the higher speed range. If more power were required, the system combined the dual sources of power for an equivalent of 108bhp. And with regenerative braking, pulling away from traffic lights

EARLY QUESTIONS

In some ways, it looked as if Toyota was using the domestic market to give the Prius a comprehensive shakedown before releasing it for export, as exchange rates were favourable, and the gap between the home and foreign launches was extraordinarily long. But making sure the car was absolutely spot-on certainly wasn't a bad idea, because being a trailblazer for a new breed of automobile, it was always going to be under the gaze of the press and public alike.

The original cylindrical form battery pack was rated with a specific output of 800W/kg. A few teething problems brought a change to a 1,000W/kg plastic-cased prismatic module produced by Panasonic in time for the 2000 season, which was not only more reliable, but also about 7kg (15lb) lighter. This was duly updated for 2004 via a metal-cased version rated at 1,300W/kg; the latest (fourth) version is much the same, but is a fraction lighter again and delivers 10W more power per kilogram.

Looking back, keeping the original car in Japan at least allowed proper monitoring of the car's performance in some of the harshest operating conditions the world has to offer. But there was probably another, more telling reason for the slow release: the early NHW10s were loss-leader machines, costing Toyota more than $10,000 in red ink on each sale. With 33,200 sales by the end of 1999 alone, and more than 50,000 cars moved by the time exports began, that's a lot of pennies! However, using the first Prius as a marketing tool, getting the car out early to make the Toyota name synonymous with hybrids from the off, was nevertheless a brilliant move.

came courtesy of energy that was otherwise wasted, further enhancing the vehicle's already impressive fuel economy figures.

ESTABLISHING THE HYBRID

In the spring of 1999, a five-year technical cooperation agreement was signed between General Motors and Toyota regarding the development of BEVs, HEVs and FCEVs. It was an ideal way of reducing R&D costs in an increasingly fickle market in which research had revealed that customers were willing to pay between 8 and 10 per cent extra for alternative power vehicles, but not much more. Almost as much as technological barriers, this is the reality of advanced development – things such as the space programme, at least in its younger days, where budgets hardly seem to matter, can justify the expense in achieving an ultimate goal, but with production cars, especially with shareholders to answer to, one has to estimate potential return and then calculate if a project is financially viable. This is why we tend to see fits and spurts of development in certain areas (usually flavour of the month with politicians who hand out R&D grants), and then everything seems to go quiet as another completely different line of research opens up.

Notwithstanding, others were trying to go it alone, particularly in Japan. While Honda was presenting its IMA mild hybrid system, and about to provide the Prius with its only real rival via the Insight, the 1999 Tokyo Motor Show was a feast of technology – Subaru had its Elten Custom on display, while Mitsubishi put forward its SUW Advance concept with a full hybrid petrol-electric drivetrain that included a CVT.

Not only was this a highly practical vehicle, it added to its 'Green' credentials by having most of its body parts made from materials that were easy to recycle.

Suzuki had the EV-Sport hybrid with a General Motors 'Generation III' EV package (complete with NiMH batteries) for the rear axle, backed up by a 393cc petrol engine for the front wheels. The same company also displayed the Pu3-Commuter with a full hybrid system incorporating a 660cc engine with idle-stop technology.

Not wanting to be outdone, Nissan gave the Tino NEO Hybrid its debut, which went on sale in limited numbers (100 only) in the spring of 2000, badged as the Tino Hybrid. This full hybrid model was powered by a 1.8-litre petrol engine, combined with compact Li-ion batteries for its single 17kW electric motor. Pricing was reasonable enough at 3,150,000 yen, although the Prius was almost 1,000,000 yen cheaper! So it wasn't particularly surprising that people in the trade were questioning the financial viability of the Prius – but with demand outstripping supply for several years, profits were just round the corner. The hybrid gamble had therefore paid off handsomely.

On the subject of Toyota, the company gave a preview of its next generation Estima (or Previa) minivan at the 1999 Tokyo Show, but the most interesting part of the design was the so-called 'THS-C' full hybrid drivetrain of this prototype, combined in this case with an electric 4WD system called 'E-Four' in Toyota speak.

In the Estima Hybrid, developed by Shigeru Matsuhashi, and which eventually made it to the marketplace in mid-2001 as the world's first hybrid minivan on general sale, the front axle was driven by a 2362cc 2AZ-FXE Atkinson-cycle engine

Cutaway drawing of the first Prius (type NHW10) by Yoshihiro Inomoto. Note the original battery pack in the rear of the vehicle. Toyota

The Tino NEO Hybrid at the 1999 Tokyo Show.
160SX/Creative Commons

and an electric motor, with the latest four-speed K110 Super CVT giving a more involving driving experience. The engine also recharged the NiMH battery pack, as did the electric motor on the rear axle, the latter using regenerative braking. This rear motor, which created the E-Four system, only kicked in under hard acceleration or slippery conditions, but gave a 4WD configuration without any mechanical connection between the front and rear wheels.

It was all very inventive, but the author, being a cynical type, often wondered if the hybrid concept was being taken too far. What is the point of having a large displacement engine coupled to an electric motor? How can excessive weight and 'Green' possibly go hand-in-hand? Battery life and replacement cost/disposal also has to be considered. Surely it was rather all to do with marketing power than ecology?

Coinciding nicely with Japan's minivan boom, the Estima Hybrid was 160kg (353lb) heavier than a regular 4WD model, which was already tipping the scales at 1,690kg (3,726lb). But the efficiency of the hybrid machine is well illustrated by the fact that it needed 5.6ltr of fuel to travel 100km, while the normal four-wheel-drive model required 9.8ltr to go the same distance.

A similar powertrain was used for the CS&S sports car concept displayed at the 2003 Frankfurt Show, as well as a

The Toyota Prius is recognized as being the first mass-production hybrid, sold in Japan from the end of 1997, with sales spreading to America and Europe in the latter part of 2000 when this updated NHW11 model was released with a more powerful petrol unit (seen here in the engine bay shot) and a new battery pack.
Toyota

Toyota's THS-II drivetrain, announced in 2003. Toyota

number of larger Toyota production models, such as the Alphard. With these big, heavy and far from aerodynamic vehicles, the hybrid system may be the only way forwards.

Meanwhile, never one to miss a marketing chance, following an 'Eco Mission' event in 1999, Toyota announced sales of the second generation (NHWII) Prius in America on Earth Day, in April 2000, although deliveries of the $20,000 vehicle didn't start filtering through Stateside until July – two months after the domestic launch, but two months before the European market debut. Nonetheless, the timing of the release of the first four-door hybrid to be made available in the USA was nothing short of immaculate.

From the outside, it looked much the same as the original Prius, except for new tyres with lower rolling resistance and more modern-looking bumpers that lacked the heavy rubbing strips of the older car – but there were significant changes to the dashboard, and more particularly under the skin.

Developed under Chief Engineer Toshihiro Oi, the new Prius featured the Toyota Hybrid Synergy Drive (HSD) system, which was basically a refined version of the THS. The main difference was in the battery pack, which was 60 per cent smaller, and also had reduced internal resistance, partly thanks to its new shape. Time would also tell us that it was a lot more reliable, too, so releasing the NHW10 Prius in limited numbers to create the ultimate field test was definitely the right thing to do.

There were other changes, too, with the INZ-FXE engine uprated to give 72bhp, and 10 per cent more power for the electric motor. This made the vehicle more suitable for export markets, where road speeds tend to be much higher than those of Japan, but emissions were said to be even lower than before, largely thanks to raising the EV-only mode's upper speed limit from 40km/h (25mph) to 64km/h (40mph).

The Daihatsu UFE-II at the 2003 Tokyo Show, with UFE standing for 'ultra fuel economy'. Fuel-powered hybrid concepts were still coming through, but only Toyota seemed willing to market them at this stage. B. Long

While Nissan signed a technical cooperation agreement with Toyota, and GM started filtering its 'Two-Mode' system on to the market (initially via diesel-electric buses), the pace of full hybrid development was relentless in Toyota City. Announced at the New York Show in April 2003, with deliveries beginning in time for the 2004 season, the third-generation Toyota Prius came with a new THS-II hybrid drive system.

This latest NHW20 Prius had a larger body than its predecessors, so power was increased to 78bhp for the familiar 1.5-litre INZ-FXE engine, while the AC synchronous electric motor was beefed up to provide 14 per cent more torque and a 50kW rating – the equivalent to 67bhp. In another important part of the equation, as well as being significantly more powerful as a stand-alone component thanks to a further reduction in internal resistance, the Panasonic NiMH battery's power was enhanced by a voltage booster in the THS-II PCU (taking output from the 270 or so volts of old to a heady 500V), so the car felt much more lively, yet still managed to give better fuel economy. In addition to improvements in the hybrid system's operational control and greater efficiency in the regenerative braking set-up, on the comfort front, the air-conditioning compressor became electric, reducing drag on the engine (like the newly adopted electric power steering pump) but also allowing it to be used without the engine running.

According to Toyota's figures, a typical petrol-engined saloon the size of the Prius had a well-to-wheel efficiency of 14 per cent. The original Prius took this to 25 per cent, and then 28 after the NHW11 was launched. Despite the bigger body, the new car could boast an overall efficiency of 32 per cent – better than FCEVs of the time.

Between 2003 and 2004, Prius sales doubled in America, and tripled in Japan. Toyota had found exactly the right formula, with awards galore and annual production increasing from 43,000 units a year to 125,000 to keep up with demand. In spite of there being 'no market for hybrids' according to some car company executives, there was actually a six-month waiting list at one point!

In March 2004, Ford signed a licence with Toyota to make its hybrid system work. With over 100 unique patents in the Ford design, this was an amicable deal for all concerned, as it completed the puzzle for Ford after five years of R&D; it also bought the Japanese company emission control technology for petrol and small diesel engines as part of the bargain. Six months later, Ford released the Escape Hybrid, the first American hybrid to go on general sale, and the world's first SUV hybrid.

Ford Chairman, Bill Ford, speaking at a news conference at the hand-over of a batch of Escape Hybrid taxis in New York, November 2005. With gas mileage 70 per cent better than a V6 petrol Escape, the hybrid model was ideal for the job. Ford

GLOSSARY OF 'GREEN' VEHICLE CLASSES AND TYPES

With so many variations on a theme, things can get confusing, especially when even the manufacturers blur the lines of demarcation. This glossary, which contains a simplified overview of vehicle classes and some examples of each breed, will help with clarification, although one should remember that some cars, even when using the strictest of definitions, will doubtless fall into two or more categories.

LEV – Low-Emission Vehicle: A series of Californian classifications (CAL LEV), although the term has also been used in Federal categories (recently becoming a required standard), as well as Europe and Asia, notably Japan. Some countries have created low-emission zones (LEZs), which have restricted vehicle access depending on their class – LEVs qualify for use in these areas without penalty.

TLEV – Transitional Low-Emission Vehicle: A national target building on the original US Tier I standards, focusing on the reduction of exhaust pollutants to an extent worthy of the NLEV badge, depending on vehicle weight and cargo capacity. Replaced by the Tier II standard in 2004.

ULEV – Ultra-Low Emissions Vehicle: In the States, the moniker is adopted for cars that release half the average emissions of their contemporaries. In Europe, the term is used to cover vehicles using electric or hydrogen power, or plug-in hybrid technology.

SULEV – Super Ultra-Low Emissions Vehicle: A category for petrol, diesel, hybrid and alternative fuel cars with very low tailpipe emissions. The stamp of approval as a SULEV brings tax breaks in the USA, so this administrative angle is its main function as far as users are concerned.

ZEV – Zero Emissions Vehicle: A classification for cars and trucks which release no harmful tailpipe gases and vapours; this means that fuel cell vehicles can be included, since water, a byproduct of FCEV powertrains, is a completely harmless emission. But in reality, battery cars need charging somehow, and hydrogen needs to be created. Even human beings need food for the fuel to do work, so true ZEVs are still a dream.

PZEV – Partial Zero Emissions Vehicle: The class for vehicles that qualify as SULEVs at the tailpipe, but also have zero evaporative emissions, and a fifteen-year warranty on emission control equipment. Longer component life is a sure way to enhance a vehicle's 'Green' credentials.

AT-PZEV – Advanced Technology Partial Zero Emissions Vehicle: A variation on the PZEV theme for cars and trucks that use alternative fuels or hybrid technology.

TZEV – Transitional Zero Emissions Vehicle: Also known as the 'enhanced AT-PZEV', this is an extension of the AT-PZEV category to include plug-in hybrids and hydrogen-powered vehicles (but not FCEVs, as these are classed as ZEVs).

HEV (or HV) – Hybrid Electric Vehicle: Also known as a full, strong, blended, power-split or series-parallel hybrid, the original Toyota Prius serves as the perfect example of an HEV, using both petrol and electric power to drive the vehicle. The original Ford Fusion Hybrid and Porsche Cayenne S Hybrid serve as other good examples. Occasionally one sees the parallel hybrid moniker being used for HEVs, but this only adds to the confusion that already exists in hybrid classification – this is a term best reserved for mild hybrids.

Mild Hybrid: Also known as a 'parallel hybrid', this particular type of mild hybrid uses a second power source (usually an electric motor) to assist the primary source, which is generally a petrol or diesel engine. Honda's IMA system, as used on cars such as the Insight, falls into this category, as does the Mercedes-Benz S400 Hybrid. (See the EREV section for another type of mild hybrid.)

Micro-Hybrid: This category covers cars with idle-stop technology on conventional IC engines. Rather than particular models, it is easier to identify a few trademark set-ups, such as the Ford 'Auto-Start-Stop' system, Kia's 'ISG' and the Mazda 'i-Stop' system.

PHEV (or PHV) – Plug-in Hybrid Vehicle: Much the same as an HEV, but with a smaller fuel tank to make space for larger battery packs and a charging system that allows the car to be charged via an outside source, thus giving the vehicle greater time in EV mode without resorting to an ICE. The Toyota Prius Plug-in Hybrid has a rather uninventive name, but it serves as a perfect example of the breed in its authentic form. (See the EREV section for another type of plug-in hybrid.)

EV – Electric Vehicle: Sometimes given the BEV moniker, standing for 'battery electric vehicle', the General Motors EV1 was the first of the modern breed to hit the headlines. Examples of typical EVs available today include the Nissan Leaf, AD Change, and the Mitsubishi i-MiEV (also badged as the Peugeot iOn and Citroën C-Zero).

NEV–Neighbourhood Electric Vehicle: Also referred to as the LSV, standing for 'low-speed vehicle', as these cars are limited to 64km/h (40mph), or the 'city electric vehicle' (CEV). Recent examples of this diverse breed include the Mahindra Reva, the ZENN, the Aixam Mega City, the Akasol Oscar, the City El, the Micro-Vett Ydea, and the GEM, although their use is restricted on many roads due to safety concerns.

HPEV – High-Performance Electric Vehicle: The description says it all. Examples would include the Venturi Fetish, the Tesla Roadster, and the SSC Ultimate Aero EV, which was sadly destined to remain a prototype.

EREV (or REEV) – Extended-Range Electric Vehicle: Also known as a Series Hybrid (or often a Mild Hybrid, which can be a little confusing), the Fisker Karma and Audi A1 e-tron serve as perfect examples of cars in this category, being EVs that use a petrol engine to charge the batteries only, not drive the machine. Various types of charging medium can be used, ranging from diesel engines to gas turbines. However, the line is blurred somewhat by cars such as the Chevrolet Volt, which can draw a certain amount of motive power from the engine, although being mainly EV-based, the car is classed as an EREV. Meanwhile, a plug-in option can extend the EV operating mode, thus creating a plug-in hybrid, albeit quite different to the PHEV described earlier in this section. More confusion!

HEHV – Human-Electric Hybrid Vehicle: An oddball category for machines that use human power with electrical assistance. The Sinclair C5 was an early attempt. They were actually raced at the 1985 British GP, when Lotus mechanics kept the crowds entertained during a heavy downpour! Today's equivalent would be the Twike or the Aerorider.

FCEV – Fuel Cell Vehicle: An EV that uses a fuel cell as its power source rather than a battery. The Honda FCX Clarity is one of the few fuel cell vehicles people may have had a chance of seeing on the road, but several manufacturers plan to launch FCEVs in the near future. These vehicles are covered at the end of the next chapter.

FFV – Flexible Fuel (Flex-Fuel) Vehicle: Rather an outsider in this section, the flex-fuel car is able to run on alternative fuels such as ethanol and methanol, which is then usually blended with petrol and drawn from the same fuel tank. Bi-fuel vehicles, such as those employing LPG, CNG or hydrogen as well as petrol (or occasionally diesel), require two separate fuel delivery systems.

The Ford Escape Hybrid E85, introduced at the start of 2006, was the world's first hybrid capable of operating on renewable ethanol-based fuel. As well as reducing oil dependence, this research vehicle cut GHG emissions by 25 per cent. Unfortunately it was never put on general sale. Ford

The Escape was a full hybrid, and at the time of its launch was far more popular than even Ford expected, being named 'Truck of the Year' in its native country. Although quite different in its detailing (including the use of an Aisin electronically controlled CVT and a NiMH battery sourced from Sanyo), the hybrid system works in a similar fashion to the Prius, having EV, petrol and combined driving modes, as well as regenerative braking.

A Mercury Mariner variant, with the same 2.3-litre Atkinson-cycle 133bhp in-line four and a 70kW motor, was duly added, along with an E85 version in January 2006: its ability to run on ethanol-rich fuels was seen as another bonus point for the Escape's 'Green' credentials. Although the Flex-Fuel model was only made as a research vehicle, the intent was good at a time when corn-based ethanol seemed like a way forwards.

All three Escape-based models made it through the early 2007 (2008 MY) facelift, with a larger 2.5-litre engine eventually finding its way on to the spec sheet, and a Mazda Tribute version augmenting the line-up. However, the E85 model remained a test vehicle, the Mercury marque faded away, and Ford ultimately turned its attention away from a future Escape PHEV to concentrate on the lighter, more compact plug-in C-MAX Energi and C-MAX Hybrid models, due for release in the 2013 season.

The European makers seemed to be sticking to diesel as the answer to reducing carbon dioxide emissions. But at the 2005 Frankfurt Show, Audi went hybrid with the 4.2-litre petrol-engined Q7 Hybrid – a full, series-parallel hybrid

Audi Q7 hybrid

09/05

LEFT: **What might have been – the 4WD Audi Q7 Hybrid SUV.** Audi

BELOW: **The third of the Daihatsu UFE prototypes that used a 660cc Kei-car engine and a pair of electric motors. This was the second Daihatsu full hybrid concept vehicle on display at the 2005 Tokyo Show, the other being the HVS sports model that had made its debut in Frankfurt a month earlier.** B. Long

with a 350bhp V8 and a 32kW motor that was planned for production, but ultimately shelved.

Meanwhile, in December 2004, General Motors announced it was joining forces with DaimlerChrysler (the company formed by the short-lived merger of Daimler-Benz and Chrysler) to develop the GM 'two-mode' full hybrid system for cars and light trucks. Not long after the Global Hybrid Cooperation agreement had been signed and sealed in the summer of 2005, BMW joined the team as well.

Prototypes were displayed at the 2005 Detroit Show, the exhibits chosen to show the transmission's adaptability, and there was also a Saab concept in 2006. By the following year, GM had already begun making two-mode transmissions at its Baltimore, Maryland facility, with the company announcing a range of future applications, all the way from FF Saturns through to Cadillac SUVs.

The two-mode transmission was a fascinating piece of technology, slotting into the drivetrain like a regular automatic transmission, yet offering all the full hybrid characteristics – motive power from an engine, electric motor or both, an idle-stop facility, and regenerative braking. The difference was in combining two 60kW motors, three planetary gear sets, four multi-plate clutches and two hydraulic oil pumps to create an electric variable transmission (or EVT) giving four fixed gear ratios and two variable ratio modes (low- and high-speed). This optimizes power delivery over a wider speed range, and combined with a V8 sporting cylinder cut-off technology (whereby 4 cylinders closed down

The energy monitor screen from the Lexus GS450h.
Toyota

The internal workings of the innovative 'Two-Mode' transmission. Unfortunately, 'Two-Mode' hybrid sales have been poor. GM

under light throttle cruising conditions), it was estimated that fuel savings could be in the region of 25 per cent.

However, trouble was brewing in the background, and in March 2007, Daimler (soon to be rid of its Chrysler ties) and BMW decided to work more closely together on another hybrid system, and eventually distanced themselves from the GM joint venture.

Notwithstanding, the GMC Yukon SUV and the Chevrolet Tahoe sister model were launched with two-mode transmissions in time for the 2008 season, followed by Cadillac Escalade, Chrysler Aspen and Dodge Durango SUVs by the

The 2007 Toyota FT-HS concept, which used a 3.5-litre V6 in a familiar Toyota hybrid arrangement, but the battery was replaced by super-capacitors to give quicker charging and enhanced performance. These so-called 'super-caps' (or 'ultra-caps' as they are also known) have been used before in the first Prius prototypes and seen in other concept vehicles, so may find their way into production one day. B. Long

end of the year, and a couple of GM pick-ups. The transmission was also used in the Mercedes-Benz ML450 Hybrid and BMW ActiveHybrid X6 models launched in 2009, but after these vehicles, the hybrid system was different for the German makers.

While all this was going on, Toyota was releasing hybrids at a good rate of knots. Having made its debut at the 2004 Detroit Show, the Lexus RX400h duly went on sale as an early 2006 model, coming with 4WD and FF drivetrains, and using established Toyota hybrid practices. This platform duly spawned Toyota Highlander, Harrier and Kluger hybrid SUVs, and was later updated into the RX450h.

The Lexus GS450h was quick to follow, being duly refined with the adoption of an Atkinson-cycle engine in 2011. As well as a number of concepts, there was also the Lexus LS600h (available in standard or long-wheelbase format) and HS250h, and several Toyota-badged cars, such as the Camry Hybrid, an updated Estima, the Sai, and the Crown Hybrid, which was transformed from a mild hybrid to a full hybrid via THS-II with the coming of the 2008 Model Year S200 series. There was even a Nissan Altima Hybrid that used Toyota hybrid technology released in November 2006.

The moment everyone had been waiting for came at the 2009 Detroit Show, when the all-new, fractionally larger NHW30 Prius made its debut. This front-wheel-drive car sported Toyota's latest hybrid synergy drive (HSD) system, which was 90 per cent new, including a bigger 1797cc Atkinson-cycle engine (rated at 99bhp) matched with a 60kW electric motor, and a NiMH battery. The larger engine, with its beefier torque output, enabled the Prius to return better fuel economy figures at higher cruising speeds.

Detail improvements included a lighter transaxle that reduced torque losses by as much as 20 per cent, a new cooling system for the PCU that allowed it to be reduced in size and weight, an electric water pump, and a new EGR system that removed all belt drives from the engine, reducing drag, and enhanced regenerative braking control.

Sales of the fourth-generation Prius started in Japan and America in May 2009, with prices actually lower than before, confirming the economy-of-scale theory mentioned earlier. Sales began in Europe in August 2009. The optional solar panel roof for powering interior HVAC systems when the car was parked up was a brilliant idea – almost as good as the Mercedes one to recycle waste exhaust heat after an engine

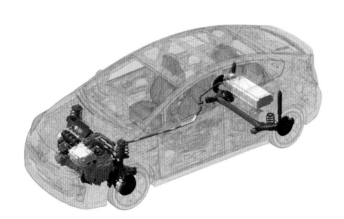

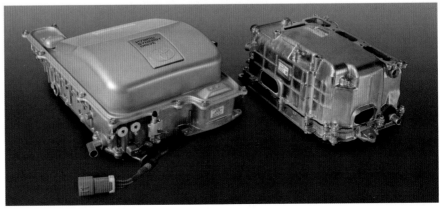

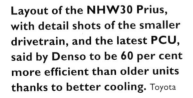

Layout of the NHW30 Prius, with detail shots of the smaller drivetrain, and the latest PCU, said by Denso to be 60 per cent more efficient than older units thanks to better cooling. Toyota

has been shut down to warm the vehicle's cockpit. In time, the closely related Auris Hybrid would also make the showrooms.

The American Council for Energy Efficient Economy (ACEEE) listed the Honda Civic GX as being kindest on the environment in 2010, as the car ran on clean-burning natural gas. Second was the Prius, which gave excellent gas mileage figures, and was also noted as being more practical to refuel than the Honda. Next was the Honda Civic Hybrid, followed by the Smart ForTwo, and the Honda Insight. Interestingly, there were no diesels in the top twelve.

On the manufacturing front in the States, thanks to the popularity of the Escape Hybrid, Ford launched a Fusion Hybrid in March 2009, along with a Mercury Milan version. These were full hybrids using 2.5-litre Atkinson-cycle petrol engines and Aisin transmissions. There was also a Lincoln MKZ variant, although it would be short-lived due to the arrival of a facelifted Fusion at the 2012 Detroit Show.

Asian countries continued to head the hybrid charge. Although the Hyundai Accent Hybrid never made it into production, the Sonata Hybrid did. First displayed at the 2008 LA Show, it eventually went on sale in 2011, sharing the same series-parallel hybrid drivetrain as the Kia Optima Hybrid – a 2359cc Atkinson-cycle petrol engine rated at 166bhp, combined with a 30kW electric motor. Also noteworthy, the Chinese BYD S6DM full hybrid SUV went on sale in time for the 2011 season.

Meanwhile in Japan, Subaru had an 'Advanced Tourer Concept' on its 2009 Tokyo Show stand. This was refined slightly for the 2011 event, becoming more practical, which hints at production-ready status. The specification is interesting, combining a direct-injection 1.6-litre turbocharged boxer engine, an electric motor with Li-ion batteries, CVT, and four-wheel drive.

Nissan displayed its Infiniti M35h (or Fuga Hybrid) at the 2010 Geneva Show, putting the car on sale in the domestic market at the end of the year. The Lexus CT200h also made its debut in Switzerland, going on sale in early 2011.

A little while later, a facelift for the Toyota Prius spawned a whole range of variations – augmenting the regular Prius, there was now an estate version (badged as the Prius v, + or α depending on the market), and a compact model with a lighter 1.5-litre drivetrain. This was based on the FT-CH concept from 2010, and eventually became the Prius c, or

The Ford Fusion picked up Motor Trend's prestigious 2010 'Car of the Year' award. Regular non-hybrid models were also built, but the magazine noted that the Fusion Hybrid was 'the crown jewel in Ford's hybrid program, and the best American-brand hybrid on the market.' Ford

The 2011 version of the Subaru Advanced Tourer Concept. Subaru has stated that it is adding a mild hybrid to the line-up in 2013. B. Long

Nissan's Fuga Hybrid powertrain, with its patented dual clutch system. The car is sold as the Infiniti M35h in the States. B. Long

ABOVE: **Porsche has also taken a part in the hybrid act in the hybrid boom in recent years.**
B. Long

LEFT: **The Toyota Aqua (or Prius c) at the 2011 Tokyo Show.** Toyota

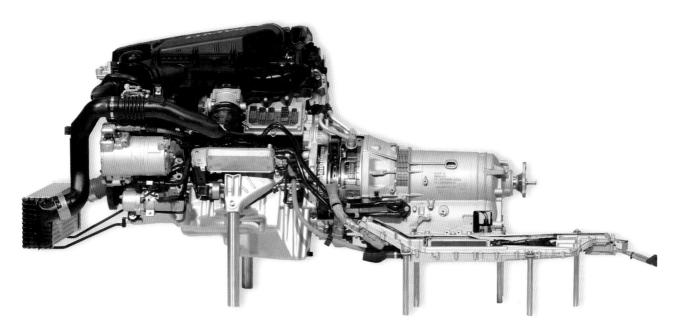

Drivetrain of the BMW ActiveHybrid 5. BMW

Aqua in Japan. The closely related Yaris Hybrid goes on sale in Europe soon, lining up alongside the British-built Auris Hybrid.

The Europeans were taking a more active interest in hybrids by now, with Porsche announcing it would create a hybrid version of the Cayenne SUV at the 2005 Frankfurt Show. It eventually went on sale in May 2010, badged as the Cayenne S Hybrid, alongside the VW Touareg Hybrid sister car, becoming the world's first supercharged hybrid (the supercharger ensuring good low-end torque), and including 'sailing' technology. The so-called sailing function shuts down the engine as soon as the throttle is lifted completely, kicking back in again as soon as the accelerator is touched. The Porsche Panamera S Hybrid, released in February 2011, uses a similar Bosch integrated motor generator (IMG) drivetrain, but it has been tweaked to better suit the vehicle's characteristics.

Jaguar unveiled a CX16 hybrid prototype at the 2011 Frankfurt Show, which looks as if it will enter production for the 2013 season, while in the following month, BMW allowed the production ActiveHybrid 5 to take a bow in

RIGHT: **Component suppliers are promoting EV technology more than ever before. This is the Mitsubishi Denki stand at the 2011 Tokyo Show, with an EV motor and an inverter closest to the camera. The inverter is used to convert battery-supplied DC power into AC electricity.** B. Long

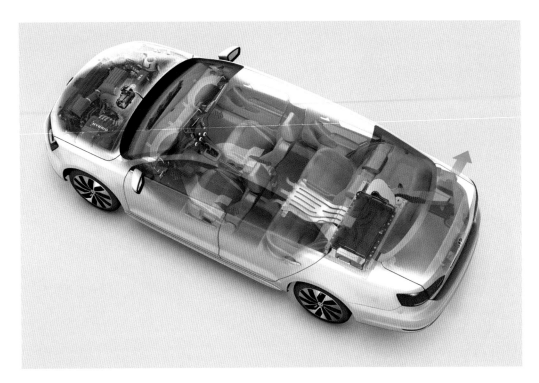

The Jetta Hybrid blends a full hybrid system with VW's highly efficient TSI petrol engine. Announced at the 2012 Detroit Show, it is due to enter production later in the year. This picture shows the battery cooling system.

Volkswagen

Tokyo. Unlike the 7-series hybrid, the 5-series version (and the 3-series to come) is a full hybrid. The ActiveHybrid 5 sports a turbocharged 2979cc straight-six, a 40kW motor linked to a Li-ion battery pack, and an eight-speed automatic transmission.

Interestingly, BMW signed up for a joint venture with the PSA Group in 2011, the two industry giants agreeing to cooperate on the development of hybrid petrol-electric cars. This extends the existing pact that sees the PSA Group supplying engines for the Mini – one of many partnerships forged in recent years, the trend being prompted by today's high development costs.

The latest hybrids, embodied in the Audi A6 Hybrid and 4WD Q5 Hybrid prototypes, seem to be working around minimal EV operation time in order to reduce battery size and weight. No doubt if one takes the number of hybrid concepts on display at Detroit and Geneva this year as a gauge, the breed will continue to evolve.

THE PLUG-IN ERA

At the inauguration of the FCVT programme (which basically took the place of the PNGV programme), George W. Bush's administration was all in favour of hydrogen as the fuel of the future. However, in 2007, the US Department of Energy announced huge funding for the development of plug-in hybrids (PHEVs) and lithium-ion batteries.

Although Toyota originally cited not having to plug into the grid as an advantage of the HEV, as in being able to use a full hybrid like any other car, the plug-in hybrid concept is becoming increasingly popular nowadays. Indeed, Toyota started testing the first of 600 modified Prius models on public roads in America, Japan and Europe in the summer of 2007 following the Bush administration's stance on PHEVs.

Basically the car can be run as an electric vehicle thanks to home charging and regenerative braking, but it can also be topped up with petrol (or diesel) when out and about, taking away all range concerns, yet allowing the car to run in EV mode that much longer. Otherwise the machine works just like a regular full hybrid.

One of the first plug-in series-parallel hybrids to go on sale came from Porsche – the 918 Spyder that was unveiled at the 2010 Geneva Show. This was a full hybrid with a powerful V8 petrol engine, electric motors on both axles, and a PDK transmission. The fluid-cooled Li-ion battery could be charged by regenerative braking or household electricity, giving a range of 26km (16 miles) as a pure EV. Considering the racing-car levels of performance of the machine, the CO_2 emissions figure of 70g/km was truly remarkable – even a regular Prius is rated at 89g/km, although the figure drops to just 49g/km for the latest plug-in version.

As it happens, the Prius Plug-in Hybrid went on sale in March 2012, sporting minor styling changes to distance the

MEASURING FUEL CONSUMPTION

We've all seen it – amazing fuel consumption figures in the headlines, followed by tiny writing which explains the measurement system used, or a disclaimer somewhere, stating that this wonderful achievement might not actually be possible in normal conditions. To allow for fair taxation and to make our car selection easier, at least for those who care enough to make comparisons before buying, we need a global standard on economy figures that are based on typical usage, averaged across the main markets. Certain areas can be chosen in each country, with a computer rigged up to the ECU in the car to record a typical day's driving. All results can be added together, averaged, and made into a rolling road programme that all governments and every manufacturer can use as a benchmark for economy and emissions, regardless of the motive power-unit. Simple.

Instead, what we have is miles per gallon in Britain and North America, with different measurement systems and the confusion over UK and US gallons, and kilometres per litre or litres per 100km in most other countries, albeit with another set of local calibrations added to establish the final numbers. For instance, the system in the EU is completely different to that used in Japan, despite both markets using kilometres and litres as the unit of measurement. Emissions are kept as a different issue in all cases, when really they should be batched together in a suitable real-life scenario.

Most countries tend to use some sort of city and highway figure, with a combined figure. Most veteran users in Europe and America will reckon on averaging the fuel consumption published against the city mode – but why should we have to assume, and have our taxes based on dreams? Surely we have a right to expect hitting the upper figure once in a while.

The Japanese '10–15 mode' system gives only one figure. The Shahyo testing team (of which I was a member) proved how foolish this system was, with figures over 40 per cent off in certain cases, both in NA and turbocharged cars. The '10–15 mode' did at least make Kei-cars look attractive on paper, which was probably part of the idea. Now, a 'JC08' system is being phased in, the new figures (still using km/ltr as a unit) generally reflecting around 10 per cent lower gas mileage, with a 15 per cent difference on the 1.3-litre Mazda Skyactiv engine.

During the Shahyo tests, it was fascinating to see an economy figure of 21.2km/ltr for the Toyota Prius, against 33.0km/ltr in the catalogue. As for the Honda Civic Hybrid, the expected 28.5km/ltr was way off the mark, with only 15.3km/ltr recorded. But therein lies the difference between figures that governments approve, and real life.

Just as this book was being put to bed, news came that Honda was being sued over publishing economy figures for the Civic Hybrid in the US that were unattainable in real-world driving. The Toyota Prius hit the headlines a while back with similar complaints – the EPA figures and those of customers were often poles apart, while there are just as many testimonials from those with more realistic expectations who are more than happy with their gas mileage. All this really does is confirm that a new, more sensible system of average expected fuel consumption is needed.

Certainly the figures that all makers release are possible to achieve under certain conditions, otherwise the manufacturers would expose themselves to people suing them all the time – but this mild form of 'Greenwashing' has to come to an end. It's like the horsepower wars of the 1960s and 1970s, when engine output figures were a joke, leading customers to stop having faith in catalogue numbers. The guides we see in brochures, adverts and on television have to reflect not what is ultimately possible, but what normal users can assume to see in an everyday scenario. This is all the more important with hybrids if one is to build up trust in the marketplace.

Similarly, the CAFE system in the States needs a more balanced approach – it's no good imposing rules that allow certain vehicles to be left out of the equation (usually the worst polluters), or badge-engineering economy cars bought from other makers, and including a few token diesels or HEVs to hit targets. As with Britain and Japan, simply taxing larger engines which are that much heavier is a shortsighted and unbalanced policy, whereas putting tax on petrol instead hits drivers in relation to their actual road use and car selection. In this way, those who own a larger car but use public transport most of the time, or work from home, are not penalized for being Greener than someone using a smaller car on a daily basis.

Plug-in hybrid drivetrains should be particularly useful for commercial vehicles. Trucks are typically mild hybrids, using regenerative braking to recoup energy that would otherwise be lost. By going the plug-in route, trucks can run in EV mode in town, and also use the larger battery capacity to power up other equipment, such as refrigerators, allowing engines to be shut down more often. B. Long

car from its more common brethren. Sold as the Prius PHV in Japan, it costs 3,200,000 yen, against 2,170,000 yen for the base Prius, although the gap is soon closed as one moves up through the grades.

Interestingly, the plug-in Prius has a Li-ion battery rather than a NiMH one, and while the battery pack actually weighs more than that of a regular Prius, it can be charged via any standard AC outlet, with no need for a fast charger. The 60kW motor works with a 650V electrical system, and combined with the new battery, allows 24km (15 miles) of driving in pure EV mode.

ABOVE: **The remarkable Porsche 918 Spyder – a full hybrid with plug-in capability. Other Porsche racing models have adopted regenerative braking in recent years, becoming mild hybrids.** Porsche

LEFT: **The Prius Plug-in Hybrid featured in some Toyota Industries Corporation promotional material. The car comes with a 1.8-litre petrol engine and a 60kW electric motor.** Toyota Industries

環境技術力で、人とクルマと街がつながる新たな社会に貢献。
Capitalizing on environmental technologies to help create a new society where people, cars and cities are connected.

人とクルマと街をつなげる「スマートモビリティシティ」。それは、低炭素社会を実現するために、私たちが目指す次世代のクルマ社会です。豊田自動織機は電動化、軽量化、省エネルギーの技術とノウハウを結集し、豊かで快適な社会づくりに貢献します。

Smart Mobility City: A city where people, cars, and cities are connected to each other. We are aiming to bring out this next generation motorized society thereby realizing a low carbon society. Toyota Industries contributing to the creation of a more prosperous and comfortable society by bringing together its technologies and know-how in the fields of electrification, weight reduction, and energy saving.

TOYOTA
株式会社 豊田自動織機
TOYOTA INDUSTRIES CORPORATION

ABOVE: **The plug-in hybrid system of the Volvo XC60.** Volvo

LEFT: **Mitsubishi's PX-MiEV II concept.** Mitsubishi

The Mitsubishi PX-MiEV plug-in SUV made its debut initially at the 2009 Tokyo Show. The hybrid system determined which of the three configurations – pure electric, engine-to-battery charging, or engine-to-wheels power – offered the most efficiency for the driving conditions. The car could drive for 48km (30 miles) as a pure EV, and judging by the refinements made to the 2011 display model and controlled press leaks, it looks as if this will be the next Outlander. Mitsubishi has been hinting for some time that it intends to make greater use of chassis electrification in the coming years.

The Honda AC-X concept, combining a 1.6-litre engine with an electric motor, may be too advanced to be taken seriously beyond a styling point of view, but the new NSX shown at Detroit certainly looks interesting, with a petrol engine for the rear axle, and in-wheel motors up front.

The Volvo XC60 concept, also displayed at the 2012 Detroit Show, goes the other way around, using a petrol engine with idle-stop technology for the front axle, and an electric motor for the rear axle. The Li-ion battery came with a plug-in facility, giving the car an EV only range of 56km (35 miles). The SUV is due to go into production within the next two years, and shows another potential way to get the best from a blended powertrain.

Also on display was the Toyota NS4 concept, with a next-generation HSD plug-in hybrid drivetrain. Apparently this was quite different to the Prius family of hybrid systems, which means we can expect something special from the engineers in Toyota City in the near future.

Meanwhile, a number of people with whom the author has come into contact following the massive earthquake that hit Japan in 2011 swear by hybrids. When fuel supplies started to run low (they even ran out in places for a while, causing queues reminiscent of the 1970s), owners were still able to get around using the electric power mode to make what petrol was left in the tank last longer. A doctor I know put a hybrid at the top of her new car list this year for that very reason. But one should also remember that the level of the disaster that caused petrol shortages also caused rolling blackouts, at a time when PHEVs and pure EVs are still anything but popular! More stress on the national grid was the last thing the country needed in the weeks following 3/11. And after all is said and done, buying a hybrid 'just in case' doesn't really make sense – one has to consider all the angles of ownership, and be sure the car suits personal needs.

While hybrid sales in general have at last reached a plateau in the States (and Japan) after years of demand outstripping supply, the 'new toy' image of the plug-in hybrid seems to have the press taking renewed interest in blended drivetrain vehicles. There's no doubt that CO_2 emissions are incredibly low on plug-in models, and with CARB pushing harder for EVs, FCEVs and PHEVs to take on an increasingly greater role in society, one can be fairly sure that the breed will continue to be developed, using electronics wizardry to increase their efficiency with each passing year.

On saying that, in many ways the diesel-electric hybrid could well be the ideal 'Green' car for the time being, especially if the diesel is sourced using third-generation bio-fuel

DIESEL-ELECTRIC LOCOMOTIVES

We've become used to the petrol-electric hybrid, but now diesel-electric models have joined the scene. Some might wonder if the system in a diesel-electric train is the same as that in a car. Well, yes and no. When compared to a full hybrid system, which is the subject of this chapter, the locomotive set-up is quite different. But if we said it was a series hybrid, using the same motive power principle as a Fisker Karma EREV, then the links between the two become somewhat closer.

The diesel-electric train, around since the 1920s, uses a diesel engine to run a generator, which then creates electricity for a series of traction motors (AC or DC) that power the loco, making the most of the torque characteristics of electric motors. There is no connection whatsoever between the diesel engine and the wheels, allowing the unit to run in an efficient rev-band, and taking away the need for a gearbox and mechanical connections to the axle sets at the same time.

Diesel engines were chosen simply because they have low overall running costs. In view of the fact that the unit only charges a generator, the large displacement is easily explained when one considers that the said generator could perhaps power 1,000 houses! The same system is often used in shipping. Interestingly, in these non-automotive applications, the two-stroke cycle is often employed, as it delivers twice as many power strokes per crankshaft revolution as an Otto-cycle ICE.

GM Electro-motive advertising from 1944. The diesel-electric drivetrain is closer to that of a strict EREV than a full hybrid. GM EMD

techniques, as even a small diesel engine should have enough low-end torque to deal efficiently with the heavier body. Add in idle-stop technology, and with a new lightweight battery pack, it would be difficult to think of a much cleaner option that offered the same level of practicality.

THE DIESEL-ELECTRIC HYBRID

The diesel-electric hybrid concept actually dates back to the 2000 Detroit Show, when the remarkably aerodynamic GM Precept made its debut. This was one of the PNGV prototypes, and while Ford and Chrysler went down the mild hybrid route, General Motors decided to build a full hybrid based around an Isuzu 1.3-litre turbo-diesel engine and two electric motors – one liquid-cooled unit from the EV1 driving the front wheels, taking the car away from traffic

lights and serving as the main source of regenerative braking energy, and a lower-powered motor that started the engine in its part of an idle-stop function, assisted it in times of hard throttle application, balanced the speeds of the crankshaft and gearbox input shaft to eliminate the need for synchros, acted as a generator for the NiMH battery pack and drove the air-conditioning compressor.

It was a beautiful piece of engineering, with forty-seven microprocessors controlling the drivetrain (deciding on when the car would run as an EV, when to kick in the engine for cruising, and also when to have the two motors assist the engine), four coolant circuits, sixteen radiators, and three voltage systems. Although it was very complicated, it looked as if GM had found a winning formula, at least if a more cost-effective bodyshell were employed, but the project was allowed to simply fade away.

RIGHT: **GM's vice chairman, Harry Pearce, with the Precept diesel-electric hybrid concept car at the 2000 Detroit Show. A FCEV version was also reported to have been built.** GM

BELOW: **Powertrain from the Mercury Meta One concept.** Ford

'Economy Mode' the initial acceleration after stopping was looked after by the electric motor, but the truck was unable to run as a pure EV. The commercial vehicle arena, be it in the States, Europe or Japan, has tended to follow this line of thinking, making good use of regenerative braking systems, but now full hybrids are starting to appear from makers worldwide.

Back on the car front, the feelings of makers everywhere were eloquently summed up by Fritz Henderson of General Motors: 'Diesel is expensive, hybrid is expensive and diesel hybrid is expensive squared.'

Meanwhile, the Eaton Corporation formed a Hybrid Power Systems unit in the year 2000, with the first result being a hybrid delivery truck for FedEx. Thanks to a combination of a smaller diesel engine and an electric motor charged through regenerative braking, on paper the E700 model introduced in 2003 cut PM by 90 per cent, NOx and other smog-causing emissions by 75 per cent, and improved fuel efficiency by 50 per cent, which naturally had a knock-on effect in lowering carbon dioxide emissions, as well as reducing oil dependency. By 2008, FedEx had been joined by UPS, Coca-Cola and Pepsico in using the Eaton HEV system.

In another line of development, the 2002 Detroit Show saw the launch of the Eaton Hydraulic Launch Assist (HLA) system. This was actually a kind of parallel system, as in

But the idea of building a diesel hybrid resurfaced nonetheless, with Ford releasing its 2.7-litre twin-turbo V6 diesel-engined Mercury Meta One concept in 2005, followed by the Reflex concept at the 2006 Detroit Show, featuring diesel power, and electricity sourced from a Li-ion battery pack and solar panels.

However, it was the Volkswagen-Audi Group that led the charge in this field. The Golf diesel-hybrid had first been exhibited at the 2008 Geneva Show, and by the summer of that year, no fewer than twenty 'Twin-Drive' prototypes were being tested on the road. The Twin-Drive featured a 1.5-litre TDI unit and an electric motor up front, plus a pair of in-wheel motors for the back. Despite fuel consumption put at 2.5ltr/100km (113mpg), the project went quiet until

The early diesel version of the VW Twin-Drive. The lack of a transmission offset a lot of the weight gain caused by the electric motor and heavy Sanyo battery pack. Some of the test cars have FF-only drivetrains, as did the petrol-engined Twin-Drive Golfs that followed. Volkswagen

mid-2011, when an updated batch of test cars was released. These lost the rear motors, which saved a lot of weight and engineering complications, and the diesel engines were changed for petrol units.

In the meantime, in 2009 SEAT had announced a plug-in Leon Twin-Drive based on the VW prototype, using a 1.4-litre TSI petrol engine and an 85kW motor. Although test drives have appeared in magazines, there is little hope of the plug-in cars – petrol or diesel – being released before 2015. Volkswagen cites the fact that electricity generation needs to become cleaner before the cars make sense. Ironically, the SEAT factory has the largest solar panel array in the whole of Spain.

Before straying too far, one cannot forget the Volkswagen L1 diesel-electric hybrid – a 2009 prototype that was ultra-low drag, ultra-low weight, but fully roadworthy. This was followed by the VW XL-1 diesel hybrid in 2011, but these were pure experiments aimed simply at seeing how far the folks in Wolfsburg could push the engineering envelope.

Then there was the plug-in Audi e-tron Spyder prototype that was presented at the 2010 Paris Salon. This blended a

LEFT: **The Audi e-tron Spyder making its debut at the 2010 Paris Salon. It seems more than a little ironic that so many hybrids are high performance and heavyweight luxury models in today's marketplace.** Audi

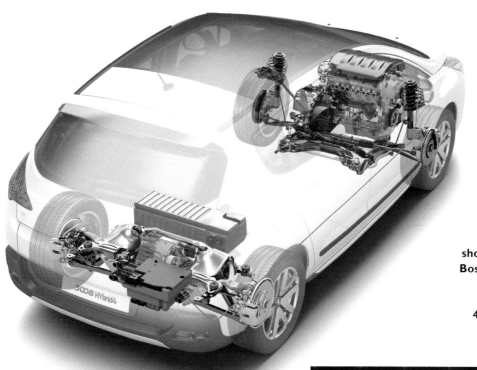

Cutaway drawing of the Peugeot 3008 Hybrid4, showing the layout devised by Bosch, and the centre console of the same vehicle. Note the Auto, Sport, ZEV and 4WD mode settings for the transmission. PSA Group

300bhp twin-turbo diesel engine with a pair of 64kW electric motors to give 249km/h (155mph) performance at the top end, stunning acceleration (thanks to what Audi called boosting, whereby the electric motors augmented engine power under hard acceleration), but carbon dioxide emissions of just 59g/km. Running in EV mode, the car had an unassisted range of 50km (31 miles), but should have been capable of covering 965km (600 miles) between fuel stops.

And so we come to the first diesel-electric hybrid that one can actually buy – the Peugeot 3008 Hybrid4. Unveiled at the 2010 Paris Salon, it went on sale in the latter part of 2011 featuring Bosch's new axle-split hybrid (AS-HEV) technology that had first been seen on the Peugeot RCZ concept of March 2010. This is a full hybrid (the world's first production model using a diesel engine), with diesel power for the front axle, and electric for the rear. Both axle sets are able to act independently, with the diesel engine and regenerative braking charging the battery, or as a pair to give what then becomes a 4WD configuration. With CO_2 emissions of 104g/km, there was also a Citroën model using the same drivetrain made available soon after, badged as the DS5.

Without doubt, despite reservations from makers that the American market may be lukewarm on the concept,

more diesel hybrids will follow. At Volvo, plug-in V70 test cars had been on the road since the end of 2009, being earmarked for 2012 production. While the V70 didn't make it to showrooms, the plug-in diesel-electric V60 Hybrid is due to go on sale in the spring of 2012.

Other examples: Hyundai pushed the diesel hybrid idea with the 'i-flow' concept in 2010. The Land Rover Range-e, another plug-in diesel-electric hybrid, was also first mooted in 2010, but its official announcement came at the 2011 Geneva Show. This is due to hit the marketplace in 2013, which should bring a 'Green' tint to the SUV breed. And at the 2012 Detroit Show, Mercedes unveiled its new diesel hybrid – the Mercedes-Benz E300 BlueTec Hybrid, which goes on sale in Europe in the second half of the year.

With rising petrol prices in America and Japan, and Europe's love of CI engines, it would be a safe bet to say diesel hybrids will be with us for some time to come.

LEFT: **The Citroën DS5 uses the same AS-HEV drivetrain as the Peugeot 3008 hybrid.** PSA Group

BELOW: **The Mercedes-Benz E300 BlueTec Hybrid, which will go on sale as an early 2013 model. It requires only 4.2ltr (0.9gal) of diesel to travel 100km (62 miles), and emits just 109g of carbon dioxide per kilometre. A plug-in S500 has been shown in the past, making one wonder if it will line up with the S400 mild hybrid.** Daimler AG

CHAPTER FIVE

PURE ELECTRIC VEHICLES AND EREVs

In a new age of mobility, in which people want to travel further and faster, as well as on the spur of the moment without any need to plan ahead, the current situation with electric vehicles was perhaps summed up perfectly by Dr Martin Winterkorn of the VW Group, speaking in October 2009:

The electric car will have a crucial impact on the future of individual mobility. We are committed to this technology at Volkswagen, and we are focused on advancing its development. However, everyone should understand very clearly that the journey to the electric car is not a sprint, rather it is a marathon.

THE BIRTH OF ELECTRIC VEHICLES

Electric vehicles (or EVs) have been around since the dawn of motoring. Indeed, the first electric car dates from 1839, when Robert Anderson took to the roads of Aberdeen in a battery-powered vehicle he'd constructed himself. Only a few notable EVs were built then, until the 1890s came

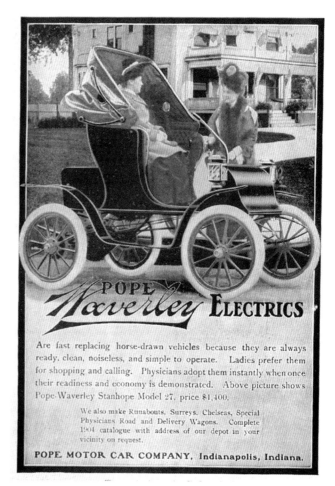

ABOVE: **A 1904 advert for the Pope-Waverley electric car.** Pope

LEFT: **The CITA electric vehicle known as 'La Jamais Contente' was the first car to pass the 100km/h (60mph) barrier. It had an alloy body shrouding two Postel-Vinay motors (as used by Paris trams) and Fulmen batteries, and rode on Michelin tyres.** Michelin

A Detroit Electric EV recharging in 1919. Library of Congress

Electric cars were all but extinct by the 1920s, although a few were built by major manufacturers in the light of wartime petrol shortages. This Peugeot VLV (voiture légère de ville, or lightweight town car) electric vehicle built during World War II is a good example. Although it looks like a three-wheeler, it actually has four wheels, just a very narrow track at the rear. Peugeot

around, by which time battery technology had made the concept feasible. The original rechargeable lead-acid battery had been invented by Gaston Planté as far back as 1859, but it was Henri Tudor of Luxembourg who made it practical in 1886.

America fell in love with the EV early on, building on the pioneering work of Thomas Davenport and William Morrison, while the first car made in Coventry – the Detroit of Britain – was the Garrard & Blumfield electric brake, built from 1894 to 1896 within the Harry Lawson empire. Patents for this machine were first filed on 14 December 1893, while in France, almost exactly five years later, the electric-powered Jeantaud driven by Count Gaston de Chasseloup-Laubat became the first official land speed record holder. By April 1899 the LSR stood at 105.9km/h (66.2mph), when Camille Jenatzy drove a streamlined electric CITA called 'La Jamais Contente' flat out on the outskirts of Paris.

By the turn of the century, however, Europeans were more enamoured by the properties of gasoline engines, and electric power took a back seat for a while. Only a few persevered with the idea, notably in America, where a survey conducted at the 1900 National Automobile Show in New York showed that people in the States preferred electric cars and steamers to petrol-engined models. This attitude, helped by easy starting and no gears to shift, as well as a complete lack of noise, vibration and exhaust fumes, allowed companies specializing in EVs to flourish, companies such as the Pope concern of Hartford (originally makers of Columbia bicycles), Baker of Cleveland, Woods of Chicago, and the Anderson Carriage Company (owners of the Detroit Electric brand).

At the same time, battery technology was taking giant steps forwards: in 1899 Waldemar Jungner invented the nickel-cadmium (NiCd, or NiCad) battery, and two years later Thomas Edison gave birth to the nickel-iron (NiFe) battery. These Edison batteries were far from cheap, but they hugely extended range and were therefore offered as an option by several EV makers.

Thomas Edison's first car was a Baker model, but he later owned a Detroit Electric, as did Henry Ford, who'd bought several for his wife, Clara. It is therefore ironic that the success of the Ford Motor Company (its establishment coming as a result of Edison's encouragement) was probably the biggest single factor in the eventual downfall of the electric car. By the 1920s, other than the likes of the Detroit Electric brand (which persevered until World War II, but by then was a shadow of its former self), they had all but disappeared on both sides of the Atlantic.

EARLY EREVs

Although we tend to have an image of extended-range electric vehicles (EREVs, or series hybrids as they are often called), being the latest in cutting-edge technology, in reality they are nothing new. Indeed, one was exhibited at the Paris Salon of 1899 – a fascinating three-wheeler by Vedovelli, Priestley & Cie of France, which had an electric motor on each back wheel, and a small petrol engine in a trailer, hooked up to a generator to charge the batteries.

Several vehicles used petrol engines as generators for electric drives in the years that followed, such as the Lohner-Porsche, the Owen Magnetic, and a number of commercials. Then suddenly, as with pure electric vehicles, shortly after the Great War, EREVs simply disappeared.

In a nutshell, the era had changed. Gasoline-powered engines, starting systems and transmissions had been refined to such an extent that the earlier advantages offered by EVs no longer made an overwhelming case for themselves in the light of the various disadvantages, such as weight (a major problem on early dirt roads after wet weather), range, and charging times, assuming one had access to electricity, which wasn't always the case in the countryside. With reduced purchase costs prompted by vehicles such as the Ford Model T (which was about a third of the price of a basic EV), enhanced reliability, an infrastructure to support gasoline-engined cars, plus cheap petrol, the fate of the first generation of electric vehicles was duly sealed, even in America, where there had been as many as twenty-five companies building EVs at the outbreak of World War I.

The Vedovelli & Priestley EREV of 1899. Poyet

THE LOHNER-PORSCHE

Born in September 1875, Professor Ferdinand Porsche would become a legend in the pre-war German motor industry, but Porsche's first car was built in Vienna, Austria – an EV called the Lohner-Porsche.

The Lohner-Porsche, first exhibited at the 1900 World's Fair in Paris (although one had been sold to an English customer beforehand), was originally a pure EV, with no fewer than sixty batteries providing power for the motors mounted in each of the four wheels. Most production cars had front-wheel drive only, but then evolution took its course.

In 1901, Porsche employed a small Daimler petrol engine to generate electricity, enabling him to reduce weight through a smaller battery pack, thus creating the Lohner-Porsche Mixte – the world's first practical EREV. It was a vehicle ahead of its time which would ultimately inspire a new generation of cars almost a century later.

In the meantime, Professor Porsche's idea was used as the basis for the design of the lunar roving vehicle (LRV) created by Boeing for NASA for use on the moon at the end of the Apollo programme. Three of the four built are still on the lunar surface.

The Lohner-Porsche. Porsche

A MINOR REVIVAL

Although a few persevered with the electric drivetrain concept – such as the Battronic Truck Company and the Henney Motor Company – and others such as AMC (American Motors) and Scottish Aviation were dipping their toe in the water, it took a bill passed by the US Congress in 1966 to revive interest in EVs and EREVs. This proposal recommended the use of electric vehicles to start reducing pollution on a nationwide scale, and caused quite a stir within the motor industry, at least initially. In reality, when it was found that the bill had no teeth, it was 'business as usual' until some proper legislation was filed decades later.

In the meantime, some fascinating concepts were put forward to save the Earth. Ford of Britain built six boxy Comuta EV prototypes in 1967, while General Motors (GM) was working on its GM 512 project in the States, building commuter vehicles with petrol, electric and hybrid powertrains. GM had also converted a Corvair into the Electrovair, with the batteries up front.

Another arm of General Motors, Opel in Germany, was working on something far more realistic for the time: the Opel Kadett Stir-Lec I. This was an interesting EREV with a Stirling engine in the tail, built in 1970. The Stirling engine, which was quiet and economical, charged the fourteen lead-acid batteries in the front of the car, with power being supplied to a single electric motor attached to a conventional back axle.

In the following year, in May, Georg von Opel drove an Opel GT converted to electrical power with Bosch motors and Varta batteries to a series of speed records at Hockenheim, no doubt inspiring the American, Dave Arthurs, to do his own conversion based on the German sports car in the late 1970s. Amazingly, after an article was published in *Mother Earth News*, 60,000 people wrote in asking for more details. Just as amazingly, the car manufacturers continued to say there was no demand for such vehicles.

Meanwhile, Victor Wouk of the California Institute of Technology (Caltech), who was heavily involved with the Henney Kilowatt EV project of 1959, along with Charlie Rosen, created an EREV based on the 1972 Buick Skylark sedan, with a Mazda rotary engine acting as the generator to recharge the batteries. Despite passing the 1976 emissions standards with ease in 1974, Erik Stork of the EPA rejected the car, citing seventy-five reasons why hybrids shouldn't qualify for R&D funding from the government as part of the Federal Clean Car Incentive Programme. To say this was a missed opportunity is a massive understatement.

Notwithstanding, EV development moved up another gear with the success of the CitiCar, produced by Sebring-Vanguard of Florida, and the Elcar, reviving a name from the past. However, moving away from the golf-cart image was crucial for general acceptance of EVs (as the failure of the Enfield 8000 in the UK had proved), and in 1975, AMC delivered over 300 electric vans for the US Postal Service to test, and the US Congress passed the Electric and Hybrid Vehicle Research, Development and Demonstration Act of 1976. This was aimed at refining electric motors, battery technology and control systems that could be used for hybrid vehicles.

As it happens, Germany had been using EVs for its post office since the 1950s, but otherwise, progress was slow in Europe on the electric vehicle front, other than the occasional conversion (such as Bedford vans made into EVs by Lucas) and working vehicles, such as milk floats and air-

This is Stir-Lec I.
And if you saw it on a highway, you'd probably think it was a standard Opel Kadett.
You'd be half right. It's got an Opel body. But it's powered by electricity. The power plant consists of 14 conventional lead-acid batteries that you could buy down at the corner. The energy from the batteries is transferred to an electric motor which in turn drives the rear wheels. And the car can tool along at speeds of up to 55 miles an hour.
While the car's running, the batteries are constantly recharged by a small Stirling engine in the rear. It's so quiet that you can hardly tell whether it's on or off. And since the Stirling is an external combustion engine (fuel is burned in a separate chamber from the engine), the exhaust has virtually no odor and pollution levels can be made very low.
Stir-Lec I is still only an experimental model. A project that Engineers at GM's Research Laboratories are working on today, to meet the demands of the future.

General Motors
Chevrolet • Pontiac • Oldsmobile • Buick • Cadillac • Opel • Fisher Body • Frigidaire • GMC Truck & Coach • Detroit Diesel • United Delco • AC Spark Plug • Allison • Electro-Motive • Earthmoving Equipment Division

An electric car that makes its own electricity.

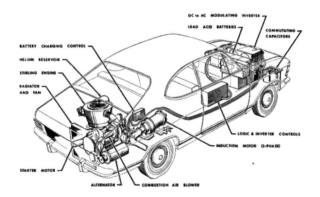

Advertising for the Opel Kadett Stir-Lec I. The Stirling engine in the tail is actually an external combustion engine. Although rarely seen (there's this car, and Nissan exhibited one in 1979, for instance), they use the alternating expansion and compression of a gas in a sealed cylinder. They are very quiet, efficient and clean, so may still yet find an application as a charging medium in an EREV. Opel

Introduced in 1947, the TAMA electric car was built by the Tachikawa Aircraft Company (the forerunner of Prince), and was in production for around four years.
Nissan

craft tractors. Early Volkswagen electric vehicles included a T2-based machine of 1973 vintage, developed alongside a hybrid model, and then a Golf EV three years later, which was put forward as a possible solution to wean the industry off fossil fuels during the oil crisis.

As for Japan, there was the 1947 TAMA, finding service as a taxi most of the time, and then a long gap before Daihatsu released the Fellow Van EV in 1968, followed by a Hijet commercial in the following year. With ten batteries on board, the Hijet minivan had a range of about 95km (60 miles).

Toyota three-wheelers were displayed at the 1970 Tokyo Show, as was the Nissan 315X runabout and the Daihatsu Fellow MAX coupé, but nothing would come of any of them, or the various concept cars from Toyota, Nissan, Mitsubishi, Daihatsu, Mazda and Suzuki that followed over the next decade, even with the backing of the Agency of Industrial Science & Technology. Toyota then tried using a gas turbine as the charging medium for an EREV based on the Century limousine. The car was exhibited at the 1975 Tokyo Show, but nothing was heard of it after this.

In reality, although General Electric (GE) had released the GE-100 in 1977, and then worked together with Chrysler to produce the sporty ETV-1 two-door coupé in 1979 (regenerative braking was used to charge the eighteen advanced Globe-Union batteries, or they could be hooked up to the home electrical system), it was probably General Motors that was pushing the EV concept the hardest, with over $20 million spent on electric vehicle research and development in the last three years of the seventies alone. There were rumours of GM EVs going into production by the middle of

the eighties, but all that ever appeared was the Electrovette prototype – a sensible hatchback based on the Chevette. If nothing else, this does explain why General Motors was ahead of the game as we entered the nineties.

With the fuel crisis era over and done with, electric vehicles were basically forgotten again, even after the formation of bodies such as the Japan Electric Vehicle Association. On saying that, there was a special EV display and public test facility at the 1987 Tokyo Motor Show (the last one held at Harumi), with cars such as the Nissan March EV-2 making their debut. One of the vehicles demonstrated was the Toyota EV-30, which was fitted with zinc-bromine (ZnBr) batteries. With an eight-hour charge time, it had a 170km (105 mile) range, almost double what the equivalent lead-acid batteries could deliver.

However, had it not been for the California Air Resources Board (CARB) introducing the Zero Emission Vehicle Mandate in 1990, which stated that a fixed percentage of electric vehicles should be included in a maker's model mix by 1998, it is probably safe to say that the only time we would get to read about EVs today would be in history books.

A NEW IMPETUS AND A FALSE START

Thanks to CARB's legislation, written in the knowledge that GM was working on a practical electric vehicle project, and the US Energy Policy Act that followed in 1992 as a result, the EV started to make a comeback, as the concept appears to offer a number of advantages from both an environmental and packaging point of view. In addition, after decades of huge conglomerates dominating the car scene, it also brought an opportunity for a flood of smaller makers to enter the industry, able to compete in an area most of the mainstream manufacturers were happy to leave well alone. This extra layer of manufacturers (the 'Small 100' as opposed to the 'Big Three' in the States) would also help increase competition.

Probably spurred on by the fact that California had forty-one smog warnings issued in 1990, to make the EV a more practical proposition, the US Department of Energy created the United States Advanced Battery Consortium (USABC) in 1991, investing more than $90 million in the development of the nickel metal hydride (NiMH) battery. With better cold weather performance and the ability to accept far more charge cycles than a traditional lead-acid battery, this was seen as a crucial part of the equation if electric vehicles were ever to stand a chance of becoming feasible in a world hooked on internal combustion engines.

In the background, however, trouble was brewing, with the American Automobile Manufacturers Association (AAMA) managing to add new wording to the ZEV Mandate, which made its legitimacy revolve around 'customer demand'. In other words, if there were no cars, there would be no customers, and therefore no demand. For those who didn't want change it was the perfect loophole, and with Roger Smith retired, the EV wasn't even that welcome at GM, as short-term profits were difficult to see on electric cars and hybrids, while the oil corporations, garages and parts suppliers would also face big losses if the EV became popular. In March 1995, the AAMA tried to hire a PR firm to deliberately play down the advantages of EVs, as 'greater consumer acceptance' was seen as a threat to the status quo, while other companies standing to lose money mounted slur campaigns.

Deliveries of the original 'Gen I' EV1s began in December 1996, but with lead-acid batteries which restricted range. This was strange, because General Motors had bought a 60 per cent stake in Ovonic to secure the NiMH battery technology invented by Stan Ovshinsky some years earlier. Only after the 'Gen II' cars were launched for 1999 did the EV1 receive the nickel metal hydride battery it deserved, and that may never have happened had it not been for a recall, when a large number of 'Gen I' models were retrofitted with the new battery pack. Not long after, GM sold its shares in Ovonic to oil colossus Texaco, which already held a 20 per cent stake in ECD – the company, founded by Ovshinsky in 1960, that could lay claim to the GM-Ovonic Battery Company as a subsidiary.

In the end a total of about 1,100 EV1s were built. Although positive lease applications numbered well over 4,000 – and

Roger Smith, GM's boss, ordered the team behind the Sunraycer solar car to start working on an electric car – a vehicle that would become the infamous EV1. With a power pack engineered by Alan Cocconi, the EV1 wasn't like a regular electric car, as it was fast, had a good range, and a practical, good-looking body. It was first shown as the Impact concept at the Los Angeles Show in January 1990, with Smith introducing it with the following words:

> *Impact is a genuine full performance machine, with capabilities that rival those of today's internal combustion cars. While we're definitely serious about Impact, about pursuing this path we're on and seeing where it leads, we're looking to our customers to tell us what they really want.*

The symbolic funeral held on 24 July 2003 for the infamous General Motors EV1. Plug In America/Creative Commons

that's after they were whittled down – supplies were kept limited, as the AAMA continued to fight CARB and the wishes of the Clinton administration, which was firmly behind EVs and HEVs.

Ultimately, in a meeting chaired by Alan C. Lloyd (later the head of the California Fuel Cell Partnership) in April 2003, CARB backed down, despite there being every sign that electric cars would be welcomed as ecology matters started making the headlines. This, combined with President George W. Bush declaring that America's future lay in hydrogen only three months earlier (by coincidence his Chief of Staff was Andrew H. Card, who was President of the AAMA from 1993 to 1998), effectively killed any hopes of there ever being mass-produced electric cars, despite a great deal of infrastructure having been put in place.

The cynical amongst us may be excused for thinking that the push on hydrogen – knowing full well that FCEVs were years, possibly decades away from being even close to ready – was simply another delaying tactic to keep internal combustion engines and the fuel they consume from being challenged.

Anyway, a symbolic funeral was held for the EV1 in July 2003, with cars being taken away from their keepers from December of that year, as General Motors refused to renew the leases. Because the cars were only leased, with no option to buy, it was easy to claw them back; the last one left in private hands was retrieved by GM in July 2004. The cars were then scrapped or decommissioned, as it saved GM having to build up an expensive stock of spares to comply with California law.

According to one official, the General Motors EV1 project was ditched due to a lack of return. But companies invest in new technology to stay ahead of the game, even taking on 'loss leaders' in the hope that things will change in the future (as Toyota did with the Prius, for instance), and production costs always come down as volume increases. Compared to the $50 million paid in 1970 for the rotary engine licence (an initial down payment, followed by additional $10 million instalments), tens of millions in R&D costs, and seven years of R&D time allocation, the EV1 project seems half-hearted. Yet while GM had the ideal opportunity to lead the way in this field of technology with the RE, the company was always going to be trying to catch up with Mazda, as well as the engineering might of Daimler-Benz, because the German company was already at an advanced stage with its own rotary unit.

Rick Wagoner, head of General Motors at the time of the EV1's cancellation, later affirmed that not giving electric vehicles and hybrids a chance was his worst mistake. The Chevrolet S-10 electric-powered pick-up with its NiMH bat-

The second generation CityStromer based on the third generation VW Golf. Volkswagen

teries was also dropped, as were the plans to build a Saturn hybrid, announced in 2006. The Saturn marque itself disappeared soon after – but there's more than a touch of irony in the fact that it was under Wagoner that the Hummer brand was being pushed hard, with new models joining the original H1.

THE ALSO-RANS

While all the fuss surrounding the GM EV1 was happening, few companies seemed to be in any great hurry to develop electric vehicles – but that's not to say there weren't any.

Realizing that more and more people were moving into urban areas, thus reducing range requirements but at the same time increasing the need for lower pollution, Volkswagen continued building on its experience with earlier EV prototypes, and released the first VW Golf CityStromer in 1989. Although it was heavy due to its lead-acid batteries, the VW engineers thought things through, and provided a diesel-fuelled heater – heating being a must in Europe, but something EVs struggled to deal with. Via a joint venture with Siemens, this was duly updated after the Golf facelift, and a total of 120 second-generation CityStromers were built between 1993 and 1996, complete with a regenerative braking set-up that uses the kinetic energy generated by the electric motor when it is not under load, or when the car is braking, to serve as a charging system.

Fascinating EREV drivetrain of the Volvo ECC concept of 1992, using a gas turbine to charge the batteries that powered the electric motor. Volvo

Meanwhile, Mercedes-Benz had an experimental 190 EV on test while BMW exhibited the E1 (with its electric motor driving the rear wheels) at the 1991 Frankfurt Show, and Renault displayed the Elektro Clio concept at the same event. Soon after, the Nissan FEV coupé, with twenty-three NiCd batteries, appeared in Tokyo alongside a Toyota Townace EV van. Interestingly, the first solar car to be classed as roadworthy in Japan also made its debut at this time: the Toyota RaRa II, although it was definitely not for sale. Indeed, being realistic, one wonders if we will ever see a solar-powered car in the showrooms, at least in our lifetime.

Skoda converted quite a few Favorits at the start of the nineties, while Volvo displayed an interesting EREV at the 1992 Paris Salon, using a gas turbine as the charging medium for its ECC concept. At the following year's Frankfurt Show, Mercedes-Benz unveiled the Vision A93 project, with one of the three prototypes being an electric vehicle. A few weeks later, in Tokyo, the Mitsubishi ESR made its debut, using a petrol engine purely to charge the twenty-eight batteries on board. This was a practical four-seater EREV capable of 190km/h (120mph), and had a Cd of just 0.25. Unfortunately, as with the Daihatsu EV Sedan (with a 660cc engine as a power generator for NiMH batteries) displayed at the same event, the idea wasn't followed through.

Hoping to cash in on an EV boom in 1994, the Reva concern was founded in India (now owned by Mahindra & Mahindra); Mitsubishi released the Libero EV for commercial use in Japan, and in the States, the Solectria Corporation made the Sunrise – an attractive four-seater coupé model with a lightweight body sporting a slippery Cd of 0.17 helping to enhance range, which was said to be 600km (375 miles).

Rare brochure for the Renaissance Tropica. Sadly, the market for electric sports cars wasn't strong enough for makers of reasonably priced machines to survive for long in the early nineties. Renaissance Cars

Being a start-up company, despite some excellent publicity, it struggled to attract enough customers, and stuck to converting Geo Metros instead.

By this time, the Dodge Caravan-based Chrysler TEVan test vehicle had been placed on the market. Most of the eighty built were sold to electricity utility firms, with the hugely inflated $120,000 sticker price and petrol at $1.40 explaining the low volume. Although the 1993 Partnership for a New Generation of Vehicles (PNGV) programme ultimately sent Chrysler in a different direction (the ESX-1 diesel-electric EREV was another false start), an updated version called the ePIC was made available for lease in July 1997.

For the battery electric vehicle (BEV) to have any chance in the marketplace, prices would have to come down in a big way. This was at least realized by Renaissance Cars of Florida, who made the Tropica sports car. However, the company fell rapidly into receivership, which was a sad event.

The CABLED (Coventry and Birmingham Low Emission Demonstrators) project was rather like an English version of the Swiss VEL programme, announced in 2009 and completed in 2012. The illustration shows an annual summary of the 2011 findings, proving that range anxieties are largely an image problem for EVs rather than a real concern with practical implications. CABLED

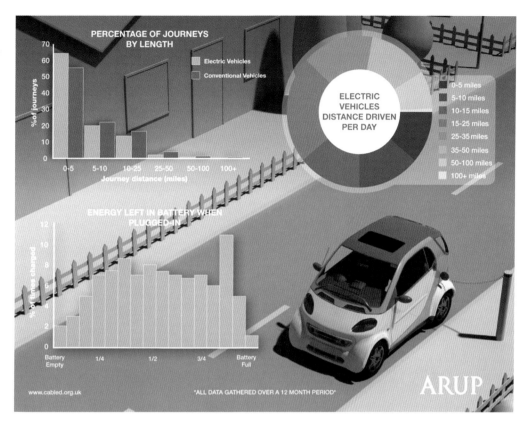

More than ever before, EVs needed to prove themselves, and it was in this respect that Switzerland came to the rescue. The Swiss government sponsored a test programme that started in 1995, choosing the town of Mendrisio to adopt EV culture as part of a long-term feasibility study named VEL1. This was replaced by VEL2 in late 2001, and VEL3 in 2005, but at least it was a serious, real-world test, with high mileages covered by 200 or so normal road users in their everyday lives. Even with steep mountains to contend with, the study showed that efficiency had improved by a substantial margin over a decade, with newer vehicles consuming two-thirds the energy of the original test fleet, which has to be a good sign.

In retrospect, the experience of the PSA Group with the Peugeot 106 Electric seemed to absolve General Motors to a great extent. Expecting to sell around 15,000 units a year, ultimately only 6,400 were sold between 1995 and 2003, the majority being bought by French government bodies. Notwithstanding, PSA remained committed to the electric car, replacing the Citroën AX EV with the reasonably priced Saxo Electrique in 1997, and adding commercials into the equation for 1998.

If nothing else, the ZEV Mandate and EV1 made Japan serious about the hybrid electric vehicle. However, they were

Publicity image for the Peugeot 106 Electric. Peugeot

The Nissan FEV-II displayed at the 1995 Tokyo Show.
Nissan

determined not to go down a single route and find it led nowhere, so development continued in other areas, with EVs getting their fair share of attention.

At the 1995 Tokyo Motor Show, Nissan exhibited the stylish FEV-II compact four-seater electric coupé, while Mitsubishi showed an EREV with a CNG-powered engine acting as a generator for the thirty batteries and electric motor. Daihatsu also had an EREV prototype called the Charade Social EV-H, using a 660cc engine to charge the batteries.

Toyota displayed the RAV4 EV that won the 1995 Scandinavian Electric Car Rally at this event, having built the car round a 1993 concept called the EV-50. The RAV4 EV was released for leasing soon after, featuring a nickel hydride battery (a first for Japan), eventually making its way to the States as a retail vehicle in 2002. Likewise, based on another

1993 concept, twenty Honda EV Plus models went on trial use during September 1997.

Back in Europe, Renault eventually joined the electric vehicle scene with the Clio EV in 1997, adding the first-generation Kangoo EV in 2004. Across the border, Fiat launched the Seicento Elettra in March 1998, which stayed in production until about 2005, and also provided the basis for a FCEV prototype. One should also remember that a number of smaller concerns were busy making EVs and converting existing vehicles. Given the importance of both the company and the base vehicle concerned, we should mention here that Broadspeed did a conversion on the Mini in 1996.

Jacques Nasser, then President of the Ford Motor Company, pictured at the 1999 Detroit Show with the TH!NK City – a lightweight, plastic-bodied zero-emission vehicle. Ford

Cutaway drawing of the Honda EV Plus. Honda

The Ford Ranger EV pick-up made an appearance in time for the US 1998 season, with around 1,500 eventually being built. Meanwhile in Japan, the tiny Toyota E-Com and Daihatsu Move EV-H (a series hybrid with a 570cc petrol engine supplying the lead-acid battery) were displayed at the 1997 Tokyo Motor Show, along with a Nissan two-seater concept that would ultimately go on sale as the Hypermini. With a full charge giving a range of 120km (75 miles), 400 were sold in 2000. The R'nessa EV was also on display, going on sale in May 1998 badged as the Altra.

All Japanese makers had EVs on display at the 1999 Tokyo Show, but the concept was still far from practical at this

Following the revival of the Venturi brand, production moved away from conventional sports cars and towards EVs. The first car was the Venturi Fetish, a limited edition 250km/h (155mph) sports car presented at the 2002 Geneva Show, but many concepts and a number of more staid production cars have followed. A Fetish II is currently being planned. Venturi

stage. Notwithstanding, with Ford having bought a majority interest in Pivco Industries of Norway, allowing them to produce the TH!NK EV in the States, electric car fans had every right to believe a new dawn had broken. Ford starting leasing the TH!NK City model in 2001, and all 350 cars available were quickly snapped up by enthusiastic Californians. This was enough to encourage Ford to announce at the 2002 LA Show that it would start selling the vehicle through dealers in the 2003 Model Year – but then the CARB decision was announced, and TH!NK was sold off to Kamcorp of Switzerland.

Having got the infrastructure in place, at least in California, the scrapping and rather public disposal of the GM EV1 set off a chain reaction. Other makers then followed suit, stopping lease renewals. Ultimately, although a few escaped to Scandinavia, a large number of Ford TH!NKs and Rangers found their way to the crusher, along with Toyota RAV4 EV (even after a two-year supply had been sold within eight months) and Honda EV Plus models.

SO WHAT'S THE BIG DEAL ABOUT EVs?

As well as the obvious zero tailpipe emissions benefit and virtually silent operation, one of the beauties of an electric car from an engineering viewpoint is the lack of moving parts in the motive power unit (increasing reliability and reducing servicing costs), and its operating efficiency, being one of the few motors that doesn't incur losses – there is no wasted movement, and the torque curve is one of the flattest imaginable across the entire rev-range. While cars with direct current (DC) motors need a basic transmission to give reverse facility, alternating current (AC) motor-powered EVs don't even need a gearbox, only a reduction gear to make the road wheels turn at a more suitable speed in relation to motor rpm, which further adds to the simplicity.

On the surface then, the EV looks like the answer to all our 'Green' prayers – but unless we have the facility to generate our own electricity via solar panels, we have to remember where the electricity comes from to recharge the machine. So we buy an EV to save the planet, and then charge it by a coal-fired, oil- or natural gas-burning power station, which burns fossil fuels and gives off all manner of greenhouse gases in huge volumes. And the bottom line is, coal will be the way most power will be generated in many countries for the foreseeable future, for although nuclear power is the way to go from both efficiency and 'clean' perspectives, public feeling against nuclear plants in the wake of the Fukushima incident in Japan in 2011 will see to it that constructing new ones will be an uphill struggle for many years. The more popular these cars become, the more stress there will be on the national grid, and the more power stations will be needed.

HOW AN ELECTRIC MOTOR WORKS

The electric motor is made up of two main components: the stator and the rotor, which turns within the stator. An electric current in a magnetic field will generate force, and by building on this basic principle via the introduction of a coil, with the current-carrying wire shaped into a position whereby it sits either side of an axle, the two forces create torque. By increasing the amount of wire (or windings) and adding a facility for electrical contacts called brushes at certain points on the rotor spindle, the rotor becomes an armature, with the result being a more uniform torque delivery.

In time – one has to remember that the electric motor dates back to the early 1800s – refinements in the creation of the magnetic field further improved efficiency, with electromagnets (or field magnets) providing the same type of magnetism as a bar magnet, but hundreds of times more powerful. Nowadays, these field magnets are usually incorporated into the stator – the motor's stationary casing.

Ultimately, the most basic AC and DC motors work in much the same way, but the wiring on the coil is different, with a commutator (which reverses the current each half revolution) being employed on the DC version to keep the rotor turning in the same direction. AC induction motors are a little different, as the electric current is induced in the armature rather than supplied to it directly, although the high current required generally rules this out from automotive use.

Indeed, most early EVs are powered by DC motors, although AC synchronous and closely related stepper motors may point the way forward, with precise speed, stop-start and rotation control allowing designers to do away with transmissions. In automotive circles, the synchronous motor (which is unusual in that the rotor has no electric current going through it) is known as a 'switched reluctance motor', or SRM, and is usually wired in three-phase configuration – that is, six poles on the stator, and four poles on the rotor, with the deliberate misalignment being the key to the SRM's advantages. As the rotor turns, different DC motor-type windings are energized in the stator, keeping the rotor turning. The SRM is rapidly finding favour in the industry, but requires an inverter to convert the direct current from the battery into alternating current.

In any case, electric motors have a very high level of mechanical efficiency – roughly 75 per cent as it happens, and sometimes more. Indeed, by eliminating the brushes (thus making what is termed a brushless motor), modern brushless DC motors can increase the efficiency to 90 per cent, which is incredibly high compared to an internal combustion engine.

The overall efficiency, of course, depends on where the electricity comes from in the first place, as generation methods vary so much, each having their own set of pros and cons attached to them, including a wide-ranging ecological impact, which naturally has more relevance in this particular book.

By the way, electric motors are rated in kW units, whereas engines use traditional brake horsepower figures. To allow you to compare outputs more readily, 1kW equates to 1.34bhp, while 1bhp is the same as 0.75kW.

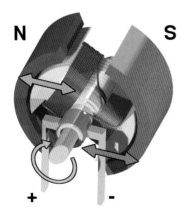 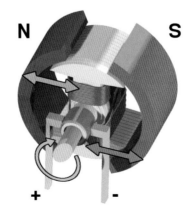 

Three illustrations showing the basic principle of how an electric motor works. Wapcaplet/Creative Commons

Adding to the conundrum, the biggest drawback with EVs, at least at the moment, is the poor range these cars provide, especially if one has a heavy right foot. And with pure EVs, there's always going to be the practical side to consider in view of this situation – as this book goes to press, there is very little in the way of public charging points, with those set up so far being nothing more than a token gesture. This basically rules out any ideas of long-distance touring, so unless an EV is to be used purely as a local commuter vehicle, doing mostly town work and recharged overnight, it doesn't really make sense as an only car.

There are also long-term running costs to take into account. Compared with a typical petrol-powered car, the EV potentially offers savings of around 70 per cent in terms of cost per mile. However, with certain electric vehicles, one has to lease battery packs. Factor this in, or the notoriously high cost of battery pack replacement if it was sold with the car, plus less-than-spectacular residual values on the vehicles themselves, and the gap soon closes.

But the EV is not to be dismissed out of hand, for the breed has many merits for urban users who cover an average or above average mileage (if only to claw back costs), and groups of engineers all over the world are committed to solving the shortcomings. Some ideas are simply not practical, even if they work well enough in theory. For example, the one put forward by the Korean Advanced Institute of Science & Technology, although it overcomes the range issue, basically calls for a whole new system with electromagnetic strips embedded in roads to generate power for EVs with special pick-ups. In fact this robs people of mobility, and would need two modern nuclear power plants just to serve it. Thankfully more practical solutions are filtering through, the use of solar power supplying the energy for charging stations being particularly appropriate.

Energy Generation and Its Impact

Thus one of the main problems with electric cars, and plug-in hybrids on charge for that matter, is that electricity needs to come from somewhere. It's no good simply saying that tailpipe emissions are zero (or at least very clean in the case of a hybrid) and the gas mileage equivalent is amazing (estimated to be twice that of the best diesel on the market), therefore we're being ecologically correct.

Power generation methods vary considerably from country to country, and the emissions released vary just as much, as we can see from the data printed in the first chapter. It may seem crazy on the face of it, but when one analyses the big picture as it stands today, depending on the country in which one lives, buying an EV actually has the potential to increase our carbon footprint rather than reduce it.

This point seems to have been missed completely by the USA. Low-interest loans approved by Congress in 2007 started being distributed by the Department of Energy in 2009, helping car companies – from the likes of Ford, through to start-ups such as Tesla and Fisker – develop EVs.

As well as backing stricter CAFE fuel consumption figures to reduce America's reliance on gasoline and – in theory – clean up the air, President Obama recently announced that his goal was to see a million EVs on the road by 2015. In addition, the state of California, whilst banning single-occupancy hybrids from the 'Pool' lane, which helped to even out traffic and therefore reduce pollution in the real world, has just announced that it wants one in seven cars to be PHEVs by 2025, and has put plans in motion to make long distances more viable through a network of charging stations.

Tax incentives that ran out for the Toyota Prius – due to high sales, the amount allocated to rebates quickly disappeared – are still available on certain US-made hybrids, but EVs get tax breaks that could add up to as much as $7,500 at the time of writing. There are also credits for converting petrol-driven machines into electric vehicles, which seems rather odd when one works out the spread of power generation feeding the national grid.

America's power generation network currently produces around a quarter of the world's total – a staggering ten billion tons – of CO_2. One wonders how many conventional cars are needed to create almost three billion tons of carbon dioxide? In reality, this figure is only so high because of coal-fired power plants. If these were replaced with greener alternatives (nuclear power, for instance, emits less than 2 per cent of the carbon dioxide released from coal-powered sites), then things start to make sense.

However, with the USA unlikely to invest in nuclear power, given the country's current finances (and a suitable excuse not to, thanks to Japan's recent events), one has to question the wisdom, given America's spread of energy generation. Studies conducted by the Oak Ridge National Laboratory (ORNL) in 2008 predict that by the year 2020, in a typical US region, PHEVs will increase carbon dioxide emissions by 42 per cent compared to a petrol-electric hybrid, while pure EVs would put even more demand on the national grid. The same study notes a 91 per cent increase in NOx emissions, and 60 per cent more sulphur dioxide released into the atmosphere. In other words, until America sorts out its long-term energy policy, there is no advantage in going down the electric car route if cleaner air is the main aim.

The same thing is true in Britain. Although power generation methods are slightly cleaner than those of America, they are not clean enough to justify all the investment in London's charging points on the 'Green' ticket. London's mayor, Boris Johnson, stated that his dream was to see 100,000 EVs on the capital's roads by 2020 – but unless the power stations are overhauled by that time, Britain's air as a whole will actually be dirtier. Ironically, incentives put forward for saving the planet by buying electric vehicles did not extend to HEVs or NEVs!

RECENT EV DEVELOPMENTS

The rising price of fuel in America, which leapt from $2 a gallon in 2004 to $3 a gallon in 2005, doubtless had the men at the helm of the 'Big Three' wishing they'd given electric cars a break, and allowed the breed to take its own course and evolve. Certainly those with hybrids on offer were able to reap the benefits of investing in 'Green' technology early on, with profits coming naturally as a result of increased volumes – the economies of scale.

In some ways, the situation was rather like the revival of the sports car, where the marketing types said they don't sell. Well, they're not likely to sell if you don't build them, but get the timing right and capture the public's imagination with the right product (as Mazda did with the MX-5 Miata), and a whole new market can be created. All it takes is a little nerve and the resolve to stick with a concept through good times and bad, and it's sure to pay dividends in the end. Toyota did it with the Prius, and after a period of losing money in the early days, couldn't stop laughing all the way to the bank as others cried in their beer, wondering how they'd given the Japanese maker such a head start. GM could have had the same kind of handsome lead with EV1, but threw away the

chance to be ahead of the game after short-term profits looked more tempting than long-term investment.

Meanwhile, 2005 was another important year for the electric car, with strong signs of public support and the twist of fate working in its favour for a change. A number of TH!NK, Ford and Toyota EVs were saved from the crusher in the States, and the 'Plug In America' group, set on cleaning up the air and gaining energy independence, furthered the cause of EV motoring.

Keio University displayed this car, the Eliica, at the 2005 Tokyo Motor Show. Developed under Professor Hiroshi Shimizu, this eight-wheeler (with in-wheel motor technology) was outrageously fast, being capable of 370km/h (230mph). B. Long

The Myers Motor NmG, a revival of the Corbin Sparrow. It has a 96km (60-mile) range, and a top speed of around 120km/h (75mph) thanks to its low weight. Myers Motors

The Tesla Roadster sent a strong message to EV doubters, including the author. This was a fast, safe and practical car, with the owner not having to make any excuses. Tesla Motors

Bolloré showed its first prototype at the 2005 Geneva Show, Dana Myers revived the Corbin Sparrow, and Commuter Cars delivered its first ultra-compact Tango to actor George Clooney. A company called EDrive Systems, a joint venture between EnergyCS and Clean-Tech, showed off its aftermarket conversion that made the Prius into a plug-in hybrid, far in advance of the showroom model.

Not long after, Subaru signed a joint venture agreement to develop EVs with Tokyo Electric (TEPCO), with the R1e, G4e and Stella EV coming as a result, while TH!NK Global was founded in March 2006, giving a lifeline to the existing Norwegian business.

The 2007 i-MiEV Sport, powered by three electric motors. B. Long

The Mitsubishi stand at the 2007 Tokyo Show, with the i-MiEV up high, allowing people to see underneath the car. As with most EVs, the underside was very flat. Domestic sales of the i-MiEV started in 2009, and had become global by the end of 2011. At the time of writing, around 18,000 had been built. Recently Mitsubishi announced it had plans to introduce six new EVs by 2015.
B. Long

Over the next few years, the EV scene suddenly came alive. Tesla, founded in California in July 2003 by Elon Musk, Martin Eberhard and Marc Tarpenning, would become a major player in the electric car world. Its first car, the Tesla Roadster 'Signature One Hundred' limited edition, sold out within three weeks of its July 2006 launch, despite a price tag exceeding $100,000.

Tesla started doing the US motor-show rounds at the end of 2006, and with an R&D grant from CARB, series-production of the Roadster started in March 2008. With a 395km (245-mile) range and crash testing completed, sales were buoyant, and a European office was opened soon after to take reservations.

Tesla was said to be the inspiration behind GM getting involved in electric cars again, with Bob Lutz pushing the concept. The first visible result was the Chevrolet Volt prototype displayed at the 2007 Detroit Show – a four-seater plug-in EREV with a 120kW electric drivetrain, and the battery power topped up whenever necessary by a 1-litre, 3-cylinder turbocharged engine. This overcame any range anxieties, but also significantly reduced emissions. There was still a lot of work to do, especially with regard to the battery pack, but as the first plug-in hybrid from a major US manufacturer, the gauntlet had well and truly been tossed.

At the 2007 Tokyo Show, Mitsubishi unveiled its i-MiEV – a practical four-door commuter, with a single electric motor working on the rear wheels. The same stand also featured the i-MiEV Sport concept, which was particularly interesting due to its unique 4WD system. The regular set-up was used for the rear axle, with one motor in the middle, but the front axle used an in-wheel motor on both hubs.

Although one pays a price in increased unsprung weight, in-wheel motors tend to make the most of an electric motor's mechanical efficiency, as the drive from the rotor is direct, reducing transmission losses. With modern sensors and electronic control systems, we can also do away with differentials and gearing to give a two- or four-wheel-drive layout with ease.

In-wheel motors are not a new idea, as the Lohner-Porsche sidebar at the start of the chapter shows, but Protean Electric has been a world leader in applying the technology in more recent years. Starting from the know-how gained during the development of an electric scooter for Peugeot,

Illustration showing the principle behind the Protean in-wheel motor. Protean

work on in-wheel motors began in earnest in 2003, ultimately leading to the Hi-Pa Drive, which made its public debut at the 2006 British International Motor Show in London. Not long after, the motors (now sporting the 'Protean Drive' moniker) were seen fitted to Volvo, Ford and Vauxhall cars, and recently, Brabus displayed Mercedes-Benz conversions on their stand at the 2011 Frankfurt Show. Schaeffler is also developing its own 'eWheel Drive' in-wheel motors.

Another big name joined the scene at this stage, with Henrik Fisker (an ex-Aston Martin man) and Bernhard Koehler forming Fisker Automotive in September 2007. Amazingly there was a prototype four-door EREV sedan on display at the 2008 Detroit Show, giving people a glimpse of what was in store, including the signature solar panel on the roof, mainly employed for powering ancillaries but ultimately giving about 320km (200 miles) of free running a year.

It would be some time before the production car, a luxury GT named the Karma, would make it to the showrooms, mainly because of the delay in EPA certification, but most of the specifications fell into place quite quickly – along with regenerative braking, the 4-cylinder turbocharged 2-litre petrol engine (sourced from GM) was employed to recharge the Li-ion batteries only, with motive power coming solely from a pair of 150kW electric motors driving the rear wheels.

The plug-in drivetrain, also used on a convertible Karma Sunset concept in 2009, was designed locally by Quantum Technologies of California, while the car itself, which finally went on sale at $95,000 after EPA certification in October 2011, was built by Valmet in Finland, chosen by the likes of Porsche.

Brabus stand at the 2011 Frankfurt Show. Protean

Cutaway drawing of the Fisker Karma. Al Gore bought one of the first Karmas. A spokesperson for the former US Vice President said: 'He believes that a global shift of the automobile fleet toward electric vehicles, accompanying a shift toward renewable-energy generation, represents an important part of a sensible strategy for solving the climate crisis.'
Fisker Automotive

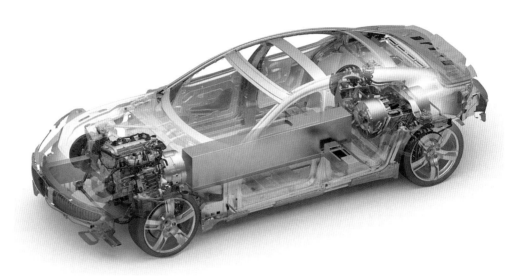

The Fisker Karma Sunset at the 2009 Detroit Show.
Fisker Automotive

The prototype Bolloré Bluecar, designed by Pininfarina, and first displayed at the 2008 Paris Salon. Note the solar panel on the roof. Other makers are looking into this as a potential range extender, or a way of powering ancillaries. If LED headlights can be developed, this will also help, as not only do they weigh less, they use substantially less energy. Bolloré

TH!NK displayed its stylish Ox concept in 2008, and Stevens delivered the first of its short-lived Zecars. But things moved up another gear when GM announced its production version of the Chevy Volt in September that year. A few days later, Pininfarina presented the B0 (or B Zero) at the 2008 Paris Salon. This was the prototype for the production Bolloré Bluecar, designed with cooperation from EDF (France's main electricity board). The car had a range of around 240km (150 miles) thanks to its highly advanced lithium metal polymer (LMP) battery pack, with its 50kW motor endowing the vehicle with an 130km/h (80mph) top speed. The solar panel on the roof of the B0 makes a lot of sense, being beautifully integrated by the Italian master coachbuilder, but it was left off the production car. Indeed, the design was toned down as a whole for production, which

is something of a shame. Notwithstanding, the Bluecar was made available for leasing in 2011.

Another car that made a splash at the 2008 Paris Salon was the South African Optimal Energy Joule. Designed by Keith Helfet, with the prototype built by Zagato, the production version of the machine was first displayed at the 2010 Geneva Show.

Renault, too, was taking an interest. As Carlos Ghosn said in Paris: 'All the pieces of the puzzle are in place for making a mass-production vehicle in the near future – battery range,

The production version of the **Optimal Energy Joule** on display at the **2010 Geneva Show.** Optimal Energy

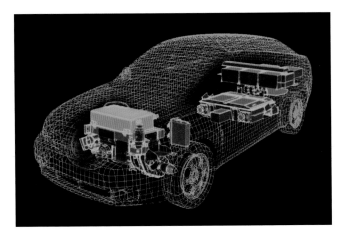

Ford announced its vehicle electrification strategy at the 2009 Detroit Show, with this BEV being a key element in the plan. Ford

optimized energy consumption, and performance and driving pleasure.' By the 2009 Frankfurt Show, less than a year later, Renault had four ZE (as in 'zero emission') cars in train: the Kangoo ZE, Fluence ZE, the Twizy and the ZOE, with all being readied for production. The Kangoo and Fluence were released at the end of 2011, with the Twizy and ZOE due out some time in 2012.

A Tesla saloon was first mooted in 2008, the 'Whitestar' project being an EREV, although the design later changed to a pure BEV configuration, thus securing Tesla's place in the electric car niche market, and orders started being taken for the $50,000 Model S in March 2009. Development continued on the Lotus Elise-based Roadster, however, with the

A batch of Mini E models gathered in Berlin in June 2009. BMW

Cutaway drawing of the Mini E showing the electric motor, control modules and transmission up front, and the battery pack in the rear. BMW

trucks that are being exported far and wide – and ironically, they're even finding favour in America.

MODERN BATTERY TECHNOLOGY

The future of EV vehicles has to lie in advances in battery technology – making them more efficient, more compact to provide better packaging options, capable of faster charging to make charging posts in parking spots a practical reality, and then being able to hold that charge for longer under load in order to increase vehicle range.

There's little doubt that these goals will be achieved in time – one has only to reflect on the way mobile phone batteries have developed in recent years, rapidly becoming smaller, lighter and able to hold power for increasingly longer periods of time. The first Motorola mobile of 1973

Roadster Sport (capable of 0–60 in a remarkable 3.7sec) being launched a few weeks earlier.

Tesla had certainly earned its spurs, and a strategic partnership was signed with Daimler AG in the middle of 2009, the German company taking a 9 per cent stake in the US EV maker. No wonder that *Advertising Age* selected Tesla as one of America's hottest brands in its review of the year.

Meanwhile the Mini E took part in field trials in 2009, but sadly the project went cold. With a 150kW motor, the car had a range of 160km (100 miles) and a top speed of 153km/h (95mph), so there's no doubt it was a practical concept. At least BMW (the owners of the Mini brand) have used the technology and experience to present a new line of BMW electric cars.

GM presented the Cadillac Converj at the 2009 Detroit Show, but Chrysler, on the other hand, threw in the towel. The 2009 Town & Country minivan EV concepts built for the US Postal Service failed to attract enough attention, and having been less than enthusiastic about electric cars for some time, Chrysler duly cancelled the ENVI programme, which had spawned a number of interesting prototypes.

It's a shame that Chrysler didn't keep with EVs a bit longer, as nearly 500,000 panel vans are sold in the States each year, and if the pricing was right, one can be sure customers would be happy to move over to electric versions. This represents the potential for a huge market that is being left untapped. On saying that, Smith Electric, who made Britain's signature milk floats (electric motors were used so as to avoid waking people up in the morning), now make electric

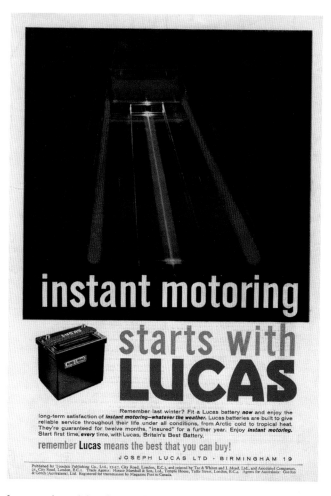

Lucas advertising from 1964. Lucas

was, by necessity, almost the size of a briefcase. Ten years later, the 8000X model was less than half the size, albeit still a weighty device, and with eight hours of standby power after ten hours of charging. Then as the 1990s rolled around, breakthroughs in technology followed one after another and one could start to recognize today's lightweight, compact phones. At under 100g, the revolutionary 1996 Motorola StarTac weighed about nine times less than the 8000X. Nowadays, with the introduction of the Willcom WX03A, standby time has increased to 300 hours in a package weighing just 40g, and physically two-thirds the size of a StarTac.

Before reviewing the evolution of the car battery, it may be useful to consider the way battery performance is measured. Electrical energy is calculated in kilowatt hours (kWh), which is a measurement of how much work can be done at the same rate within an hour. This isn't the same as a kilowatt (a kW, or 1000 watts), as this is a unit of power generated or used, as seen in engine specifications in the former case, and household electricity bills in the latter.

The typical lead-acid battery that we've all grown up with has been with us since the nineteenth century. It's fine for conventional car applications, as it only looks after a limited number of fairly low-load tasks, so its size and weight is acceptable from a packaging point of view. But for every kilogramme of a traditional lead-acid battery, only 0.02kWh of energy is delivered, so when powering a drivetrain, a lot of batteries are required – and the more that are needed, the more weight, which limits performance, or one can choose to reduce the vehicle range, which has a detrimental effect on practicality.

Nickel-cadmium batteries were far superior in their performance, but cost was prohibitive at the turn of the century. Realizing this, Waldemar Jungner, who invented the NiCd battery, starting working on a more cost-effective nickel-iron version – but Thomas Edison beat the Swede to the marketplace with a workable NiFe battery. Ultimately, thanks to refinements in design and manufacturing techniques, the NiCd battery would become a part of everyday life. Despite suffering from 'memory effect' (a loss of efficiency caused by recharging without discharging first), the nickel-cadmium battery was also used on several modern EVs.

It was obvious, however, that if the electric vehicle was ever to have a chance of competing with conventional IC-engined cars, new battery technology would be needed. Ford brought out the sodium-sulphur (NaS) battery in the sixties, which displayed exceptional energy density. The Ford Ecostar van of the early 1990s was the first real use of NaS batteries, followed by a Suzuki hybrid in 1993, but it was always going to be rare due to high operating temperatures;

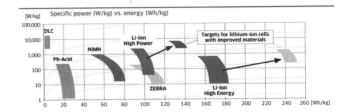

Bosch data showing that Li-ion batteries deliver the most promising energy and power potential. Toyota and BMW have recently joined forces developing Li-ion technology. Bosch

it would ultimately end up being used mainly in utility storage applications. Likewise, the zinc-bromine (ZnBr) battery, developed by Exxon in the early seventies, offered a high level of performance and excellent shelf life, but was also destined not to catch on in automotive circles.

The next big thing was the nickel metal hydride (NiMH) battery, which was similar to a NiCd one, except the cadmium used for the negative electrode was replaced with a hydrogen-absorbing alloy. With five times the power delivery of a lead-acid battery per kilogramme, vastly superior cold weather performance, and the ability to accept up to three times as many charge cycles, this was obviously the way forward.

As it happens, the NiMH battery had started life in 1967, with Daimler-Benz sponsoring most of its early development. Around twenty years later, it became a practical battery thanks to the work of Kurt Buschow and Johannes Willems, and was then further refined by Stan Ovshinsky of Ovonic. General Motors then bought a majority stake in the Ovonic battery business, but the technology was used sparingly – almost too sparingly according to some critics, who have pointed out that GM's shares were ultimately bought by oil giant Texaco, which then became owned by Chevron. In 2003 the Cobasys name started being used on Ovonic batteries and licensing agreements, although unthinkably, in February 2012, the business was bought by BASF after the American company filed for bankruptcy.

Whether Ovonic was unlucky or sabotaged, as some conspiracy theory people believe, technology has since moved on again, with the GS Yuasa concern in Japan refining the positive electrode design. The latest NiMH batteries are highly efficient yet far more friendly to the environment in the way they are made.

Meanwhile, the lithium-ion (Li-ion, or LIB) battery came of age, also having been in development for several decades. M. Stanley Whittingham invented it whilst working for Exxon, and indeed it was Exxon that ultimately marketed the first rechargeable Li-ion battery in the mid-1970s – button cells for watches.

Dozens of electrode combinations were duly tried to make the Li-ion battery safer, and eventually, in 1985, Akira Yoshino of Asahi Kasei replaced the lithium metal anode with a carbonaceous material infused with lithium ions, and used lithium cobalt oxide for the cathode. This provided the basis for the modern Li-ion battery, which Sony first put on the market in June 1991, although refinements have been taking place ever since, including the introduction of lithium polymer (LiPo, or LMP) batteries, which are cheaper to make and easier to shape.

The main advantage of the Li-ion battery is its low weight in relation to its power output, along with elimination of 'memory effect', and its ability to adopt different shapes to perfectly suit its application. It also has a relatively low self-discharge rate, but constant charging tends to reduce efficiency and service life, albeit over a reasonable period of time. As it happens, many EV batteries use a lithium iron phosphate cathode, which reduces performance but enhances safety, increases the average number of charging cycles possible, and generally gives the battery a longer useful life.

Research carried out by Dr Gerbrand Cedar and his team at the Massachusetts Institute of Technology (MIT) has the potential to significantly reduce charging times. By altering the surface structure of lithium iron phosphate electrodes, ions are released and absorbed one hundred times faster than normal, meaning that a mobile phone battery can be charged in as little as ten seconds. Development work is ongoing in adapting MIT's technology for use with EV batteries, while Professor Harold Kung of Northwestern University is following another line of research on smaller cells that could perhaps be adapted to suit EVs at a later date, and Subaru published a paper on the subject in 2011.

Fast charging is possible with many existing batteries, of course, but it does tend to have a detrimental effect on service life. Some research has shown that constant fast charging can shorten battery life to just three years in certain cases. Considering that at the moment, typical EV batteries take six to ten hours to charge fully at safe limits, this is a very exciting breakthrough, which makes the electric vehicle a far more practical proposition.

At the same time, Altair Nanotechnologies came up with 'NanoSafe' batteries that have an anode coated with lithium-titanate oxide (LTO) nanocrystals. Developed for electric utility companies and the US and UK military, the faster charging capability with only a marginal rise in temperature, combined with greater stability under stress, is another step forwards. So far, Toshiba seems to have made best use of

Detail shot of the Li-ion battery from the Chevy Volt. GM

lithium-titanate (LiTi) battery technology, marketing its SCiB line – rechargeable batteries originally released for laptop PC applications in March 2008, but which have since already found service in Mitsubishi and Honda electric vehicles.

With lithium relatively cheap (which is ironic, considering the expense of contemporary lithium-based batteries), fairly easy to come by (it is usually extracted from brine pools, mainly in South America – limited cobalt supplies present more of a headache in the long term) and recyclable, one can safely assume that it is only a matter of time before someone combines all the technological advances and makes a com-

The 360V 24kWh Li-ion battery pack from the Nissan Leaf, made by the Automotive Energy Supply Corporation (AESC), a joint venture between Nissan and the NEC Corporation. B. Long

pact, lightweight Li-ion battery that will serve EV manufacturers well until a new discovery spawns another generation of energy storage.

Meanwhile, new additions to the scene include the potassium-ion (K-ion) battery, first invented in 1999 and likely to provide an ideal EV power source at some stage, especially now that researchers at Stanford University have come up with an inexpensive cathode with high performance combined with the potential of 40,000 charging cycles. Another newcomer is the lithium-sulphur (LiS) battery, which promises high voltage and lower weight; it is used on the Mercedes F125 FCEV concept.

As well as improvements in efficiency and lowering costs, positive steps are also being made in weight reduction. Indeed, only a few months before this book was being finished, a team of American scientists claimed to have made the world's lightest material, formed by a metallic micro-lattice with an incredibly low density. Ten times lighter than styrofoam, it is already being earmarked for use as a battery electrode, which could help cut EV weight by a significant amount.

Nevertheless there is still work that needs to be done in more mundane areas of science to capitalize on the mechanical efficiency of electric motors. For instance, we need to increase charging efficiency, which currently stands at about 90 per

cent: this means that for every 10kWh pumped into the battery, we can only rely on being able to use around 9kWh of it, give or take a few per cent.

EVs TODAY

After a series of false starts – which must often have left casual observers wondering if in fact manufacturers were really making a full effort with EVs or just using them for

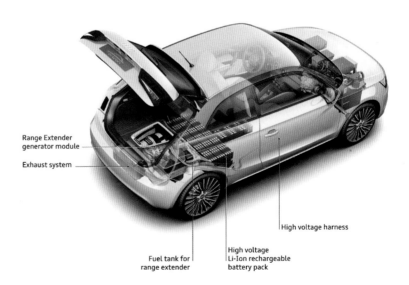

Range Extender generator module

Exhaust system

High voltage harness

Fuel tank for range extender

High voltage Li-Ion rechargeable battery pack

The Audi A1 e-tron EREV, with its petrol-powered 254cc single-rotor Wankel unit hooked up to a generator as a range extender. The advantages of an RE (rotary engine) are its compact size, low weight, and smooth, almost silent running. Audi

TOP: **The TH!NK (the red car in the centre) was made at Valmet from December 2009 – but sadly the Norwegian company has now gone bankrupt. As can be seen, Valmet was also busy building the Porsche Cayman and the Garia LSV EV (right) – and it tried its hand at creating its own EV: the Eva concept, which made its debut at the 2010 Geneva Show.** Valmet

MIDDLE: **Modern electric cars bring with them a new generation of driver information. This screen is from the BMW ActiveE concept.** BMW

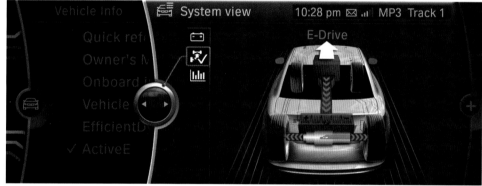

PR and marketing hype – a few years into the new millennium the electric car and the technology that powered it at long last came of age. Audi's stand at the 2009 Frankfurt Show brought electric car culture in Europe close to reality with the e-tron prototype. Developed under Peter Kainz, this fully operational sports car concept had four motors (one for each wheel) to give 230kW (the equivalent of 313bhp) and phenomenal torque. Combined with the lightweight ASF frame and plastic panels, the 4WD e-tron could cover the 0–60 dash in 4.8sec.

A few months later, a second prototype appeared at the 2010 Detroit Show with a more modest, rear-wheel-drive specification. It also featured a new style of heat pump: heating might be considered a minor concern in the overall concept of a new model, but people do tend to like to stay warm whilst driving, and this can present a problem in electric vehicles. The Audi e-tron heater was designed to cause less of a power drain than the conventional convector type (electric air-conditioning compressors are the norm on HEVs, but use even more power). Chevrolet was the first to pioneer the idea, introducing it on the ill-fated S-10 pick-up truck.

Pininfarina's earlier Nido concept was revisited in 2010, gaining electric power along the way. Pininfarina

Commemorating the expansion at BMW's Leipzig plant, to mark the occasion, Chairman Norbert Reithofer was joined by Chancellor Merkel. The ActiveE model can be seen on the right. BMW

Keeping up the pace, the Audi A1 e-tron EREV was exhibited at the 2010 Geneva Show, using a state-of-the-art single-rotor Wankel engine as the charging medium. In October 2011, a test fleet of twenty cars was delivered to drivers in Munich: the data gathered from this programme will help in the development of production models.

The use of a rotary engine as an EREV generator has naturally been investigated by Mazda (*Autocar* reported it in 2008), and AVL Powertrain Engineering has also considered the idea, with the smooth, lightweight RE looking a good option. Even more exotic, Jaguar used gas turbines for recharging on its 2010 C-X75 concept.

BMW was becoming more involved with the EV movement, too: the ActiveE was launched at the 2010 Detroit Show, based on the 1-series coupé body, and a test fleet of 100 cars was ultimately built for evaluation in Europe, the USA and China at the start of 2011. It was obvious the Munich company was serious about EVs after it expanded its Leipzig plant solely for electric car production. The i3 (or MCV as it was originally known), an exotic carbon-fibre-bodied vehicle, should roll off the lines soon, possibly coming in both pure EV and EREV guises.

Not to be outdone, Volkswagen announced its Golf Blue e-motion in May 2010. The car duly did the show circuit, both in Europe and America, revealing selective regeneration as a new piece of technology, with four modes ranging from freewheeling to maximum charge. The 85kW model is scheduled to go into production in 2014.

Another interesting EREV launched at around this time was the Proton EMAS, which made its debut at the 2010 Geneva Show. Although this remained only a concept, it spawned the Lotus Ethos from Lotus Engineering. This had

Cutaway drawing and powerplant of the VW Golf Blue e-motion. Volkswagen

a 1.2-litre Flex-Fuel engine as a range extender, and is due to go on sale in 2014.

Meanwhile the Nissan Leaf, displaying a vague resemblance to the Note Adidas prototype at the 2005 Tokyo Show, was declared production-ready at the 2009 Tokyo Show. Sales of the Nissan Leaf battery electric vehicle, with regenerative braking and its 80kW AC motor driving the front wheels, started in the USA and Japan in December 2010. Demand increased rapidly, so much so in fact that there are plans to build the car in America from the end of 2012, and in England from 2013.

Incidentally, although the Leaf is currently available on the domestic market for a very reasonable 3,000,000 yen after a 780,000 yen government credit, a fast charger currently costs around 500,000 yen! It used to be double that, however, so things are bound to become more sensible in time – and more practical, too, because vehicle-to-home (V2H) technology is also being developed, allowing the Leaf to power a house – the 24kWh Li-ion battery would give an average household two days' worth of electricity. The car can then be charged at off-peak times, and with solar power in the equation, it all starts to make sense, especially after the huge earthquake that rocked Japan in 2011 highlighted that the car still needed the power of the national grid. With the price of all manner of home charger installations for EVs in general setting the internet alight as a subject far and wide, one can only hope cost-effective integration comes soon.

As it happens, Mitsubishi has just brought out the 'MiEV power box' – a useful quick-charging device that allows power to be transferred from the vehicle's battery to the box, which could then be carried anywhere it was needed.

The Nissan Leaf secured all three major 'Car of the Year' awards in Japan. Regular charging of the Leaf's Li-ion battery pack takes eight hours, while the fast charge takes thirty minutes. Nissan

The Honda Fit EV, and a close-up of its mode switches. With only a single transmission speed, the modes control throttle response in this case, and have a bearing on battery life – the faster the response, the sportier the feeling, but it also shortens the range. Honda

Thanks to its proven Tesla drivetrain being ready for installation straight away, testing of the plug-in Toyota RAV4 EV began in July 2010, and is due to go into production some time in 2012. In a sign of the times, it's interesting to note that Toyota takes on mostly electrical engineers at staff inductions nowadays. Toyota

This would be ideal for camping or emergencies: if the car battery had been fully charged beforehand the box could provide a day's worth of electricity for an average house.

While all this was going on, Honda released its Fit EV. It made its debut at the 2010 LA Show and testing started a year later, with part of the programme being a joint project with the Guangzhou Automobile Group of China. With a 153km (95-mile) range from its Li-ion battery pack, a useful-sized body, and a 92kW motor with 'Sport', 'Normal' and 'Eco' modes to improve throttle response, it would seem to be a very practical proposition. It is scheduled to go on sale in the summer of 2012.

Over in the States, Tesla displayed its 1,000th Roadster at the 2010 Detroit Show, with global sales now a reality for the American company. Toyota duly invested $50 million in Tesla, with Akio Toyoda singing its praises and giving the go-ahead for joint development on a new version of the RAV4 EV. By the end of the year, Tesla had secured the old NUMMI plant (once shared by GM and Toyota) to produce its Model S saloon, and Panasonic threw another $30 million into the pot.

General Motors has stated that electrification of power-trains will increase directly in line with the passage of time. There is no sign that petrol cars will be abandoned, in reality, but hybrids and vehicles powered by alternative fuels are sure to filter on to the marketplace, with EVs and EREVs further reducing oil dependence. It appears that the long-term goal is finally to harness fuel cell technology.

En route to achieving that target, production of the Chevrolet Volt began on 31 March 2010, with sales starting officially in November. The plug-in Volt builds on GM's earlier EV1 experience, reducing battery space by two-thirds, thanks to the EREV (Voltec in GM speak) configuration. Motive power is provided by two electric motors (rated at 111kW for the primary unit and 54kW for the secondary), with the smaller Li-ion battery recharged by a 1.4-litre NA Opel petrol engine when necessary. In addition, the engine could be called upon to assist the motors at high speeds or if hard acceleration were needed, although the drivetrain was basically EV-based to ensure a top smog rating.

The Volt looks like a conventional four-seater hatch, which is good from a marketing point of view. At $40,000, its pricing is also very competitive, especially after a Federal tax credit for electric vehicles.

However, after a battery leak caused a fire in one of the NHTSA crash test cars, three weeks after it was hit in a heavy side impact, once again EVs had an uphill battle to fight.

The Chevrolet Volt with its unusual T-shaped battery pack. This is one of the Li-ion battery's advantages – its ability to mould to a desired shape allows designers more freedom. With traditional batteries, the layout has to be set around them. GM

Ford's Global Director of Electrification, Nancy Gioia, charges the Ford Focus Electric at its unveiling in New York in January 2011.
Stuart Ramson/Ford

But a suitable fix to protect the casings was soon found, and the problem was sorted once and for all. Global sales followed, although in Europe the Volt was also given the Opel Ampera nametag (or Vauxhall badges for Britain), on sale from March 2011, while in Australia, the Holden brand will be used. With sales extending beyond US borders, General Motors was hoping to sell 60,000 units a year – and with high levels of customer satisfaction reported in the States, it could well work out that way.

In the meantime, Ford unveiled its Focus Electric model in January 2011, announcing at the event that it planned

to release five EVs in the near future. This particular BEV uses a proven drivetrain from Magna International of Canada, incorporating a 100kW motor in this case (commercial vehicles such as the Transit Electric employ an Azure Dynamics set-up). Combined with a 23kWh Li-ion battery, it gives more than enough performance in the real world. Although Ford has also ventured down the full hybrid path, it has stayed away from the EREV formula, as its engineers are not convinced that batteries can deliver enough power whenever it is required – they experienced power fade and a lack of responsiveness at times during the testing of Ford's

The Tazzari Zero Speedster. Tazzari

The lightweight Myers Duo. Myers Motors

ABOVE: **The COMS concept from Toyota Auto Body. Makers have been showing prototypes like this for decades (often too futuristic, and therefore not taken seriously), with compact dimensions reducing weight.** B. Long

The Chevrolet EN-V electric commuter vehicle. Although the top speed is only 48km/h (30mph), well-to-wheel carbon dioxide emissions are 10 per cent of those for a typical car. B. Long

BELOW: **The BMW stand was dominated by its electric car technology, with the i3 and i8 concepts taking centre stage. The EV has come of age...** B. Long

The Tokyo Show always has more than its fair share of EVs on display. With electric cars in general taking off in the showrooms, the 2011 event had a bumper crop, along with demonstration runs for the public. Here is a selection of what was there.

Readers should also be aware of the huge number of stands promoting information technology (IT), to the point where one can rightfully question what the purpose of a vehicle actually is. Personally, the author feels the link between automobiles and the IT world is simply not needed, adding unnecessary weight, cost and complication.

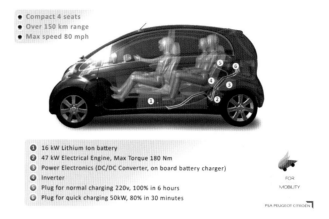

- Compact 4 seats
- Over 150 km range
- Max speed 80 mph

❶ 16 kW Lithium Ion battery
❷ 47 kW Electrical Engine, Max Torque 180 Nm
❸ Power Electronics (DC/DC Converter, on board battery charger)
❹ Inverter
❺ Plug for normal charging 220v, 100% in 6 hours
❻ Plug for quick charging 50kW, 80% in 30 minutes

FOR MOBILITY

PSA PEUGEOT CITROËN

ABOVE & BELOW: The Mitsubishi i-MiEV was put on sale as the Peugeot 'iOn' and Citroën 'C-Zero' in September 2010. These useful illustrations show the drivetrain packaging and charging sequence for the Li-ion battery. PSA Group

Business end of the Toyota FT-EV III – the third car in this compact BEV series that dates back to 2009. B. Long

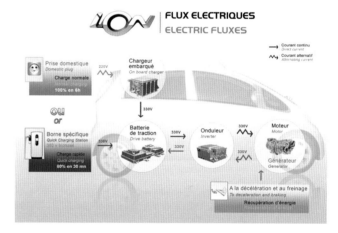

fuel cell vehicles with a series hybrid set-up, convincing them to stick with a full hybrid or pure BEV configuration. Interesting…

By this time, the 'Small 100' was making an impact around the world. To give an idea of the activity, the Tazzari Group of Italy launched the €20,000 Zero in 2009 (with a Speedster version due to go on sale any minute), the Mia Electric went into production in France, while the Dynasty IT Sedan was made in Canada. China's battery makers, BYD, released the F3DM EREV and practical e6 estate, the Wheego LiFe hit showrooms, and the rapid Evelio K1, Electric Lightning GT, Electrocity Nemesis and Delta Motorsport E-4 coupé put EVs in the supercar league. CODA started selling its car in America, Myers added the Duo to its range, and machines such as the Bolloré Bluecar, Optimal Energy Joule and Mahindra Reva came of age.

Mitsubishi Fuso's first EV truck, called the E-CELL. Hino also displayed an EV concept. Getting trucks to move towards electric power seems to make a lot of sense from a 'Green' point of view. Fuso

Volvo's **C30 Electric** with its Siemens motor in the foreground. *Volvo*

Advertisement for the **Nissan Leaf Nismo RC racer**, which made its debut at the New York Show in April 2011. More than a publicity stunt, the car is being used as a rolling laboratory. It even tackled Pike's Peak, while Ikuo Hanawa set a new EV record for the hill climb using a Yokohama-sponsored machine. Japan is serious about developing the electric car. *Nissan*

SIM-Drive of Japan unveiled the innovative SIM-001 in March 2011, with its in-wheel motors allowing for 2WD, 4WD or 8WD configurations in the future. Supervised by Professor Hiroshi Shimizu, the project holds promise, as SIM-001 had a 0–60 time of 4.8sec, and a range of over 290km (180 miles). A lighter 2012 version, complete with a stronger battery, recently improved range by around 25 per cent. SIM-Drive Corporation

Production cars based on conventional mass-produced models, such as the Mitsubishi i-MiEV (Lancer and Colt MiEV models have also been made), the Tata Indica Vista EV, Renault Fluence ZE, Volvo C30 Electric, SEAT Altea XL Electric Ecomotive, Westfield Sport E, Toyota RAV4 EV plug-in SUV, the limited run Subaru Stella EV and the Mercedes Vito E-Cell van, show just how diverse the EV market has become.

With sales of the Karma EREV about to commence, Fisker unveiled the Surf, a wagon version of the Karma, at the 2011 Frankfurt Show. Due to go into production in 2013, it was announced at the same event that Fisker would be

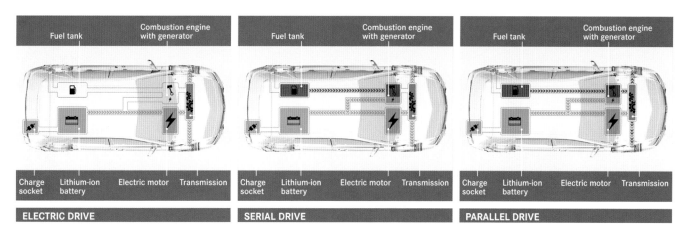

Concept B-Class E-CELL PLUS

ELECTRIC DRIVE | SERIAL DRIVE | PARALLEL DRIVE

ABOVE: **The Mercedes-Benz B-Class E-Cell Plus concept made its debut at the 2011 Frankfurt Show, using a 1-litre turbocharged engine to create an EREV. Looking at the drivetrain, in many ways this is a full hybrid, but with the EV and EREV modes being given priority, rather like the Chevrolet Volt. Six months later, in Geneva, the electric version of the AMG SLS was unveiled, with production cited for 2013. Exciting times lay ahead...** Daimler AG

RIGHT: **The compact plug-in Smart Electric Drive took a bow in 2006, but this new version based on the ForTwo and featuring a 55kw (70bhp) Tesla drivetrain, made its debut at the 2011 Frankfurt Show. This is the advert from the time of the Tokyo Show, held a few weeks later, with a glimpse of the Forvision EV concept in the lower right-hand corner.** Smart

sourcing its turbocharged engines from BMW in the future. And many people were anxious to see the 'N-Series' plug-in hybrid that will be built at the old GM plant in Delaware.

Ultimately, after an uncertain era, and with the benefit of modern batteries, control systems (ironically being developed faster thanks to the upsurge in full hybrids and the technology that powers them) and charging devices, it looks as if the EV is now here to stay, with makers continuing to produce concept vehicles, falling into categories ranging from the viable to the far-fetched.

The Kia Naimo, which made its debut in April 2011, is a good example of the new breed of EVs that await us some time in the near future, while the Tokyo Show was positively bristling with electric concept cars, from the Volkswagen Nils and Bulli, to Honda's EV-STER and Micro Commuter, the Suzuki Swift EV Hybrid EREV model, and the Toyota FT-EV III. As well as the Leaf (in standard and racing guise), Nissan also displayed the ESFLOW sports EV, and the Town-

Manche Weihnachtswünsche gibt es nur einmal.

Some Christmas wishes are one-of-a-kind.

An amusing Christmas card from Audi, proclaiming that the R8 e-tron is going into production. Who says 'Green' technology has to be boring? Audi

Andere kommen in Serie. Der Audi R8 e-tron.

Others are available in series production. The Audi R8 e-tron.

Nothing more than a distant dream only a decade ago – electric cars having prime space in shop windows. This is a Fisker display at Harrods in London, pictured in January 2012. Fisker Automotive

pod and Pivo3 town cars using electric power at the Tokyo event, the latter with an in-wheel motor (IWM) system.

Tesla unveiled its Model X SUV prototype in February 2012, completing its EV range, as the Roadster had been updated (albeit now sold out in America) and the beautiful Model S saloon was about to enter the series-production phase. Production of the Model X was due to start in late 2013, with 2WD, 4WD and 4WD high-power layouts, along with 60 and 85kWh battery options.

Conversions still pop up, too, with the lightweight Citroën C1 proving a popular base car in Europe, while Phoenix Motorcars of California employ Altair batteries to transform SsangYong vehicles; the SUT pick-up holds particular appeal for business users. As for EREVs, VIA Motors will soon start making SUVs and pick-ups based on 'Big Three' models for private use, having restricted supplies to business users in the past. With Bob Lutz now on board at VIA, the future holds promise.

ABOVE: **Some recent models, like this Tesla Model S saloon, for instance, will start to win over buyers who've previously viewed EVs as quirky. Global sales have also helped enhance the Tesla brand image.**
Tesla Motors

RIGHT: **Nissan displayed an Infiniti electric sports car concept at the 2012 Geneva Show, while Hyundai offered this I-oniq EREV.** Hyundai

CHAPTER SIX

ALTERNATIVE POWER

Alternative power is probably the area where we will be able to find examples of the closest thing to a 'zero carbon' engine in the real world, although practicality issues – and possibly political ones, too, if the truth be told – are delaying development in certain fields that could provide part of the answer to reducing our carbon footprint.

Anything that contains energy can be regarded as a fuel – even a bar of chocolate! But while we wouldn't use a Snickers bar to power a car (although, ironically, cocoa bean shells are being used more and more in the creation of biomass energy), there are still plenty of alternative fuels to consider, along with the powerplants that make use of them.

Granted, most of these alternative power options don't come with the elegant solution of some of the latest bio-fuels, using the wonders of nature to cancel out the harm done by burning the end product, but many of them are available now, and each offers a number of benefits that may help in the short to mid-term. Looking further ahead, like the so-called 'third generation' bio-fuels, the fuel cell vehicle (FCV) may yet provide us with the ultimate long-term answer for our transportation needs.

LPG AND NATURAL GAS

Liquid petroleum gas (or LPG – a mixture of hydrocarbons, with propane as its main ingredient, combined with small amounts of ethane and butane in transport applications) and natural gas (CNG or LNG) can both be used in spark-ignition engines, subject to certain modifications.

As it happens, the natural gas alternative is difficult to source in many countries, with the UK having just fourteen service stations with gas refilling facilities, although Germany has over 800, and some stockbrokers with a keen eye on the futures market are forecasting a potential boom in the States. For the time being at least, due to the ease of fuel storage and cost, LPG (or Autogas) is by far the most popular choice for automotive applications.

LPG is relatively easy to liquefy under pressure, and the tank required can usually be fitted in the luggage compartment without affecting practicality to any great extent.

There are often conversions where a car is capable of running on either petrol or LPG, although this simply adds complexity and weight.

LPG, as the name implies, generally comes from refining crude oil. This puts a question mark over the long-term sustainability of the fuel, but the fact that the amount of crude needed to produce 100ltr (22gal) of liquid petroleum gas gives only 63ltr (14gal) of diesel (or about 76ltr/16.5gal of gasoline) means that oil reserves can be made to last longer – at least in theory. By now, however, you will have realized that nothing is straightforward when it comes to 'Green' issues, and the higher fuel consumption of LPG-powered cars in relation to pump volume sadly cancels out a lot of this benefit.

LPG can also be extracted from so-called 'wet' natural gas, sourced from oil or gas streams as they emerge from the earth, and more than half of the world's LPG is made this way. With natural gas fields scattered far and wide, all over the world (and often in places where crude is extracted, making good use of oil company facilities), it starts to make sense as a low-cost alternative fuel.

This book is concerned with the 'Green' angle of the fuel, of course, and here liquid petroleum gas displays a number of

A Ford Transit topping up with LPG in Britain. Ford

An LPG storage tank and dispenser in America, one of many installed as part of the Texas Propane Fleets project, to fuel school buses and other public service vehicles as part of a clean energy incentive.

Texas Propane Fleets/The Railroad Commission of Texas

plus and minus points. LPG has a high octane rating (around 105 RON, with 120 RON not uncommon), and burns to give off very low levels of PM and volatile organic compound (VOC) emissions, thanks to the way in which it can readily mix with air prior to combustion. It gives off lower levels of NOx when compared to petrol units at the kind of engine revs generally used in everyday situations, but higher emissions at lean mixture calibrations.

A mixed picture is presented with CO as well, but LPG can't compete with diesel in this respect in any case, although cold-start emissions are exemplary. Also, the level and type of HC emissions are not particularly harmful, and the release of chemicals such as benzene and butadiene is minimal. Better still, the sealed fuel system promotes zero evaporative losses, and the potential to lower CO_2 emissions by as much as 35 per cent compared with petrol engines is another bonus.

However, while LPG is about half the price of petrol nowadays, the lower energy density of the alternative fuel means an increase in consumption of around 30 per cent in terms of litres per mile. With the cost of converting the car, one can see why only those covering high mileages ever consider LPG as a viable option, despite the promise of lower emissions to help the planet – although those who live or work in Britain's capital could benefit, as most LPG-powered vehicles would be exempt from the London Congestion Charge. Ironically, the conversion cost could basically be recouped within a year, having done nothing to reduce gridlock in the city! But then, since when has any legislation been intro-

duced to actually – much less successfully – serve its stated purpose?

Australia is quite keen on LPG, with the government giving incentives to owners to convert from petrol to liquid gas. The country estimates a 15 per cent reduction in GHG emissions, and exhaust gases are said to contain twenty fewer toxic air pollutants. With an abundant supply of natural gas situated off the north coast Down Under, it would appear to make a lot of sense as an alternative to fossil fuels for this particular country.

At the start of 2012, LPG at $0.71 per litre is literally half the price of petrol and diesel in Australia's metropolitan areas, and still significantly cheaper in the countryside – $1.08 against $1.64 for premium unleaded and $1.63 for diesel. Five years ago, the price differential was even more in favour of LPG, being 45 per cent the price of traditional fuels in the cities.

Italy, Poland and South Korea are also big supporters of LPG, these countries accounting for a fair percentage of the ten million LPG-powered cars currently thought to be on the road (there are estimated to be about 100,000 cars and vans running on LPG in the UK), while Japan's ubiquitous taxis are almost exclusively run on LPG, explaining why so much of this particular fuel is used in Japan in relation to the amount of vehicles registered. There's actually a theory in Japan that the clean burning reduces engine stress, making power units last longer, which is another ecological bonus.

Interestingly, with so much focus being on 'Green' technology at the 2011 Tokyo Motor Show, companies involved with LPG were given far more prominence than ever before.

Brochure from the 2011 Tokyo Motor Show promoting Japanese and Korean LPG vehicles. The car shown on the cover is the Hyundai i40 Tourer – like Japan, Korea is very keen on liquid petroleum gas, with LPG conversions commonplace on the Asian mainland. Hyundai also released the world's first full hybrid to use an LPG-electric drivetrain – the Avante LPi Hybrid, which went on sale in Korea in July 2009.

Japan LPG Vehicle Promotion Association

An advert for Autogas from IndianOil. IndianOil

Prince Gas noted that their electronically controlled bi-fuel system could be applied to almost any vehicle, and while few private users would be tempted to invest (it would take a long time to recoup the initial outlay for low-mileage users), with the cost of LPG 40 per cent lower than petrol (85 yen per litre, against around 145 yen), it was doubtless of special appeal to those running fleets of smaller delivery vans.

Prince Gas was also working on a prototype diesel-LPG model at the time of the event, while an Iwate concern was offering LPG conversions on the Toyota Prius. In addition, virtually all the Japanese makers clubbed together with Hyundai to have a joint stand promoting LPG vehicles and other machines running on the fuel. Unlike hydrogen, which was once fancied by Mazda as a perfect alternative to gasoline until refuelling logistics came into play, with over 1,800 places to buy LPG in Japan, the infrastructure was already in place.

Ford's marketing manager for alternative fuel vehicles, Mike McCabe, delivering a natural gas-powered Expedition to the Atlanta Checker Cab Company. The taxi firm had a fleet of seventy Crown Victorias already running on CNG. Recently, with petrol prices at an all-time high in the States, the 'Big Three' have started to introduce a new range of bi-fuel CNG vehicles, with gas-guzzling pick-up trucks seen as an ideal starting point. Ford

Many manufacturers, past and present, have offered off-the-shelf bi-fuel cars that run on LPG and petrol (sometimes exclusively LPG), including the likes of Peugeot, Renault, Citroën, Fiat, Ford, Rover, Opel, VW, Skoda, Volvo and Saab from Europe, Ford and Chevrolet of America, Toyota, Daihatsu, Mazda, Suzuki, Tata, GM India, Hyundai and Daewoo from Asia, and Holden of Australia.

As it happens, a recent Holden project from Holden Special Vehicles (HSV – the factory tuning shop) has brought a novel LPG development to light. The majority of HSV vehicles are now available with a special induction system from Orbital Autogas Systems of New South Wales, Australia, which injects the LPG into the combustion chamber as a liquid rather than a vapour. Called liquid phase injection (or LPi), it allows for cooler combustion and superior metering, leading to a 13 per cent reduction in carbon dioxide emissions whilst maintaining the engine performance HSV fans have come to expect.

Ironically, having once been hailed as a saviour, LPG is being slowly pushed to one side as a fuel of the future, with compressed natural gas (CNG) becoming a better option in the eyes of many scientists. This is basically a mixture of gases, comprised of around 80 per cent methane with propane, ethane and butane making up the remainder, compressed to less than 1 per cent the volume it occupies at atmospheric pressure. LNG, as opposed to LPG, is much the same thing as CNG, but the gas has been liquefied.

According to the Indian Academy of Sciences, compared with traditional fuels, CNG has the potential to reduce certain hydrocarbons by as much as 90 per cent, carbon monoxide by 80 per cent, NOx emissions by up to 40 per cent, and CO_2 by 25 per cent. Indeed, CNG is credited with having the lowest CO_2 emission levels of all commercially available fuels.

But the main thing seems to be the promise of lower running costs once the fairly high initial investment has been made. A lot depends on the type of mileage one covers (the higher, the better) and location as to whether these costs can be clawed back – LPG has recently become very expensive in India, for instance (in line with rising popularity, by amazing coincidence!), while CNG is still fairly cheap, as long as one can source it.

New ECUs have overcome the old trait for CNG power loss phases, but one still has to put up with larger fuel tanks compared with LPG. In reality, though, unless one is converting a small economy car, the tank packaging problem is no worse than having to deal with a hybrid motor and all its control systems, and with the majority of vehicles on sale today, with huge luggage compartments or seven-seater bodies, the space issue fades into insignificance in comparison with the initial conversion costs.

FUELLING IDEAS FROM THE PAST

What is recognized as the world's first car, the French Cugnot of the late eighteenth century, was steam-powered – a giant three-wheeled contraption as inefficient as it was big. But there were others, offered as an alternative to the horse-drawn carriage at the height of the Industrial Revolution, and then more practical road car models for everyday use at the turn of the twentieth century. America led the way in this field, with Stanley, Locomobile and Doble each finding their fair share of success with steamers before the breed died out; only a handful of working vehicles – such as steam rollers used in road construction – were left to carry the flame beyond the 1920s.

The difficulties involved in securing petrol and diesel during World War I led a number of people to convert their vehicles to run on town gas. This usually involved fitting a large balloon-like bag on the roof to contain the gas. Looking at pictures of old buses, in particular, one can often spot these 'gas bag' machines, the larger bodies making the mounting of the fabric bags – huge, by necessity, as town gas couldn't be compressed and remain useful in an automotive application – that much easier.

Seeing no end in sight to the Great War, a 1918 copy of *Illustrated World* predicted that the car of the 1920s would be running on compressed coal gas, with four storage bottles under the rear floor and one in each of the running boards.

Fortunately the conflict did come to an end, and although gas bags disappeared overnight, there then followed a second exciting era of experimentation with man-made fuels,

The Trevithick & Vivian London steam carriage of 1803. The man sitting up front gives an idea of the vast scale of the beast. Wikimedia Commons

some of which are being hailed as a possible fuel of the future today, several decades further down the line. But this section focuses on the more bizarre plans to keep man mobile via alternative fuels, and surely the best of these surfaced during the hard times of the 1930s.

Bags containing gas were being fitted to the roofs of vehicles once again as austerity measures kicked in, although some opted for compressed natural gas (CNG) contained in tanks, for both practicality's sake and a neater appearance. However, it was wood gas that started to make an impression in the years leading up to and during World War II.

Without doubt, wood burners (the 'Holzbrenner' in German, or 'gazo' in French) have to be the least eco-friendly alternative fuel of all time – or are they? After all, the majority of the wood being burnt is waste. But if every road user in the world switched to wood burners, there would be no forests left in a very short space of time, when really we could do with planting a few more trees. If the first generation bio-fuels had become the financial goldmine they were once predicted to be, one can only guess what those worrying about deforestation at the time would have to say!

A Mercedes-Benz type 170VG from 1943, equipped with a wood gasification system. Daimler AG

In 1958, Ford built a number of scale models representing concepts for the future. One of them was a creation called the Nucleon, powered by a small nuclear reactor on the flat rear deck! At least the emissions would have been low, but there were a lot of practical issues to consider with nuclear power which had obviously escaped consideration. Such is the beauty of a concept car. Ford

Even so, the wood burner is, in itself, an interesting concept. The principle dates back to the mid-1800s, when the wood gasification process (heating a carbon-containing organic material in an oxygen-limited environment to a temperature hot enough that it releases a combustible gas, usually consisting mainly of hydrogen) was used to produce syngas for street lighting and cooking needs in big cities.

Engineer Georges Imbert (born in 1884 in the disputed Alsace-Lorraine region of France, so officially German at the time) duly developed a scaled-down generator suitable for motor vehicles, which went on sale across Europe in 1931. Most owners skimmed the cylinder head to raise the compression ratio (to make up for the 30 per cent drop in power, as the energy density of petrol is significantly higher than that of wood gas), and ignition timing had to be advanced a touch, but other than the plumbing and the fixing of 350kg (770lb) of metal to the car, very little was needed in the way of modifications. With petrol rationing but wood in plentiful supply, it seemed an ideal solution.

By the time that World War II was in full swing, Germany had 500,000 wood burners in service, with over a million worldwide, mostly in Europe, but spread as far afield as America, Australia and parts of Asia.

A range of about 100km (60 miles) and a top speed of roughly 80km/h (50mph) sounds antiquated by the standards of the day, but check the specifications of the majority of today's EVs, and if you consider how much time has passed since the end of World War II, the package starts to look like a feasible mode of transport.

As a result, in 1957 the Swedish government, in conjunction with Volvo on the transport front, set up a research programme to investigate the possibilities of the country converting to wood gas in times of fuel shortages. Sweden has no oil but is blessed with plenty of forests, and with the Cold War closing in on Sweden's borders, it was certainly something worth considering.

Once the generator is up and running, gasification emissions are on a par with those of burning natural gas, so it's reasonably eco-friendly with low hydrocarbon emissions, although CO levels are high. Maintenance levels are high, too, making it far from useful for everyday use unless one has a lot of time or a boilerman ready to hand. Research continued, however, and wood gas technology spawned a small but enthusiastic band of followers, and not only in poor countries. Ultimately a study was published in 1986 by the Food & Agriculture Organization of the United Nations looking at wood gas as a fuel. It concluded, rather damningly:

It is clear that the technology can have a future role in oil-importing countries as an emergency option, even though Sweden appears to be the only country which has officially taken the decision to make preparations for a conversion of vehicles to wood-gas operation. By all probability wood gas will not have a future as a regular engine fuel.

THE HYDROGEN OPTION

It is interesting to reflect that the gasification process used in wood-burner cars of the World War II era produced high concentrations of hydrogen – enough to run vehicles without any other fuel source. Just after the war, the USAF was considering ways of using liquid hydrogen as a fuel for aircraft, and NASA has employed it for many years in its space programme. As well as being used in a number of industrial applications, including oil refining, now the gas is being looked at as an alternative fuel for cars once again.

In the 2003 State of the Union address, President George W. Bush said:

In this century, the greatest environmental progress will come about not through endless lawsuits or command-and-control regulations, but through technology and innovation. Tonight I am proposing $1.2 billion in research funding so that America can lead the world in developing clean, hydrogen-powered automobiles. A single chemical reaction between

At regular atmospheric pressures and temperatures, hydrogen appears as an odourless gas (H_2), but becomes a liquid (LH_2) once cooled and pressurized. It has a very high octane rating (over 130 RON), but its characteristics are such that only when mixed with another fuel (such as the air-gasoline charge in a petrol engine) does it possess good anti-knock properties. Also, as compared with petrol, it has a low energy density by volume; even when compressed or converted to a liquid (LH_2 giving the ideal comparison with petrol, the energy delivered being almost exactly four times less per litre), conventional storage tanks tend to be cumbersome. And while hydrogen burns to give no carbon emissions, only NOx and water vapour, the flame also burns very quickly and at very high temperatures. These are just a few of the main reasons why for so long car manufacturers have steered away from machines using only hydrogen as a fuel.

As it happens, the world's first internal combustion engine, designed and built by Isaac de Rivaz in 1804, used

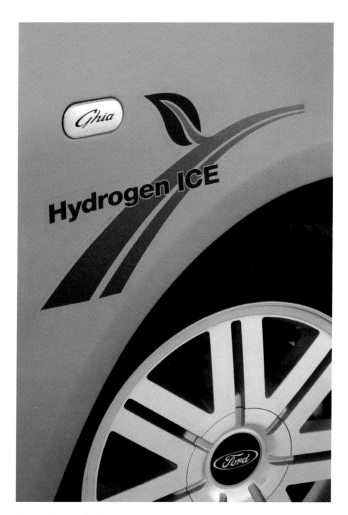

Focusing on hydrogen. Ford

hydrogen and oxygen generates energy, which can be used to power a car, producing only water, not exhaust fumes. With a new national commitment, our scientists and engineers will overcome obstacles to taking these cars from laboratory to showroom, so that the first car driven by a child born today could be powered by hydrogen, and pollution-free.

Although hydrogen (H) is the simplest and most common of all the elements, it is rarely found on its own – it generally has to be manufactured. In America, for instance, almost all hydrogen is gained from the steam reforming of natural gas (consisting mainly of methane, CH_4), but companies such as HyperSolar, harnessing solar power to create hydrogen from waste water, and electrolysis using wind power for electrical generation, could provide a perfect 'Green' solution for the long term.

A hydrogen fuel dispenser – the first in the US to be fed by an industrial pipeline, pictured in 2011. Toyota

The front-wheel-drive 1991 F100 MPV developed by Daimler-Benz engineers. Although hydrogen was used as fuel for the 6-cylinder engine, solar panels on the roof provided electrical power, with a novel feature added – an automatic interior cooling fan, which would start up whether the car was being driven or not. Daimler AG

The rotary-engined Mazda HR-X2, which made its debut at the 1993 Tokyo Show. Mazda

hydrogen gas as a fuel, so the idea is hardly new! Strangely, though, few persisted, and it wasn't really until World War II that conversions were made in any quantities – the Russian GAZ concern building as many as 200 trucks to run on hydrogen in 1941.

As with wood burners, the end of hostilities brought the end for the immediate need to source alternative fuels, and only a small number of people recognized the beauty of hydrogen. In America, the work of Roger E. Billings was at the forefront of using hydrogen as a fuel, not just in automo-

biles, but housing, too. One car he converted in 1972 actually cleaned the air, with negative HC and CO values coming from the exhaust pipe. Over in Japan, from the mid-1970s onwards, the Tokyo-based Musashi Institute of Technology built a number of concept vehicles running on hydrogen, while Germany's BMW and Mercedes-Benz had bi-fuel models based on the 5-series and W123-series, respectively; Mercedes also offered a bi-fuel panel van from 1984.

As we moved into the 1990s, Mercedes was once again pushing hydrogen as a feasible option in the world of alternative fuels, displaying its 6-cylinder F100 MPV concept at the 1991 Detroit Show. Meanwhile, Mazda was putting the final touches to its rotary-engined HR-X, readying it for

One of the hydrogen-powered RX-8s at the 2003 Tokyo Show. B. Long

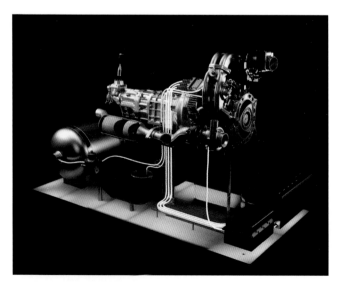

The Mazda RE set up to run on hydrogen. Ford

its debut at the 29th Tokyo Motor Show. The four-seater HR-X2 came at the following Tokyo Show, which opened in October 1993, powered by a 13B twin-rotor RE developing 130bhp. This was at a time when the normally aspirated petrol 13B rotary unit was pumping out 148bhp.

At the end of the 1990s, BMW introduced a 7-series model to run on liquid hydrogen (the 1999 750hL was actually a bi-fuel model, as was the later 745h), the large boot providing a good home for the LH_2 tank. The new Mini was displayed at the 2001 Frankfurt Show with a bi-fuel option, and Ford brought out the P2000 with a 2-litre engine modified to run on hydrogen – the first of several LH_2 vehicles from the US giant. Russia's GAZ and Norway's TH!NK also launched cars suitable for hydrogen fuels, but Mazda proved to be the staunchest supporter of hydrogen without the use of fuel cells.

A rotary-engined MX-5 Miata convertible was built with a hydrogen tank providing the only fuel for the vehicle, a perfect test-bed for comparison to the showroom MX-5 and another prototype with electrical power. Being about 10bhp down on power but considerably heavier, the hydrogen car couldn't compete with the stock vehicle in terms of performance (the 0–60 time went from 9.4 to exactly 13sec), but it was still much better than the 21.5sec needed for the EV to complete the same task. As for refuelling, on the hydrogen car it took about fifteen minutes to fill the metal hydride tanks (chosen for safety), against several hours to recharge batteries.

Then came the RX-8 Hydrogen RE of October 2003 with its new 'Renesis' rotary, delivering 210bhp on petrol and 109bhp on hydrogen. This was a switchable bi-fuel car, capable of running on either petrol or hydrogen mode at the touch of a button thanks to separate injectors for the two fuel systems. Driving on public roads began in late 2004, and a number of prototypes were duly leased to the Hiroshima local government for real-world testing, which revealed a range of about 100km (60 miles) in hydrogen mode.

As it happens, the RE is well suited to the use of hydrogen as a fuel, as its design overcomes a lot of the combustion difficulties associated with hydrogen and conventional internal combustion engines. For one thing, the exhaust phase takes place in a different area to the intake phase, thus avoiding backfires caused by premature ignition, while the motion of the rotor encourages better mixing of the hydrogen and air charge, made that much better by pre-mixing when the engine is running at low loads in hydrogen mode. Lean-burn and EGR technology combined with the standard three-way cat to keep NOx emissions in check, while carbon dioxide levels were zero.

The Mazda project sadly came to a premature end, excus-

The opening of the **BMW CleanEnergy exhibition, July 2007. BMW** has done a huge amount of R&D work on hydrogen-powered ICEs (building several one-off prototype units as well as converting production engines) and hydrogen fuel storage systems. BMW

es being fired off in all directions to avoid commitment – and now the rotary engine itself looks as if it is set for retirement. One of the main hurdles seemed to be range and the related infrastructure that would be needed for refuelling.

In reality, using regular-sized fuel tanks, even with older storage technology – modern lightweight and cheap to produce H_2-binding metal-organic framework (or MOF) compounds make high-density storage of hydrogen more practical than ever before – range problems only come into play when compared with petrol and diesel vehicles.

Ultimately, no one seems to be moaning about the poor range of EVs, simply because they come with a 'Green' badge. And as we've proved, because of the rather less than eco electrical generation methods employed from country to country, a lot of this image is nothing more than veneer until global energy policies are updated. Add in the fact that more than half of the Americans who drive to work cover less than 64km (40 miles) a day in a round trip (almost twice the European average), and as a commuter vehicle, it doesn't seem to be too big a problem to overcome in view of the ecological benefits to be gained.

One can therefore conclude that in Japan, hydrogen power was ultimately a victim of bureaucracy. Granted, the initial costs would be fairly high, but no one is saying that an entire transport system needs changing overnight.

Therefore, especially given the fact that a handful of refuelling sites already exist in the Tokyo Bay area (in addition to those built in Hiroshima), the excuse that the infrastructure wasn't in place simply isn't valid, as the present EV culture boom is going to put so much strain on the electricity generation grid – already operating near maximum output – that new power stations will have to be built in the near future if those nuclear plants closed for the time being (following concerns brought to light in 2011) stay closed.

Where to place these power stations, and what type of energy they adopt to generate electricity, are questions that have no easy answers (balancing sustainability and commitment to the Kyoto Protocol with the fears of local residents), but at least there are people in the right places with vested interests to make sure that something happens – the same old friends of heavyweights who were missing in the fight to adopt hydrogen power. And compared to the 'Smart City' concepts on display at the 2011 Tokyo Show, calling for entire urban areas to be created from scratch, a few hydrogen refuelling sites really don't seem so difficult.

At least Mazda's hard work has not gone to waste, for Norway has taken up the gauntlet, and the RX-8s used in field trials now run in Scandinavia on the 'HyNor' corridor. Norway uses mainly hydro-electric power generation, and with electrolysis, can make as much hydrogen as it needs to fuel up the entire country's fleet of vehicles, both cleanly and relatively cheaply once all the initial infrastructure is in place. Rather than take the easy route, though, and stay with short-term conventionalism, Norway has made the investment, and shown the world a true alternative.

In America, California and Florida have set the ball in motion, setting up a number of hydrogen refuelling stations, and others are popping up slowly but surely in Canada, Denmark, Sweden, Korea, Great Britain and mainland Europe, with – as one might expect – Germany heading the charge. However, most of these service stations will probably find they are used by customers driving fuel cell vehicles rather than cars with converted internal combustion engines.

WATER AS FUEL

The idea of water as a fuel may sound far-fetched, but it could be the fascinating breakthrough we've all been waiting for. So why are so few people taking it seriously? What appears to be the problem is that it seems too good to be true. It's almost shockingly simple in principle, but the basic chemistry all makes sense, and there are many benefits to the system – ultra-low emissions, low running costs (albeit after a sometimes hefty initial investment) linked to a sustainable fuel supply, and the advantage of being an 'on-demand' system, meaning that the storage of volatile gases isn't an issue.

A number of accessory shops already sell so-called HHO (or oxyhydrogen) cells to improve the gas mileage of regular petrol engines: the hydrogen is introduced into the intake manifold along with the normal air-fuel charge to make for a leaner mixture, and electrolysis is used to break the atomic bonds in electrolyte or distilled water to create two parts hydrogen and one part oxygen. Furthermore a number of academic research centres support the idea of hydrogen fuel enhancement for internal combustion engines, using some form of hydrogen injection to augment the regular fuel-injection system – the hydrogen makes petrol burn more effectively by extending the lean limit of combustion, thereby enhancing fuel consumption and reducing emission levels.

But according to Stanley Meyer, the true HHO fuel cell is not a fuel enhancer – it can use water from just about any source to provide the only fuel needed to run a vehicle. According to his various US patents, Meyer used his HHO cell as a capacitor, and employed a very high-voltage electrical system, so it's quite a different set-up to the DIY kits on sale all over America right now. Some are convinced Meyer's invention can work, pointing to a buggy he built that proves HHO technology is feasible, but sadly an Ohio courtroom thought otherwise, and convicted Meyer of fraud. He died in 1998 aged fifty-seven, and as yet, no one has managed to translate his patents into a working prototype – perhaps not surprisingly, given the conflict with the laws of thermodynamics.

So there we have it: myth, not helped by the discrediting of Meyer's work, the use of the 'Brown's Gas' moniker (Yull Brown's name for oxyhydrogen, which causes yet more confusion, as Brown's work was also surrounded in controversy) and Jules Verne novels, and undisputed fact. Evidently cars do not run on water, but they can use water to create a gas that will enhance fuel consumption on regular engines – but didn't Etienne Lenoir's 'Hippomobile' successfully run through the centre of Paris using electrolysis to generate hydrogen as the sole fuel source for its single-cylinder, two-stroke engine back in 1863? The plot thickens…

THE GAS TURBINE

The gas turbine was a fascinating piece of technology adopted as a possible form of motive power for cars by a number of makers, although one that was ultimately destined to be relegated to the history books before its full potential could be realized.

Rover of Britain was perhaps the strongest supporter of the gas turbine engine, as the company had done a great deal of top secret development work refining Frank Whittle's jet engine during the war years. Following the end of hostilities, Spen King and Frank Bell got to work on the concept of a gas-turbine-powered road car. The first prototype engine

Renault's Étoile Filante pictured at Bonneville Salt Flats in September 1956. The gas turbine engine produced 270bhp at 28,000rpm, propelling the slippery vehicle to a recorded top speed of 309km/h (193mph). Renault

The FRP-bodied 1958 Ford La Galaxie concept. The front end is said to have been the inspiration for Chrysler's turbine car. Ford

was up and running in February 1947, but it would be three years before a gas turbine car was seen. Announced to the press in March 1950, the Rover 'JET 1' was duly developed into a number of interesting road-car prototypes, ending with the T4 of 1961 vintage.

But that wasn't the end, because 1963 saw the debut of the Rover-BRM racer, driven in the Le Mans 24-hour race that year for demonstration purposes. This elegant machine, rated at 150bhp, was finally campaigned properly at Le Mans in 1965, with Jackie Stewart and Graham Hill coming home in tenth overall. While that spelt the end of the gas turbine car at Solihull, the project ultimately led to the formation of Noel Penny Turbines, founded by Rover's Noel Penny in 1972.

The simplicity, smooth running, and clean-burning characteristics (on a wide range of fuels) of the gas turbine charmed other car manufacturers into investigating its advantages further, most notably General Motors (with their typically futuristic 'Firebird' series), Chrysler, Fiat and Renault.

The racing world also embraced this new technology for a time, with the STP-Paxton Turbocar single-seater making its debut at the 1967 Indianapolis 500, and providing Lotus with the inspiration to make a turbine car – the Lotus 56, which lasted into the 1971 season. By this time, the Howmet TX sports prototype had entered the scene, competing in 1968, and winning a couple of minor races along the way. One of the two original Howmet TX coupés was then used to set new LSR records for gas turbine cars, clocking up six FIA records in August 1970 before a deserved retirement.

The 1963 Chrysler turbine car was the closest there ever was to a production gas turbine automobile, with fifty-five being built. Chrysler

Mitsubishi, Nissan and Toyota also experimented with the gas turbine in 1970. However, production costs, combined with turbine lag (a 1 to 2sec delay after initial throttle application), the long-term practicality issue (regular servicing, for instance) and high fuel consumption (something that certainly had to be considered in the seventies) put an end to its development. Until quite recently, that is, because in 1984 GM presented its striking Chevrolet Express concept car, with a top speed of 240km/h (150mph). As it happens, the US DOE funded some of the General Motors and Ford research into gas turbines, while Japan's MITI, encouraged by Kyocera's work on ceramics ideally suited to AGTs (advanced gas turbine engines), supported Toyota, Nissan and Mitsubishi. Sadly, cost and reliability silenced the idea of gas turbines in automotive applications yet again.

The exotic Jaguar C-X75. The gas turbines, which can be seen through the rear window and weigh only 35kg (77lb) each, use their exhaust pressure to drive the generator that tops up the lithium-ion battery pack. Because the turbines reach their operating speed and temperature in seconds, they can be used in short bursts without compromising fuel consumption. Jaguar

Nevertheless, Volvo (which had been working on gas turbine engines for nearly as long as Rover) brought out its ECC (environmental concept car) model at the 1992 Paris Salon, using a small, 76bhp gas turbine engine as a generator to charge the electric motor system. This extended vehicle range to over 645km (400 miles), with exceptionally low emission levels – and nor was turbine lag an issue, since the gas turbine engine was not being used as the main form of motive power.

All went quiet again until the 2010 Paris Salon, when Jaguar displayed its C-X75 concept car powered by an electric motor by SR Drives, with a pair of lightweight Bladon micro jet engines used as generator drives. With a funding grant from the British government, Bladon hoped to continue development in order to produce 'the world's first commercially viable – and environmentally friendly – gas turbine generator designed specifically for automotive applications.'

On the subject of jet engines, a note here on kerosene is relevant. Jet fuel is kerosene's most common use, but in the immediate post-war years, a number of cars in Europe were converted to run on kerosene, which wasn't taxed as heavily. The fuel crisis era of the 1970s brought forth the thought of using kerosene once more, with Saab-Valmet (Saab's Finnish arm, which later became Valmet Automotive) producing the bi-fuel Saab 99 GL 'Petro' model in limited numbers from 1979 onwards, able to run on petrol, kero-

sene or turpentine. In addition to the 3,756 'Petro' Saabs, a few Finnish-built Talbot Horizons also carried this conversion (around 2,400, constructed between 1980 and 1984).

The idea of steam cars also surfaced once again in the 1970s, with Saab, Nissan, and the British designer Peter Pellandine all trying to revive the concept, but it was Enginion AG of Berlin (out of IAV GmbH) which came closest to giving steam technology a comeback. A prototype 'EZEE' two-stroke unit was tested in a Skoda saloon, with the concept duly presented at the 2001 SAE World Congress. However, despite being supported by Volkswagen, market research led Enginion to drop the idea of powering a car, and to adopt its 'Steamcell' engine for other purposes. Today it is mainly used as an auxiliary power unit (APU), or in cooling, heating and power (CHP) applications.

CARS RUNNING ON AIR

Cars capable of running on air may sound crazy, but they do actually exist – and not only in museums, because examples of the breed (automotive and, more particularly, locomotive) date back to the second half of the nineteenth century, but also in the current marketplace. Depending on where you live, you could actually go out and buy one of these machines today, and several 'big name' car manufacturers are looking into ways of bringing this technology to showrooms in the near future.

While certain machines use compressed air only as a form of motive power, such as the interesting experimental Toyota KU:RIN, the majority of cars that run on air inevitably use another generator of some sort (such as a small petrol engine, for instance) to run a compressor, otherwise the vehicle's range is next to nothing.

It should be noted that the compressed air is not employed as a fuel. Instead, cars using compressed air technology (sometimes referred to as pneumatic motor technology) tend to use expansion of gas to move a piston rather than igniting the air, so therefore work on a similar fashion to traditional steam engines. Indeed, the basic operational theory is based on the rapid expansion of air one sees when supercooled air is exposed to ambient temperatures – or heat to speed up the process. The science is simple, and storing the air is a lot less worrisome than storing hydrogen (despite being kept at pressures of up to 4500psi!), and emissions, at least from the prime mover unit, are basically non-existent.

The latest practical air engine to hit the headlines, and validated by Ricardo (adding a great deal of viability to the project), is the Dearman Engine, which runs on cryogenic liquid air. The liquid air expands as a gas as soon as it is exposed to the ambient temperatures inside the cylinder,

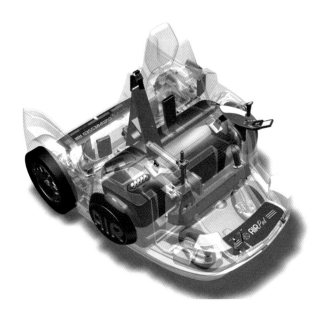

Basic layout of the AIRPod – one of the most promising attempts at harnessing air as a power source. MDI

The MDI AIRPod. MDI

pushing down the piston for a power stroke; cold air is the only by-product. There are hopes that Ricardo and Peter Dearman working as a team can bring the technology 'closer towards commercial maturity'.

Without doubt, Guy Legre's Motor Development International (MDI) concern has been at the forefront of developing this technology, prompting the Tata Group of India to sign a licensing agreement in February 2007 that promised R&D resources for the French company.

The MDI range of petrol-air hybrid commuter vehicles uses the expansion of compressed air heated by solar power (an electric compressor starts the car and compresses the air again once it has driven the pistons in the tiny engine), which promises exceptionally clean emission levels. Other specifications were also promising, with 56km/h (35mph) possible on pure air, or a 145km/h (90mph) top speed if the petrol engine kicked in to heat the air, exceptionally long service intervals, and a fair range, too.

Naturally, with several prototypes being road-tested and Tata's support bringing the possibilities of mass production ever closer, the MDI air car created quite a buzz. From early

2008 deposits were taken in the US for 2010 deliveries, and there were said to be more than fifty parties interested in licensing MDI technology.

However, at the end of 2009, Tata, with the Nano looking like a safer bet, took a step back from the MDI project, their engineers unable to overcome a number of technical problems, particularly one of limited range: plans for production therefore met with a serious setback. Zero Pollution Motors, who were promoting MDI vehicles in the States, has withdrawn their support, and only the Australian distributor seems to remain hopeful of the future.

Notwithstanding, MDI has continued to work hard behind the scenes, recently announcing a revised version

The Honda Air concept vehicle produced by the Honda Advanced Design studio in California. Honda

of the AIRPod model with a larger carbon-fibre air tank. A novel bonus of the cool, clean air from the exhaust is that it can be channelled off and used for air conditioning. Perhaps 2012 will be MDI's year, a decade after the air car's debut.

Other compressed-air car makers have also been faced with more than their fair share of woes, with the French team behind K'Airmobiles giving up on their project due to technical difficulties, a Spanish company tied up in legal wrangling, and the Energine Corporation of Korea having its CEO arrested for making exaggerated claims regarding its hybrid compressed air/electric vehicle.

The Quasiturbine – a rotary air engine – has had a number of patents applied to it, but is still being refined, becoming more and more simple as design work continues; while

The SolarWorld GT on a leg of its epic tour.
Bochum University

the Sarich orbital engine (invented by Aussie, Ralph Sarich), capable of running on compressed air or steam, has yet to prove itself as a viable project. With four decades having passed since the Sarich engine first surfaced, it is unlikely to see the light of day now. Incidentally, Sarich is behind LPG specialists Orbital Autogas Systems.

The Honda Air concept, presented at the 2010 LA Auto Show and using 'turbo-vacuums and external airflow to regenerate tank pressure', is just as unlikely ever to find its way into the showrooms, although it is gratifying to see some of the big name manufacturers play with the idea of compressed air as a power source for road cars.

SOLAR POWER

We've looked at water and air, and concluded that possibilities exist, albeit remote ones at the moment. But making use of another element, solar power from the sun, is surely an area where current technology must be close to allowing us to produce a vehicle capable of running on nothing more than the sun's rays?

As it happens, a SolarWorld GT (built to a design by Bochum University of Applied Sciences in Germany) was making its way round the world as this book was being completed. But despite the PR success of the SolarWorld machine, in reality one wonders why so little progress has been made in this field, given the extensive use of solar energy in housing nowadays, not to mention decades of experience in building project cars in universities and R&D departments worldwide – the first practical solar car (the 'BP Solar Trek') having been built in 1982.

The photovoltaic (PV) solar cell, generally made from selected semi-conductor materials (such as silicon, for

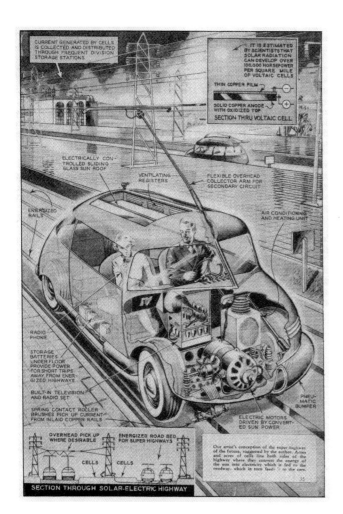

A twist on the solar power theme illustrated in a copy of *Modern Mechanix*, dating from 1940. It just goes to show that harnessing the power of the sun has been around for a long time, with the science in place for decades.

Modern Mechanix

The Mackay solar car that took part in the 2001 World Solar Challenge, which started in Darwin and finished in Adelaide. Toyota

instance) that can convert sunlight into electricity, has to be one of the cleanest, most renewable of all our power sources when it comes to relatively low-level energy requirements. The manufacturing process is such that careful calculations taking a long-term view would be needed to see if a city could be powered by solar panels as a true 'Green' option, but for a lightweight vehicle, an array of PV cells can provide more than enough power for effective propulsion once hooked up to an electric motor.

As yet, only promotional events such as the World Solar Challenge and the North American Solar Challenge have managed to put solar cars on the map. The first World Solar Challenge race, held in 1987, was won by the 'Sunraycer' developed by General Motors (GM), AeroVironment (AV) and the Hughes Aircraft Company – three real heavyweights in the technology stakes – at an average speed of 67km/h (42mph). The next car arrived at the finishing post a whole two days later, giving some idea of the difference in class compared to the rest of the field, but the 2009 winner averaged 100km/h (62mph), built by Japan's Tokai University using a fraction of GM's $2 million budget in real terms.

This just goes to show the progress made in this field, but – discounting the likes of the 2006 Venturi Eclectic, and the Antro Solo, which ultimately relies on pedal power as much as the sun – as this book goes to press, very little of the knowledge is being translated into marketable automotive technology that can be used on a daily basis.

One notable exception is the work of Solar Electrical Vehicles of California, founded in 2005 by Greg Johanson: their concept replaces the roof of the Toyota Prius with a custom-made PV cell array, allowing the vehicle to run up to an additional 48km (30 miles) a day in EV mode. Given the low power output available from solar cells at the moment, which requires a car to be in the sun almost constantly, and

the lack of suitable storage batteries – the added weight being the last thing a solar car needs in view of the aforementioned lack of power generation from current generation PV cells – perhaps the range extender application is the best we can expect in the short term.

However, as an electrical source for fuel cells, PV cells start to make sense. We are also seeing mainstream makers eyeing up solar power for driving electrical accessories, as seen on the GM Cadillac Provoq concept, for instance. With the big names taking an interest in solar cells, definite advantages in water consumption (plugging into the national grid for power calls for huge amounts of water, while PV cells only use a small amount during production) and electronics technology moving at a frightening pace, who knows what is possible within the next ten years?

FUEL CELL VEHICLES

A statement from the US Department of Energy in 2011 reads as follows:

> *Hydrogen has the potential to revolutionize transportation and, possibly, our entire energy system. The simplest and most abundant element in the universe, hydrogen, can be produced from fossil fuels and biomass and even by electrolyzing water. Producing hydrogen with renewable energy and using it in fuel cell vehicles holds the promise of virtually pollution-free transportation, and independence from imported petroleum.*

A Honda FC car prototype pictured at a hydrogen production and supply stand in California in the summer of 2001. Now, over a decade later, fuel cell fever is at last starting to take hold. Note the solar panels behind the vehicle. Honda

A historic photo taken in Stuttgart in December 1997. From left to right: Alex Trotman (Ford), Jurgen E. Schrempp (Daimler-Benz) and Firoz Rasul (Ballard Power Systems), agreeing to join forces on the development of fuel cell technology. Ford

Conventional fuel cell vehicles (FCEVs), as opposed to those carrying the 'HHO fuel cell' moniker discussed earlier in the chapter, are considered the way forward by many car manufacturers. The author was lucky enough to test one of these machines in prototype form at the Honda R&D centre in Japan about a decade ago, and can confirm that it feels much like any other car, but with a whooshing noise and nothing much else coming from the motive power unit. It was the latest thing, and FCEVs are almost inevitably thought of as carrying the latest in leading-edge technology.

However, the basic idea dates back to the mid-1800s – it's only in recent years that fuel cells have started to hit the headlines, being taken seriously in the automotive sector both directly and indirectly, because a glance at the Chevron and ExxonMobil websites soon reveals that even 'Big Oil' is anxious to take a part in fielding this technology.

As it happens, the ExxonMobil concept is quite different to the regular fuel cell approach, using traditional fossil fuels such as petrol and diesel to create hydrogen (in effect, a scaled-down version of a commercial hydrogen-making plant). The majority of modern fuel cells tend to turn towards hydrogen-rich alcohols such as propanol (C_3H_7OH), methanol (CH_3OH) or ethanol (C_2H_5OH) as the hydrogen carrier, or to store compressed gas in an onboard tank in the luggage compartment.

The principle behind the fuel cell was first revealed in the 'gas battery' invented by the English scientist, Sir William Grove, in 1839. Whilst experimenting with electrolysis, with the earlier work of Sir Humphry Davy in mind, he found that the process of breaking up the elements contained in water

by electricity could be reversed. Grove put a bottle filled with hydrogen and a bottle filled with oxygen in a solution of sulphuric acid. A naturally occurring electrical current began to flow between the platinum electrodes inserted in the bottles, and the gases were duly converted into water.

Progress was slow thereafter, as other, more practical forms of energy were developed, but Dr Francis Bacon of Britain's Cambridge University made a real breakthrough in 1932, producing the first alkaline fuel cell (AFC) after replacing the costly platinum electrodes with nickel gauze, and the sulphuric acid with a less corrosive solution of potassium hydroxide. However, a quarter of a century would pass before Bacon could harness enough power to make a practical fuel cell.

In the meantime, over in the States, NASA and General Electric (GE) were hard at work on their own fuel cell in the fifties – a proton-exchange membrane fuel cell (PEMFC), which worked on much the same electrochemical reaction principle as other fuel cells, but the PEMFC is split by a special electrolyte membrane, with hydrogen on the anode side catalytically split into protons and electrons. The protons travel through the membrane to the cathode to give the current, while oxygen on the cathode side reacts with the hydrogen to give water as a by-product. Controlling the flow of this water, to keep the solid membrane neither too wet nor too dry, presented a real technical hurdle.

As it happens, Pratt & Whitney ultimately gained the NASA business for fuel cells on manned spacecraft, perfecting Bacon's AFC during the sixties. The USSR was also working on FC technology, using its own version for the Russian space programme.

Back on Earth, Harry Karl Ihrig of Allis-Chalmers (the famous American agricultural equipment manufacturer) combined over 1,000 cells to make an FC stack that was powerful enough to move a vehicle. Given the Allis-Chalmers link, it's perhaps not surprising that it was actually a farm tractor that can claim the honour of being the first fuel cell vehicle (FCEV), demonstrated in the autumn of 1959.

General Motors made an experimental van in 1966, running on power produced by a Union Carbide PEMFC, which, like most other fuel cells that followed, converted hydrogen and oxygen into water, creating electricity and a little heat in the process. Despite the fact that the hydrogen could be stored quite readily in tanks (or even produced onboard a vehicle) and oxygen was drawn from the air we breathe, expense and technical problems kept fuel cells out of the automotive arena for some years.

In fact it wasn't until a few breakthroughs came together in the 1980s that the idea of an FC road car became truly feasible. Spurred on by the California 'Zero Emission Vehi-

BASIC FUEL CELL VARIATIONS

There are many variations on the fuel cell theme, but it will pay briefly to review the most common types, along with the main differences, advantages and disadvantages, as well as a few notes on carrier fuels where applicable.

The **Alkaline Fuel Cell (AFC)** principle made the FC a practical alternative to conventional powerplants. The advantage over the 'gas battery' was cost-performance, with cheaper and less corrosive materials being employed. As for emissions, while the water given off is clean enough to drink (a situation NASA has used to its advantage in space missions), the cell can easily be 'poisoned' by even small traces of CO_2, making pure oxygen a better bet than regular air. This adds cost and naturally reduces the practicality angle from a road transportation viewpoint.

Proton-Exchange Membrane Fuel Cell (PEMFC): This cell brought rocket science to the automotive world, becoming known as the polymer electrolyte membrane fuel cell as time rolled on (also recognized by the PEMFC acronym, making life easy). In addition to giving high output and short reaction times to demands, the only emissions are water and heat, and operating temperatures are low.

For years, cost was a bigger problem for the PEMFC than its weakness against fuel impurities. Recent innovations, such as the introduction of cheaper platinum alloys for catalysts, and the replacement of machined graphite electrodes to carry the platinum coating with carbonfibre composite plates (sealed by flowing methane over them at very high temperatures to deposit carbon on them), keeps the PEM fuel cell alive, the robust carbon-fibre items weighing half and costing a fifth of their graphite counterparts.

Direct-Methanol Fuel Cell (DMFC): A variation on the PEMFC theme, using methanol mixed with a little water as a hydrogen carrier, to be broken down on the anode side to give positively charged hydrogen and carbon dioxide. While this type of FC gives off water and carbon dioxide as byproducts, compared with hydrogen gas, ease of storage is a major advantage. On the down side, the voltage given is not so high, partly due to the use of a weak solution of methanol. There are cells that get round this problem by reforming the methanol via steam to give hydrogen before being fed into the cell. These so-called reformed methanol fuel cell (RMFC) and indirect methanol fuel cell (IMFC) systems also give off carbon dioxide and water, but are generally more compact.

Incidentally, propanol was used as the source of hydrogen for FC units for many years, since it was able to generate a higher voltage than methanol in the majority of alcohol-based fuel cells. However, methanol is finding favour more recently due to its relatively 'Green' and cost-effective way of manufacture – certain methods used in its creation being able to cancel out any CO_2 emissions from the FC itself.

Ethanol is another option as a hydrogen carrier, as it is less corrosive and has a higher energy density than methanol.

Direct-Ethanol Fuel Cell (DEFC): This works much like a DMFC unit, giving off carbon dioxide (which can be offset in the ethanol creation process) and water, and can take advantage of modern technology such as alkali anion exchange membranes (AAEMs), which allow non-noble metals such as iron, nickel and cobalt to take the place of platinum – the traditional but costly catalyst for the oxidation of methanol's and ethanol's organic molecules.

If efficiency is the prime concern, three years ago, scientists at the Brookhaven National Laboratory (attached to the US Department of Energy) announced a new catalyst – a network of platinum and rhodium atoms on carbon-supported tin dioxide nanoparticles: not only could this reduce the ethanol perfectly, it could also oxidize the resulting molecules at room temperature.

Solid Oxide Fuel Cell (SOFC): This cell employs a solid oxide or ceramic electrolyte membrane to separate the anode and the cathode. This promises better long-term efficiency, greater freedom on the choice of fuels, and low production costs, but the higher operating temperature can be a serious disadvantage, both from an insulation and cooling point of view, as well as longer starting times. As it happens, all fuel cell and hydrogen-powered cars can experience starting difficulties in cold weather.

An SOFC uses the non-porous electrolyte to carry negatively charged oxygen ions from the anode to the cathode, while a proton-conducting solid oxide fuel cell (PC-SOFC) transports protons across instead, allowing the operating temperature to be reduced. Emissions from SOFC units include water (steam), trace amounts of nitrogen oxides and sulphur oxides, and a small amount of carbon dioxide.

Phosphoric Acid Fuel Cell (PAFC): The PAFC uses orthophosphoric acid as the electrolyte, and is less susceptible to CO_2 poisoning than an AFC unit. However, despite this, and the fact that it gives off water and heat as its only emissions, it is rarely seen in automotive applications – the platinum-coated graphite electrodes making it too costly, allied to a weakness against carbon monoxide poisoning.

There are many other types of fuel cell, but most are for industrial use. One should keep a look-out for the further development of the zinc-air battery, as well as the direct borohydride fuel cell (DBFC) – a variation on the AFC theme, with promising power outputs and cheaper construction materials. In addition, any hydrogen that results as a by-product can be directed to a tank for use in another type of fuel cell.

BMW has been working on PEM fuel cells since 1997. These pictures show the first (left) and second generation versions. At the end of 2011, BMW announced it was joining forces with General Motors in FC research and development. Interestingly, many of the company's working vehicles inside the factory were powered by fuel cells. BMW

cle' mandate of 1990 that encouraged the development of alternatives to the internal combustion engine, even then techno-freaks had to wait until 1993 before a Canadian company, Ballard, launched the first marketable fuel cell for passenger transport – a compact PEMFC unit that found its roots in the early NASA/GE experiments, by now carrying the polymer electrolyte membrane fuel cell moniker. Interestingly, Ballard sold its interests in this field of technology in 2007 to Ford and Daimler AG, both companies having invested heavily in Dr Geoffrey Ballard's firm since the 1990s.

In the years leading up to the new millennium, Mercedes-Benz, General Motors and Toyota led the way in fuel cell vehicle technology, tending to concentrate their efforts on the PEMFC unit. The Mercedes NECAR 1 van of April 1994 vintage gave birth to a series of NECAR prototypes, with the 1997 NECAR 3 using an onboard methanol reformer. GM built a fuel cell version of the EV1, also featuring a methanol reformer, as well as a couple of Opels, while Toyota had its 'FCEV' series (later given the 'FCHV' moniker).

Renault and Mazda also produced examples of FCEVs, with Ford, Honda, Nissan and Daihatsu joining the fray in 1999. The line of Honda 'FCX' prototypes, using Ballard PEM technology, showed real commitment to fuel cell cars by the Japanese maker, while Hyundai, Chrysler, the PSA Group and Volkswagen started displaying concept cars from 2000

The Honda FCX-V2 platform from 1999. Its methanol reformer and fuel stacks were so compact that engineers were able to position them under the floor, immediately overcoming many of the packaging problems one associates with hydrogen-powered vehicles. Honda

The Ford Focus FC5 was launched at the 2000 Detroit Show, the 'FC5' moniker referring to the TH!NK fifth-generation fuel-cell unit that the vehicle employed. The car used methanol as a fuel, which was then converted into hydrogen by an onboard reformer before entering the FC. Ford parted company with TH!NK in 2003. Ford

onwards. Interestingly, Volkswagen was experimenting with the SOFC unit, as well as the more common PEM power-plant. The FC regulars were joined by Mitsubishi and Lada in 2001, Suzuki and Fiat in 2003, and Audi in 2004, meaning virtually all the heavyweights in the industry had made an attempt to jump on the fuel cell bandwagon as the new century dawned.

Meanwhile, smaller concerns such as Microcab Industries (supported by Coventry University) were launching their own FCEVs – the H4 made its debut in 2005, along with the Norwegian TH!NK, and the Agni and Reva models from Asia. As it happens, it was another minor player, Hywet of Denmark, that offered the first commercially available fuel cell car. Launched at €27,000 in July 2007, the compact two-seater had a top speed of 80km/h (50mph) and a 160km (100-mile) range.

However, despite the promise of excellent emissions performance of the fuel cell, with CO_2 levels reckoned by the US DOE to be 55 per cent those of a conventional ICE in well-to-wheel calculations – and that's with a fairly inefficient way of sourcing hydrogen – it looks as if cost will be the enemy for some time yet.

Even in 2007, by which time the price of manufacturing fuel cells had dropped by around 80 per cent compared with the start of the decade, an FC-powered bus still cost as much as five times the price of an equivalent diesel model.

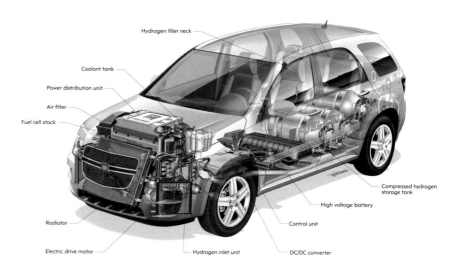

The Chevrolet Equinox starred in a testing programme called 'Project Driveway' in 2007, leading to long-term loans of updated models to members of the public beginning in 2010. GM hopes to have the vehicle in production by 2015. GM

Add in the fact that most scientists will tell you that a regular battery offers greater efficiency, and these two factors are the main reasons why the Obama administration in the USA keeps blowing hot and cold on fuel cell technology, cutting research funding, then bringing it back, only to cut it again.

As we look around today, it seems that the fuel cell car's future lies with Mercedes-Benz and Honda, and possibly Toyota if its 2011 Tokyo Show exhibits are anything to go

The 'Clean Energy Partnership' fleet pictured in front of an Aral/BP hydrogen service station in Berlin in July 2006. From left to right: a BMW 745h bi-fuel model, a Mercedes A-Class F-Cell, a Ford Focus FCV, an Opel HydroGen3 fuel cell car, and a VW Touran HyMotion, with a Ballard Mark 902 fuel cell and NiMH battery pack. Volkswagen

An FCX Clarity model being built by Honda in June 2008. The model was available for lease to customers in Japan, America and Europe. Honda

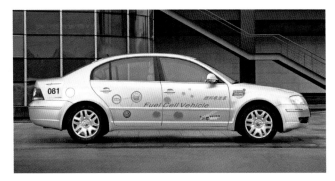

The VW Passat Lingyu FCEV, developed in partnership with scientists from Tongji University. Having made its debut at the 2008 Beijing Olympics, the model was then used in a test programme in the USA. Volkswagen

The Toyota FCV-R concept was unveiled at the 2011 Tokyo Show, and then went on a tour of America and Europe, stopping off at all the major car exhibitions. There are plans to put the vehicle in production by 2015. B. Long

by. With more than three million miles of road testing and proving already behind the FCEV, one has a right to wonder why so few are standing by the FC concept beyond commercial and material handling vehicle makers.

In reality, more than technical problems delaying production, it comes down to what a car can be sold for in the showrooms. Toyota seems to think US customers would stand for a $50,000 price tag, but are unlikely to be willing to stump up more than that. Naturally, fuel cell vehicles will benefit from the new technology being applied to today's hybrid cars and EVs, particularly in the dedicated drives and storage battery fields, which will help reduce development costs. In turn, these savings and higher volumes on component manufacturing will doubtless bring the cost per unit

down to reasonable levels. After years of slow progress on the fuel cell car, the appliance of science which is making the current breed of electric vehicle a practical proposition is sure to speed up FCEV development.

Meanwhile Daihatsu, helped by Toyota's funding, is investigating a so-called 'PMfLFC' concept – the initials standing for precious metal-free liquid-feed fuel cell, which uses high-density hydrazine hydrate as a liquid fuel. If all goes to plan, this will reduce FC sizes, as well as pricing. What was being tackled by small teams on the limited budgets allocated to fringe projects is now being handled by mainstream R&D departments, with the promise of spreading costs across a wider product range, making the investment and effort that much more worthwhile.

The current financial situation doesn't make bold moves any easier, however, with one Japanese executive saying to me recently that moving vehicles in the States results in a loss on every sale due to the outrageous strength of the yen (or the weakness of other currencies, depending on which way you look at it). This leaves little for R&D budgets, and the same lack of a slush fund is true across the industry, no matter which country is picked on as an example. But sticking with the fuel cell concept, and clearing just one or two technological hurdles, could make the difference between FC cars becoming a reality, or being a missed opportunity.

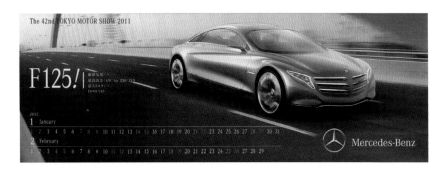

The gullwing F125 concept vehicle was the exhibit that attracted the most attention on the Mercedes-Benz stand at the 2011 Tokyo Show. Although this particular FCEV won't be available for the foreseeable future, Mercedes built a test fleet of B-Class F-Cell models in 2010. The latest fuel cells, whilst being more compact, offered higher output, better cold start performance, and superior range (400km/250 miles). There are plans to retail the B-Class F-Cell in 2014, which would make it the first FC car to be offered for sale by a mainstream maker. Daimler AG

CHAPTER SEVEN

THE BODY BEAUTIFUL

We've already stated that there is unlikely ever to be a true zero-carbon car, certainly not in the foreseeable future, one of the main reasons being that the typical mainstream buyer is, generally speaking, more interested in projecting their own image than saving the planet. Outside its simple role of getting people from A to B, the car is basically a fashion statement – nevertheless careful body design, material usage and component matching can have a huge effect on reducing our carbon footprint.

REDUCING VEHICLE WEIGHT

Regarding weight, the physics are simple: the heavier the vehicle, the more powerful the engine that is required to meet benchmark performance – or in the real world outside

R&D centres, the existing power-unit has to work that much harder, which has an equally detrimental effect on fuel consumption. Expressed another way, the lighter the machine becomes, the more the power-to-weight ratio improves, making the energy released by the engine that much more efficient in relative terms. But whichever way you look at it, the bottom line is that additional weight wastes fuel.

Here are some interesting figures which effectively put this last paragraph into perspective: in an automobile weighing 1,000kg (2,205lb), to achieve a realistic 0–60mph time of 10sec, at least 99bhp would need to be at your disposal. In a car with a 1,500kg (3,310lb) kerb weight, the requirement goes up to 152bhp, and at 2,000kg (4,410lb), 218bhp. In other words, for every 10kg (22lb) the vehicle carries, at least one horsepower is wasted, as it could be used for something more productive than pulling the body along. Alternatively, on a lighter car, the power-unit could be downsized without any loss of performance. At the same time, for every additional 100kg (220lb) of bulk, on average, we can generally add about 4 per cent to the existing fuel consumption figure.

Not realistic in today's world, but the Suminoe Flying Feather, seen here at the 1954 Tokyo Show, displays many of the ideal characteristics for a 'Green' car – a compact vehicle with ultra low weight, a small frontal area, a frugal engine, and tyres with a low rolling resistance. We've known the way forward for more than half a century, but better times soon made us forget the need to conserve energy. Yutaka Katayama

Racing cars have employed weight reduction techniques ever since the dawn of motoring. Rather than using the principle of less weight to allow vehicles to go faster, in road cars it can be used to save fuel. Daimler AG

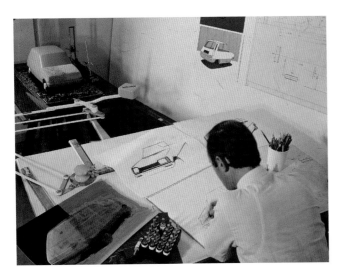

Car design has always been a question of compromise. But at least there was a little more freedom in the old days, before safety and emissions rules became so strict. This picture shows the lightweight Renault 5 taking shape before its late 1971 launch. Renault

In a racing car, weight-saving techniques can be translated into extra speed on the track, as one doesn't have to worry about fuel consumption. Look at any old racer from the early twentieth century, and we see an absolute minimum of bodywork, along with drilled chassis rails to save a few grams here and there. Windscreens are tiny, and in the case of the Silver Arrows of the 1930s, even the paint was removed! Lightweight alloys on the body, as well as drivetrain and chassis components, dropped the kerb weight yet further. Evolution called for smaller machines, and in sports car racing, homologation specials such as the Ferrari 250GTO and the Porsche Carrera RS, which were stripped of everything but the bare essentials needed to drive. Then space-age materials such as carbon-fibre were introduced into the equation, in an arena where cost is a minor issue in the fight against the sworn enemy – weight.

On a road car, it's not really that simple. People tend to like things such as air conditioning, electric windows and stereo units with a huge array of speakers, not to mention the basics that are the first things to go in a track racer, such as passenger seats, carpets and sound insulation material. Indeed, noise, vibration and harshness (NVH) control is a major consideration in a modern road car, almost on a par with safety concerns if some of the television advertisements are to be believed!

In reality, meeting safety regulations is probably the number one cause of middle-age spread in a car, followed by the gadgets and equipment levels that today's custom-ers feel they can't live without, emission and NVH control measures, and the use of materials that are chosen first and foremost to keep production costs in check.

As such, we can blame nanny states, fashion and bean counters for the fact that the base BMW Mini of today is very nearly twice the weight of the BMC Mini of 1959, with an engine having twice the displacement. Nor is the situation that much different on the latest versions of the Volkswagen Beetle and Fiat 500, when comparing them to their predecessors of the fifties.

Creating a balance is what it's all about at the end of the day, with more and more importance being put on 'Green' credentials nowadays. So we have a situation where engineers and designers cut weight wherever they can in order to save fuel (and therefore reduce emissions) and enhance performance, whilst at the same time meeting all the necessary regulations without destroying the 'feel' of their product and incurring the wrath of the accountants. Nor must they upset the marketing types, for that matter, because they set the final selling price on a car during the concept development stages – it's not as simple as making something the way you want, figuring out the cost once it's finished, and then putting a mark-up on the end figure.

We should also bear in mind that however hard the engineers work, probably the most effective form of weight

The VW Nils gullwing concept weighs just 460kg (1,014lb), yet it offers full weather protection, a modicum of luggage space, and can cruise at 130km/h (80mph) with a 15kW electric motor. It would surely suit the needs of many who only use a car to go to the local shops or a sports club. B. Long

reduction can be achieved through our own sensible choice of vehicle for daily use. The current boom in Japan, tailing off slightly after a decade of hot sales, is for the so-called 'one box' – what Americans would class as a minivan, despite there being very little relation to 'mini' in the overall dimensions. From experience, one can safely say that most of the time there's only one child bouncing around in the back, and long journeys with more than four people are extremely rare. So why drive a seven-seater shaped like a brick and as heavy as the *Queen Mary*, when a compact saloon would be more suitable for the daily routine? It's the same as going back and forth to three different supermarkets trying to save a few pennies, having to fold seats to find luggage space,

and wasting fuel running around in a vehicle more suited to a commercial firm.

Take a look around any motor show, and you will see that nearly all the future concept vehicles are tiny. Effective downsizing – introducing a vehicle line smaller than its predecessor – is definitely the way forwards, although we only ever seem to have witnessed the phenomenon during the fuel crisis of the 1970s. Even the Ford Thunderbird, a symbol of carefree America, went from 2,047kg (4,514lb) in 1972 to 1,480kg (3,263lb) in 1980. Suddenly, small economical cars from Japan, having once been laughed at by the usual 'experts' in the local bar, became all the rage, and the Toyota Corolla joined the Volkswagen Beetle in the ecologist's hall

BALANCING REAL-WORLD SAFETY WITH ECOLOGY

Not so long ago there was a report concerning a lady who, after seeing a bad road accident, made her husband sell his nearly new open sports car and buy an old saloon from a certain Scandinavian maker. It was big and heavy, and came with a truly enviable reputation for safety – but this reputation was established when the car was new, and the model they chose was several generations behind on body design (and airbag and seatbelt design, for that matter). Add in the nimble handling and superior braking of the sports car to better avoid an accident in the first place (a lighter body augmenting the suspension components to reduce reaction times to driver input), and the convertible would have probably been the safer vehicle in most scenarios.

Those who have changed to big SUVs for 'safety' have also failed to read NHTSA statistics, where a high centre of gravity is blamed for 36 per cent of the 280,000 rollover incidents reported annually in the States – about the same as rollover accidents caused by driving whilst under the influence of drink or drugs, and significantly more than those caused by weather conditions. Image, combined with a little knowledge – as opposed to a deep understanding of the physics of a car accident – can be a dangerous thing!

Therefore size and weight isn't directly related to safety – so it's ironic that the US market has demanded that vehicles are tested in a certain way, and only those that pass are declared 'safe' enough for American citizens – for many years, bigger bodies gave a simple solution to meeting Federal regulations. This may or may not be another form of latent protectionism, but it certainly excludes a lot of 'Green' models on the market, which no one in their right mind would use on a highway anyway, whilst nothing is said about the personal safety of motorcyclists.

Bikers simply don't have huge bumpers, crumple zones, side beams, front airbags, side airbags, curtain airbags or rollover

strengthening to protect them – not even seatbelts (or a helmet, for that matter, in certain states!). Those who enjoy classic cars also do without many of the things vehicles have to have by law nowadays. It's called freedom of choice, and in the car world, this freedom of choice could save several hundred kilos in excess weight – a figure that would have a startling effect on handling. It would also help fuel economy, or even allow a downsizing of power-units, both coming with resulting benefits for the environment.

And how often do cars, especially those with a sensible track-to-height ratio, roll over in relation to miles travelled? Personally, I'd rather have a lighter machine. And if I had to keep the weight for whatever reason, I'd prefer to have the extra sheet metal around the suspension mounting points to give the vehicle a chance of handling better, or at least improve the weight distribution to an ideal 50:50 – to me, this is safer than moving the car's centre of gravity further away from the ground.

For sure, a certain level of safety should be built into all vehicles – I'm not suggesting we abandon everything to save a few grams of carbon dioxide entering the atmosphere. But we seem to have taken things to extremes, with Europe following America's lead, yet at the same time allowing loopholes to appear that make a joke of the current strict rules on mainstream machines, and crash testing carried out at totally unrealistic speeds. It's like saying we should all walk around dressed like NFL football players, just in case somebody bumps into us on the street at walking pace – but expect a broken leg regardless of the body armour you're wearing if one party is running. A proper study is needed worldwide on the true benefits of certain safety features, and, after working out the percentages, seeing whether regulations can be adjusted to save weight.

Oil-crisis-induced downsizing: the 1972 (left) and 1980 Ford Thunderbirds compared, with the two ladies giving an excellent idea of scale. We may never see such dramatic moves again, in part due to our own buying habits, which tend to scare marketing men away from taking chances on big changes. As long as we continue to choose cars, SUVs, minivans and pick-ups that are far larger than we actually need, manufacturers will keep making them, as the investment needed to develop cars is huge nowadays – makers will instinctively tread a proven path rather than take a gamble. Ford

of fame. With so many other large cars on the road today, downsizing is probably seen as a risky move by the marketing men, as people tend to base value on quantity rather than quality. But somebody must be brave, and make the first move.

The RX-7

The third generation (FD) Mazda RX-7 was one of the finest examples of weight saving ever seen in a mass-production road car, with 'Operation Zero' taking its inspiration from the Hiroshima company's racing programme and the Mitsubishi Zero – the fighter aircraft from World War II.

The author's old FD-series RX-7. B. Long

The Mitsubishi Zero was famous for its lightweight but strong construction, so Mazda's engineers actually studied one that was being restored at the time of the FD project. Duly inspired, starting in October 1988, Operation Zero called for every part on the drawing board to be analysed, then a reduction of its mass to a bare minimum, redesigning it so as not to lose its primary function and strength.

Cost also had to be borne in mind, so materials such as thermoplastics and aluminium were used extensively (as an example, the aluminium bonnet saved 8kg/18lb compared to a steel item), but smaller glass areas were adopted to save 9kg (20lb), and flange welding – made cost-effective by robotics – allowed a thinner-gauge steel to be used than for spot welding for the main shell without a loss of strength. Even the alloy wheels were 'squeeze cast' – a technique often used in the aviation industry to save weight.

After six sessions spent reviewing each and every component, from suspension parts to wiring lengths, from the drilled aluminium pedal-set to the lightweight seats and interior trim, and even the use of aluminium alloy for the car's jack and handle, Operation Zero shed a total of 110kg (243lb) between late 1988 and signing off the final designs.

MATERIALS

The materials used to produce a vehicle body depend to a great extent on the car's market positioning, as a regular family hatchback has a certain bracket on pricing within which customers expect such a vehicle type to fall. Therefore, any thoughts of using light but expensive materials such as carbon-fibre to reduce weight by a few kilos have to be forgotten. Volume considerations also come into play, so glass-fibre doesn't make sense either (it's only really suitable for short-run production), meaning we come back to dependably reliable steel. Such is the case with so many projects.

Material Weight Comparison

The following table shows a material's typical weight (expressed as a percentage of a block of mild steel measuring 25cm/10in on all sides – something easy to visualize) and its ultimate tensile strength. It also shows the cost (expressed as a percentage of mild steel) of certain metals commonly used in car body production, plus a couple of interesting alternatives for reference.

	Weight	Strength (UTS)	Cost
Mild steel (1018)	100%	63,800psi/440MPa	100%
HT steel (4130)	99%	97,200psi/670MPa	132%
Stainless steel	101%	73,200psi/505MPa	375%
Galvanized steel	102%	79,800psi/550MPa	120%
Aluminium alloy	35%	45,000psi/310MPa	113%
Magnesium alloy	23%	31,900psi/220MPa	212%
Titanium alloy	57%	138,000psi/951MPa	950%

Some of these prices fluctuate due to market demands. For instance, the cost of steel has gone up faster than aluminium, and demand for stainless steel (particularly in China) has pushed its price up far beyond its real worth. A lot also depends on grades and processing – bar, sheets and so on – but these prices should give a fair representation of current (2012) sheet pricing in Europe.

We can therefore conclude that the choice of panel material is not as straightforward as selecting the lightest, thus reducing weight to save fuel and improve vehicle dynamics, but a combination of factors: these include – but are not limited to – the ease of forming (including tooling costs) balanced with overall strength in a given application (where the difference between a material's ability to withstand tensile stress and bending stress has to be taken into account), the ease of incorporation into the manufacturing process (welding or bonding, as well as finishing, including known imperfections that certain materials have when they come out of a press or mould, and the ease of painting), the ability to withstand everyday knocks, the ease of recycling, and the resistance to corrosion, before and after any potential treatment. While the engineers work through this selection

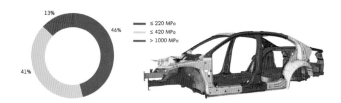

The use of different strength steels in a VW Jetta body.
Volkswagen

process, other departments are consulted to ensure that the initial cost per piece is acceptable based on expected volume forecasts, and replacement and potential repair costs are kept reasonable in relation to market positioning – insurance companies play a far larger part in vehicle design that one imagines.

Steel is cheap and easy to recycle, and being an alloy, it means that there are plenty of grades to choose from, all the way from basic mild (or low-carbon) steel, through to common high-tensile variations (produced with varying amounts of nickel, chromium, molybdenum, vanadium, tungsten and other elements added during the manufacturing process), and the latest ultra-high-tensile steels (UHTS or UHSS), like boron steel, which has an ultimate tensile strength rating of around 200,000psi (1,380MPa).

Adding carbon to steel makes it harder, but it also makes it more difficult to form and weld. This also has to be considered on the stronger steels, as pressing tools struggle to cope with difficult shapes on less ductile metals. This is why, despite the fact that thinner gauges can be used, offering the distinct advantage of the same strength being gained for less weight, the use of ultra-strong steels is still fairly new to the car world, with makers turning to them for the first time in this century.

UHSS is generally around four times harder than regular high-tensile steel, as well as being significantly stronger and stiffer in sheet form. Indeed, with boron steel, one can usually reckon on using metal at least 10 per cent thinner than normal, and up to 15 per cent thinner in places. This can save a great deal of bulk, even on a lightweight sports car such as the original Mazda MX-5, with the basic bodyshell tipping the scales at an ultra-light 200kg (440lb). On a large saloon, the savings can be far greater.

Boron steel is about as far as one can go within practical limits, employing it in pillar, sill and scuttle areas where strength is of paramount concern. Porsche was one of the first to use it, on the 2002 Model Year Cayenne SUV, with Mercedes-Benz and Volvo not far behind. Meanwhile GM,

Steel bodies are the accepted norm for cars, but rust is a problem. For the 1976 season, Porsche introduced a galvanized steel body for the 911 – a move the rest of the industry was quick to react to, thus making shells last longer. Porsche

first thinking of using composites and aluminium to reduce bulk on its showcase hybrid model, finally settled on boron steel to give the best balance between weight, performance and cost for the Chevrolet Volt.

As it happens, Mazda recently adopted a 261,000psi (1800MPa) rated steel for the bumper beams on its new CX-5 model – the simple component shape lending itself to the use of the strongest steel employed in the automotive field so far. These new beams, developed in collaboration with Sumitomo Metal Industries and the Aisin Takaoka Company, are 20 per cent stronger than normal and save 4.8kg (11lb). As well as the ecology angle, saving weight at a car's extremities has a huge effect on handling (in particular, sharper dynamic responses can be guaranteed), so two very real benefits are achieved thanks to this new technology.

Of course, steel rusts, as we all know too well (especially fans of Italian cars from the 1970s and 1980s), and older protection methods such as wax and underseal add weight. Besides which, underseal is far from a long-term measure – it actually needs stripping off and replacing fairly often, as it becomes porous. What does this have to do with 'Green' technology? Well, as we pointed out in the first chapter, it takes a lot more energy to build a new car than keep an old one serviceable.

Galvanizing is a cost-effective way to lengthen the useful life of steel – adding a light coating of zinc to the steel, either by electro-plating or by dipping selected areas or a whole car body in a bath of molten zinc.

The hot-dip galvanizing principle has been around for more than two centuries, but it wasn't until the 1970s that car factories finally started using galvanized steel for bodywork, despite it being easy to work with, and having definite benefits for the end user in comparison to the 10kg (22lb) average weight gain when galvanizing a complete bodyshell.

The Germans led the field, with Porsche, for instance, introducing galvanized steel for the entire 911 shell in time for the 1976 season (at least for the domestic market – the Americans had to wait a while longer due to the limited supply of the special Thyssen steel), with selected galvanizing on the 924. Other manufacturers soon followed suit, although it has been noted that the level of protection offered by zinc plating differs from maker to maker, and not all offer galvanized panels by any means.

Steels that are naturally resistant to corrosion are also available. Stainless steel, as we know it today, was invented

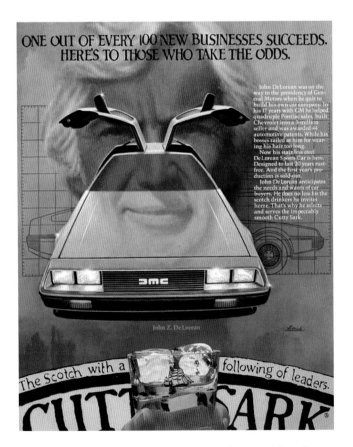

The stainless-steel-bodied DeLorean featured in a Cutty Sark whisky advert from the early 1980s. Cutty Sark

WHEN LIGHTWEIGHT BECOMES TOO LIGHT

There are actually times when engineers go too far in their quest to save weight. Certain old British sports cars had a terrible reputation caused by chassis flexing, for instance, and scuttle shake was common in convertibles. But in recent years, the problem has resurfaced in a number of Japanese models made for the domestic market.

It seems the testing codes are different for export machines, where regulations, speeds and other conditions dictate a very rigid body. Those that stay at home are expected to lead an easy life (if one excludes traffic jams, that is), and the so-called 'Weight Tax' encourages designers to creep in just below a certain limit to avoid customers having to pay a rather hefty bill.

Japanese buyers expect air conditioning – in all fairness it's difficult to live without it in summer – and all the electrical goodies one can think of, plus automatic transmission, PAS, and so on. At the same time they don't want to pay the tax, and expect an ultra-competitive sticker price to boot. Savings have to be made somewhere, and the body strength suffers. Unwittingly (one assumes, although it could always be an underhand scheme to keep selling new cars at a faster rate!), the 'Weight Tax' therefore dramatically shortens the useful life of a vehicle. In this particular case, lowering weight is the exact opposite of 'Green' thinking. Thankfully, having been around since 1971, it looks as if it will be abandoned in the near future.

When Mercedes-Benz adopted aluminium alloy for the 450SLC 5.0's engine block, wheels, bonnet, bootlid, rear bulkhead and bumpers, it saved a total of 126kg (278lb). This picture was taken at the 1977 Frankfurt Show, when the 5-litre car made its debut. Daimler AG

just before World War I, and contains a high chromium content to give it its resistance to corrosion. Also known as inox steel, some are putting it forward as the best alternative to aluminium or high-strength low-alloy (HSLA) steels due to its excellent anti-fatigue properties (a useful factor in a car body, which gets hammered and twisted countless times every year) and crashworthiness. This, combined with its ability to fight off the dreaded tin-worm, should make it the ideal choice – but unfortunately it isn't so easy to work, and it is now very costly. Of the few cars built with a stainless-steel body, the DeLorean was the best-known example.

One of the beauties of steel is its recyclability, and there's no doubt that recycling can reduce our carbon footprint. In America, the steel industry has been recycling for over 150 years, long before it became fashionable. And with steel it

The Audi ASF, as presented at the 1993 Frankfurt Show. Audi

makes sense – recycling saves 75 per cent of the energy it would take to create a fresh batch from raw materials, the latter including 1,135kg (2,503lb) of iron ore, 635kg (1,400lb) of coal and 55kg (121lb) of limestone to make just one tonne of new metal.

Moving on to aluminium alloy, this was quite a common choice for bodywork on quality sports cars after World War II, but very rare on saloons, other than in the production of lightweight engines, transmission casings and suspension components. Slowly but surely, aluminium was selected for bonnets, and sometimes bootlids and door skins – usually on top-end sports models initially. There was also the occasional concept vehicle here and there, and the Honda NSX sports car – but it's fair to say that Audi was the first to introduce a complete aluminium monocoque body on a mainstream production saloon.

Audi had been studying the plus and minus points of aluminium bodies since 1984, releasing a prototype based on the Audi 100 at the 1985 Hanover Fair. The German firm found there were a number of technical problems to deal with, especially on the manufacturing front, with specialized welding, riveting and bonding techniques having to be developed, as well as new treatment technologies, before aluminium could be declared suitable for a saloon with a high-class image.

Eventually, the Audi ASF concept (with ASF standing for 'Audi space frame') was unveiled with a polished body at the 1993 Frankfurt Show, held that year in September. This used an aluminium frame to which the high-tensile aluminium

Ford's original P2000 research vehicle was unveiled at the 1998 Detroit Show. Powered by a 1.2-litre CIDI diesel engine and weighing about 40 per cent less than the standard Ford Taurus, thanks to the extensive use of aluminium, titanium, magnesium and carbon-fibre, the car delivered some exceptional economy figures. Later P2000s would employ hydrogen as a fuel. Ford

The X350-type Jaguar XJ made good use of aluminium to reduce weight. This helped the big car save fuel, and feel a lot sharper on the road. Jaguar

panels would be attached, and was duly translated into the Audi A8 production car, which made its debut at the Geneva Show in the following spring. The body, at 249kg (549lb), is said to be 239kg (527lb) lighter than the steel equivalent.

Audi then proved that it was possible to build a high-volume aluminium-bodied car at reasonable cost with the 1999 A2, based on the Al2 concept car first displayed at the 1997 Frankfurt Show. A slightly different approach was taken with this second generation ASF, using fewer parts and making others do more functions, leading to a body that weighed in at just 156kg (344lb) – 43 per cent less than an equivalent steel shell. At the same time, laser-beam welding was introduced and robotics were employed to a far greater extent, reducing production time and improving quality.

Even the Americans, who had shown very little interest in weight reduction beyond the fuel crisis years, were starting to take a part in these developments. The worthy Partnership for a New Generation of Vehicles (PNGV) challenge was established in 1993 by the Bill Clinton administration and the auto industry to help move forward the creation of affordable, fuel-efficient, low-emission vehicles capable of meeting all customer needs. Concept cars, such as the 1998 Ford P2000, were born out of the PNGV challenge and sported aluminium bodies, and a number of 'Big Three' run-of-the-mill production saloons and SUVs gained alloy bonnets, bootlids and tailgates.

The Jaguar XJ, having become a real heavyweight after years of safety regulations adding bulk, was revitalized thanks to a stressed all-aluminium alloy body on the X350 of 2003 vintage. Aviation industry adhesives and self-piercing rivets (SPRs) were used in the production of the shell, which

The new Range Rover Evoque uses aluminium for the bonnet and roof, and composite plastics for the tailgate, keeping the car's centre of gravity as low as possible – a key factor in enhancing handling and safety. B. Long

was 40 per cent lighter than a steel version. Another 'Green' element for the 'Big Cat' was the fact that more than half the structure was built using recycled aluminium (there is no difference in the quality of recycled aluminium compared to a fresh batch, and recycling aluminium requires less than 5 per cent of the energy required to make it from bauxite ore), saving over three tonnes of carbon dioxide going into the atmosphere for every XJ produced.

Aluminium bodies are still fairly rare, but they are starting to come on-line via a number of makers now, with the undoubted potential for many more to come. There is also a growing trend for mixing steel and aluminium panels to get the best of both worlds – something previously unheard of due to the extreme difficulty in welding the two metals together.

Mazda was the first to come up with a process using friction to join the two metals, using the technology on the company's RX-8 and MX-5 (NC-type) sports cars. BMW went a different route with the 2004 Model Year E60 5-series, using adhesives and rivets to bond the metals.

Interestingly, the Munich-based manufacturer chose aluminium alloy for the front structure (from the bulkhead forward) and steel for the rest of the shell, reducing weight but at the same time balancing weight distribution, which is never easy on an FR machine. Despite being bigger than earlier 5-series models, the aluminium section allowed the bodyshell to be 20kg (44lb) lighter than before. Mitsubishi also went beyond the norm, making the most of the weight

distribution benefits of aluminium by using it for the roof panel on its Outlander SUV and later models of the Lancer Evolution.

There are those who will point out that body repairs are not as easy as they are with steel shells and panelwork, but technology is evolving all the time in line with experience, and as aluminium bodies become more commonplace, the quality and number of repair facilities is sure to improve.

According to a 2011 study by the University of Aachen in Germany and the European Aluminium Association (the EAA), the average car body can safely shed 40 per cent of its weight by replacing steel with aluminium in selected areas. On a larger vehicle, this could translate into fuel savings of up to 10 per cent, which has to be considered worthwhile.

Add in the findings of a Ford study conducted by Jim de Vries in 2009 – which concluded that from a manufacturing point of view, compared with steel and two forms of SMC plastic (glass- and carbon-fibre-reinforced), aluminium offered the best cost-performance ratio in terms of weight saved – and one wonders why there aren't more aluminium cars on the road as a result. To a great extent, insurance company input is restricting advances, as they want cheap replacement costs first and foremost.

Magnesium alloy body panels have been used on racers, such as the 'Silver Arrows' models of the fifties. But we also saw what happened to the 300SLR that was involved in the 1955 Le Mans disaster – the fire intensity was made that much worse due to the burning characteristics of the lightweight 'Elektron' material. This safety factor, expense, its lack of resistance to even the smallest of car park knocks, and salt corrosion concerns have kept magnesium out of the picture for a long time, although there are now thoughts of applying a thin coating of aluminium to the magnesium alloy sheet. While a number of manufacturers use magnesium alloy for road wheels and certain mechanical components to reduce weight, we shall have to wait and see if anyone is brave enough to bring out the first magnesium alloy-bodied production car.

Having considered the metals traditionally used in car bodies, it's time to look at plastics, resins and composites – an area of technology developing on an almost daily basis. Graphene, for instance, broke cover in 2011, and having been declared 200 times stronger than structural steel, may find its way into the hearts of coachbuilders in the future, while some of the other options have been around for many years.

Fibreglass, also known as FRP or GRP, is old news nowadays, a composite material formed by reinforcing plastic with a fibre mat. The fibres contained within certain high-performance glass-fibres, such as S-Glass, whilst ten times the cost of the common E-Glass ones, have tensile strength

PRODUCTION TECHNIQUES

Modern factories, at least in the so-called developed nations, look nothing like they did in the fifties. In fact, as far as some of the smaller makers are concerned, they look nothing like they did in the seventies and early eighties! Although one quickly notices the robots spot-welding bodyshells, replacing the teams of men who used to gas weld the panel joints, one of the biggest areas of change is in the paint shop.

When the author was in the trade in his younger days, it was common to use cellulose paint to spray a car. Plumes of coloured spray would be created in the process; sometimes the air was so thick you could hardly see across the garage! This was basically a huge volume of VOCs being released into the atmosphere, undoing all the good work of lightweight panel selection, and explains why cellulose paint is slowly being outlawed in so many countries.

Nowadays, virtually all the major manufacturers have turned their back on all types of solvent-based paints and have opted for water-based paints. These are basically the same in many respects – they use the same pigments and the binder is similar,

子どもたちに青空を。

「自由な移動の喜び」を子どもたちの未来へ、青空とともに。
Hondaは、クルマやバイク、太陽電池などをつくる幅ひろい力をいかし、環境のために情熱を注ぎ続けます。

走りの楽しさと低炭素をいろいろな"Honda"で。
ハイブリッド、EV、燃料電池電気自動車を、カーナビやエネルギー技術で支える。

Hondaでいちばん使われているクルマを電気で。
「フィットEVコンセプト」、すべての人に新しい"移動の喜び"を、研究は今日も続いている。

働くバイクを電気で動かし、世の中を変えていく。
電動バイクのたしかな未来は、出前や配達で走り回るEV-neoから始まる。

太陽電池などでHonda製の電気をつくる。
Hondaは、電気を使うものだけでなく、電気をつくる技術も進化させる。

環境にやさしいグリーンファクトリーを育てる。
省エネ・省資源、日本の全工場で廃棄物の社外埋め立て処分が「ゼロ」を続ける。

1976年来の"ふるさとの森づくり"をこれからも。
近くに豊かな"鎮守の森"のような自然の緑をHondaの施設で育てる。

BLUE SKIES FOR OUR CHILDREN

Hondaは、2011年、「自由な移動の喜び」と「豊かで持続可能な社会」の実現をHonda環境ビジョンとして定めました。1970年代、当時最も厳しい排出ガス規制とされた米国マスキー法のクリアにチャレンジしたHondaの技術者は、子どもたちの青空を残したいという思いからも、果敢に取り組みました。「自由な移動の喜び」を次世代(our children)に伝えていきたい、だからこそ、豊かで持続可能な社会(blue skies)を実現させたいという、これまでも、これからも変わらないHondaの環境への取り組みに対する思い、それがこのスローガンに込められました。

ABOVE: Honda has pledged to clean up car production from the raw material stage through to a vehicle's end of life. Honda

BELOW: Modern paint facilities in Toyota's Altona Plant in Australia. Today, spraying cars is a far more eco-friendly exercise than it was in the past. Toyota

but the carrier is water. Yes, it takes longer to dry, but the impact on the environment is negligible compared to finishes such as cellulose, two-pack and COB paint.

As well as using more eco-friendly paint materials, besides improvements in the management of waste-water, oil and solvents, modern manufacturing practices are reducing CO_2 emissions year on year. For example, Subaru recently announced that it had cut the release of carbon dioxide at its Gunma plant by 25 per cent compared with 1990 levels, partly through revised factory heating methods, and in mid-2011, Honda set itself a challenging goal to reduce global CO_2 emissions in both the production phase and supply chain; a few months later, Volkswagen announced it was attempting to make production 25 per cent more environmentally compatible by 2018. In another example of 'Green' thinking, a few years ago, Mazda recycled some of its old plant to make a new line at the Hiroshima factory without incurring any extra costs and waste.

properties approaching carbon-fibre standards, although the finished product (usually moulded in wooden moulds) is ultimately nowhere near as strong or light when comparing sheets of the same thickness. Its advantage is that it costs about the same as mild steel in its cheapest form, it doesn't require pressing tools (which are very expensive to produce – typically around seven to eight times more than moulds), and, being plastic-based, it certainly doesn't rust.

The original Chevrolet Corvette of 1953 was one of the first and best known cars to use fibreglass for its bodywork, Owens-Corning having perfected the fibre strands before World War II. Indeed, the 1946 Owens-Corning-built Stout Scarab Project Y prototype can probably lay claim to being the very first fibreglass-bodied car.

A very early Chevrolet Corvette, featuring a fibreglass body. GM

BODY PANELS FROM PLANTS

As it happens, the first plastic, Parkesine, invented in 1862, was made using plant cellulose. Celluloid, also an organic polymer, followed soon after. The idea of making plastics from natural materials rather than petrochemicals is therefore far from new – indeed, the very origins of plastics can be found in plant life.

With steel being rapidly vacuumed up by the war effort, in August 1941, Henry Ford (thanks to Lowell E. Overly of Ford's Soybean Laboratory) was there with an answer as monumental as the Model T. A contemporary issue of *Popular Mechanics* described the low-key debut with the following prose:

> When Henry Ford recently unveiled his plastic car, the result of twelve years of research, he gave the world a glimpse of the automobile of tomorrow, its tough panels moulded under hydraulic pressure of 1,500psi from a recipe that calls for 70 per cent of cellulose fibres from wheat straw, hemp and sisal plus 30 per cent resin binder. The only steel in the car is its tubular welded frame. The plastic car weighs a ton, 1,000 pounds lighter than a comparable steel car.

In a stroke, Ford had reduced weight by 35 per cent, and as the man himself demonstrated, had given buyers panels that a swinging axe would bounce off. Then, of course, the clouds of war darkened on America to the same extent as Europe, and the idea was brushed to one side – and once the conflict ended, the so-called 'Hemp Car' had as good as been forgotten. No one even knows what happened to it.

In the 1990s several concept cars were made using recycled materials (other than recycled steel, that is), such as the Volvo ECC and Mazda HR-X2, but it took seventy years for the idea presented by Ford to resurface as 'new' technology.

Now a number of manufacturers are starting to consider the advantages of panelwork made from organic materials, as so ably outlined by Henry Ford. For the present, they are seen in concept cars such as the 2010 Honda Air with its vegetable-based polymer panels – but BMW are known to be seriously evaluating similar materials with a view to using them for production. Who knows, soon we may be debating the merits of recyclable versus biodegradable panels.

Henry Ford with the 'Hemp Car' he presented in 1941. Ford actually had a plastic bootlid fitted to his own car so that he could personally demonstrate its strength with a lumberjack's axe! As it happens, Ford was dedicated to environmental issues and waste reduction, such as recycling. Indeed, even the wood used in shipping crates was cut in such a way that it could be used for roofs or floorboards. The great man once said: 'It isn't possible to get something from nothing, but it is possible to get something from what was once considered nothing.' Ford

ABOVE: **'Green' trim materials used on the Citroën C4, including recycled plastics. Most makers are following similar paths. For example, in its latest sustainability report, Ford stated that it was focusing efforts on using as many recycled, renewable and lightweight materials as possible in its vehicle lines.** Citroën

LEFT: **Markings found on plastics nowadays aid recycling, with polyethylene terephthalate (PET or PETE), high-density polyethylene (HDPE), polyvinyl chloride (V or PVC), low-density polyethylene (LDPE), polypropylene (PP), polystyrene (PS), and others that fail to fall within the other six groups.** US DoE

In the case of the Chevrolet, FRP was something new and exciting, adding kudos and saving steel supplies for other, more mundane vehicles, but rather more practical considerations led others to use it. Documents pertaining to the Daimler SP250 project noted that 3,000 bodies a year seems to be the tipping point where investing in tooling for steel bodies makes more sense.

Nissan had difficulties stabilizing FRP, and had abandoned it by 1960, while Auto Union is known to have looked into using it during 1954 and decided against the move until the 1980s, when new technology gave plastic-based composites new appeal. Notwithstanding, for low-volume production runs, and applications where panel shapes were changed on a regular basis, fibreglass was the material of choice, explaining why so many of the smaller makers of the 1960s and 1970s (including the likes of Lotus and Rochdale) opted for it.

Although FRP cannot be recycled, at least the glass used in making the fibre strands can be sourced from bottle banks. However, newer composites and plastics have rapidly been replacing fibreglass in the automotive world since the 1980s.

It is in plastics that so many variations are seen, although only a few are of any real use in car bodies. Plastics are basically synthetic polymers, largely employing petrochemicals as a base in today's industry, although some use organic ingredients in their make-up. This latter point is interesting from a 'Green' angle, and is looked at in more detail in the accompanying sidebar.

Thermoplastics can be easily re-formed with the application of heat (making them easier to recycle – PET bottles being a good example), whereas thermosetting polymers use a chemical reaction so a piece maintains its shape as soon as it is set. Ultimately, however, they are both plastics, and both groups come with a wide variety of properties, such as differences in weight and strength, and the way they react to certain chemicals.

Ironically it was probably the US bumper regulations of the mid-1970s that accelerated the use of plastics (as opposed to GRP) for body panels. Moving away from separate bumper blades, Porsche used polyurethane skins to cover the nose and tail of the 928, introduced at the 1977 Geneva Show. Nowadays, polypropylene thermoplastic is a more popular choice, but either way, today's plastic car components are always marked up as one of seven category types ready for the afterlife – the recycling of plastic saves twice the energy it takes to incinerate it.

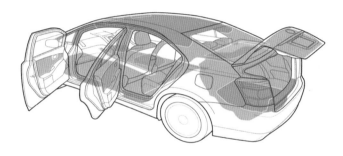

Total Ecological Plastic coverage
approx. 80% of interior surface

New Ecological Plastic coverage

In 2011, Toyota announced that it will be using sugar-cane-derived plastics for a number of its interior surfaces. Toyota

At a fraction of the price of even the cheapest carbon-fibre, thermoset SMC (sheet-moulded composite) plastic is also finding favour with automobile manufacturers, giving a good balance of strength and lightweight characteristics – and, of course, it doesn't rust. Generally, SMC is made up of widely available calcium carbonate (almost half by volume), 25 per cent resin, 25 per cent glass reinforcement (which can be replaced or augmented by carbon fibres), and a small amount of other elements, although the mix can be varied to suit the application.

It can be heated and moulded with ease to form unstressed panels such as doorskins, bonnets and bootlids. Mazda used it for the first MX-5 Miata hardtop, which tipped the scales at 22kg (48lb). Granted, the sizes aren't exactly the same, but compare this to 42kg (93lb) for a steel one off the R107 Mercedes SL, and one begins to see the benefits.

Plastics will doubtless be used more and more, with Ford using a special hybrid plastic for the front bulkhead on its latest Taurus, for instance, and Chrysler building the CCV concept, employing fully recyclable PET resin panels glued to a steel chassis, though with an eye on future production under the Daimler-Benz merger the project was put on hold. This glass-reinforced PET plastic, known as Impet

Hi, was also seen on the Dodge ESX2 and Plymouth Pronto Spyder concepts, and can now be bought through Ticona.

Aptera (formally Accelerated Composites) was working on an interesting idea that combined E-Glass matting with epoxy resin and sandwich technology to create a reasonably priced LITE (standing for lightweight, impact-resistant, total cost-reducing and efficient) composite body panel material that was three times stronger than automotive steel, but weighed 30 per cent less. Although Aptera went bankrupt in 2011, it remains to be seen whether Energetx Composites,

The Dodge ESX2 concept of 1998 used a glass-reinforced PET plastic material called 'Impet Hi' for its bodywork. It was half the weight of a Dodge Intrepid with a traditional body, and also halved the upfront investment necessary for tooling. Meanwhile, across town, GM's Saturn brand was making extensive use of thermoplastics for body panels on its early models. Chrysler

The Aptera, whilst displaying exceptional aerodynamics, was also to have showcased a new form of composite body construction. Sadly, Aptera was declared bankrupt before the company had a chance to bring the concept to market. Aptera

Daihatsu's D-X concept of 2011, with interchangeable resin panels to give four different bodywork variations for the same car. Daihatsu

who were to produce Aptera bodies, will be able to market the new material.

Exotic synthetic aramides (aromatic polyamides) such as Kevlar, invented by DuPont in 1971, and five times stronger than steel, weight for weight, will likely remain in the upper echelons of the aerospace industry or in military and law enforcement applications, as carbon-fibre sheet reinforced by Kevlar fibres costs half as much again as regular carbon-fibre, which is already considered expensive by most people.

Although one of the first examples of using Kevlar composite for car bodywork dates back to the Audi Sport Quattro of 1984, this was hardly a mass-production vehicle (just 224 of these Group B homologation specials were made),

and it is far more likely to be seen employed on armoured cars than family saloons.

Whenever one calls to mind space-age and composite racing-car materials, one inevitably thinks of carbon-fibre. Also known as carbon-fibre reinforced plastic (or CFRP), carbon-fibre is significantly lighter than steel but around ten times stronger, and therefore able to absorb over twice the energy of steel in a typical collision. It is seen in small quantities on top-end sports cars, but rarely full bodies.

There is a simple reason for this. Unfortunately, even though prices are coming down rapidly thanks to innovative companies such as Toray (the cost today is ten times less than it was a decade ago, but still ten times higher than steel!), space-age materials are simply not suitable for mainstream mass-production vehicles as yet – the cost would be too high, pushing the car's selling price beyond what most customers would be willing to pay.

Indeed, before coming up with its new 'aRTM' (advanced Resin Transfer Moulding) technique, which has at least made things a little more realistic, Volkswagen estimated a twenty-fold increase in manufacturing costs if carbon-fibre was used to replace steel on one of its concept vehicles. Tesla, too, concluded that aluminium bodywork made more sense than carbon-fibre in cost-performance terms, the US manufacturer deciding to move across to alloy coachwork in the transition from the Roadster sports car to the Model S saloon; it also replaced a number of earlier CFRP parts on the Roadster, with cheaper SMC versions in areas where the strength and stiffness of carbon-fibre wasn't required.

Even so, aircraft makers are starting to turn to the material, which is usually made by some form of moulding, such

MATERIAL WEIGHT COMPARISON

This table shows the typical weight of carbon-fibre (shown as a percentage based on various pieces of 1018 mild steel bar measuring the same) and the material's ultimate tensile strength. It also shows the estimated cost, expressed as a percentage of mild steel to put things into perspective.

	Weight	Strength (UTS)	Cost
Mild steel	100%	63,800psi/440MPa	100%
Carbon-fibre	18%	441,000psi/3040MPa	965%

It should be remembered that there are many types of carbon-fibre. Some variants, those baked at around 1,500°C, are rated at up to 820,000psi/5650MPa.

A carbon-fibre roof panel being made for the BMW M3. Toyota uses plastics on some of its cars fitted with panoramic roofs – with plastic having a specific density of roughly half that of glass, the weight saving is 40 per cent. BMW

as RTM, and baking. This lends itself to short production runs, with quicker, cheaper shape changes possible compared to cars built up using traditional pressing tools.

Low-volume cars such as the Mercedes-Benz SLR McLaren and GTA Spano use a lot of carbon-fibre, while BMW specified it for the roof on the M3 CSL, reducing overall weight and lowering the vehicle's centre of gravity. Cars like the Chevy Corvette and Dodge Viper have used it, as have the Ford GT and certain Mustang variants.

Maybe some day carbon-fibre bonnets, generally only offered by aftermarket suppliers at this stage, will become as common as aluminium items. Although it is far from straightforward to recycle, it is achievable, and given the strength and weight-saving benefits, one can only hope that new techniques are found to make carbon-fibre more accessible to the motor industry. After all, reducing a body-in-white (BIW) to two-thirds the bulk has a huge effect on fuel consumption.

As it happens, a lot of weight was saved in the transition from bodies being bolted to separate chassis frames to the use of unit construction (or monocoque) steel bodies. Although the innovative 1922 Lancia Lambda can lay claim to being the first monocoque car, it was really cars such as the Chrysler Airflow, Citroën Traction Avant and Opel Olympia of the mid-1930s which made the manufacturing technique fashionable. Even then, it wasn't until the early sixties that its use was widespread throughout the industry, partly because of its lack of suitability on smaller volumes and the restrictions it placed on minor design changes.

With most of the cars we see on the road today having a unit body, and the aforementioned balance required on material selection, one has to wonder if any weight can be saved on the multitude of plain vanilla saloons in the real world, given current safety regulations. But here, computer technology can give us the 'Green' angle, with modern CAD/CAM programmes able to place strength in just the right places, reducing all excess in the body architecture.

The latest programmes, helped by the rapid advances in supercomputer technology and data handling, are thousands of times more effective, to the point of suggesting different types and different gauges of steel (including the increasing use of lamination) to be employed in specific locations, all to save a few grams here and there without compromising bodyshell strength.

The Teewave AR1 electric vehicle was displayed on the Toray stand at the 2011 Tokyo Show. Designed by Gordon Murray, the two-seater sports car used an all-carbon-fibre body, keeping the weight down to just 846kg (1,865lb) – around 420kg (926lb) less than the same vehicle would weigh if steel coachwork had been employed. Gordon Murray Design

The 1934 Chrysler Airflow – an early monocoque-bodied vehicle, and one that started a worldwide trend on aerodynamic styling. Chrysler

THE PORSCHE FLA

The Porsche FLA two-door, four-seater hatchback was a rare, shining example of 'Green' thinking from the 1970s, its eco credentials accomplished not only by lowering weight, but in particular by providing a longer service life – something on which metal choice, or selection of plastics or composites, can have a huge bearing.

Introduced at the 1973 Frankfurt Show, a time during which Porsche research indicated that 12 million cars were being scrapped annually having served an average of just ten years on the road, the FLA (or 'Long Life Car') was at the spearhead of a fresh line of thought that had taken eighty years to evolve. As Henry Ford once so eloquently said: 'Thinking is the hardest work there is, which is probably why so few engage in it.'

To make the FLA last longer than the norm, Porsche employed a rust-proof steel chassis and aluminium bodywork. This stemmed corrosion, and it also reduced weight, allowing a lazy engine to be fitted – its 75bhp was low for a 2.5-litre unit, but this lack of stress would enhance longevity. In the same vein, the engine was linked to a three-speed automatic gearbox to reduce the amount of driving at high revs, thus reducing wear and tear on the whole drivetrain. The Fuchs alloy wheels were another weight-saving measure.

Even after the car's useful life came to an end, Porsche's engineers had thought about recycling, with the extensive use of aluminium, as plastic recycling techniques hadn't been properly developed at the time. Naturally the FLA concept wasn't liked within the industry, and the oil crisis gave an ideal opportunity to shift attention to fuel consumption instead of longevity. The exercise at least gave rise to Porsche leading the way in the adoption of galvanized steel panels for production vehicles.

The Porsche FLA at the 1973 Frankfurt Show.
Porsche

The teardrop shape of the rear-engined Auto Union was a perfect example of pre-war aerodynamics, but the design would never suit a road car! Audi

AERODYNAMICS

What shape is an arrowhead? What shape is a bullet? For that matter, what shape is a ship's bow? The importance of aerodynamics has been known since long before man invented the automobile, but only recently have designers made a concerted effort to reduce air resistance (or drag) on production-car bodies. Indeed, before the 1980s, while it was common enough to see streamlining in racing and sports cars, few saloons received the kind of detailed design work they garner today.

According to the US Department of Energy's current figures, in an average car, overcoming wind resistance can account for 4 per cent of fuel consumption at town speeds, rising to 16 per cent at a highway pace. This can be explained by the fact that drag can increase by as much as eight times as a vehicle doubles its speed. Saying that everyone should drive slowly isn't realistic (even though Japan seems to thinks it is!), so aerodynamics come into play. Reducing a vehicle's coefficient of drag (expressed as a Cd figure in brochures) can increase its energy efficiency, and therefore make it more eco-friendly as a result.

Unfortunately, this area of automotive design – like so many others – is largely a huge compromise. A body shaped like Concorde would be ideal for cutting through the air and reducing wind noise to a minimum, but it simply isn't practical for an average road car. We have to balance things like the packaging of drivetrain components, passenger accommodation and ergonomics, luggage space, global safety regulations, limits of material properties, and last, but certainly not least, fashion trends. At the same time, this all needs combining within reasonable dimensions that one has come to expect for a certain vehicle class.

The ideal scenario is to get a motor vehicle to look as close to an aeroplane as possible. Some of the best aerodynamics in the early post-war years were seen on cars from companies with strong aero-industry links, such as Saab (seen here) and Bristol. Saab

as the Citroën DS. But vehicles like this were the exception rather than norm. Not until the shockwaves created by the first Ford Sierra, launched in the autumn of 1982, did aero-dynamics really catch the attention of the general public, spurring designers on to try that little bit harder.

Basically, one is looking for a small frontal area, and a smooth airflow up over the bonnet and around the wings. The sides should contain the gentlest of curves, and prefer-ably taper inwards at the back of the vehicle. The wind-screen should be curved at the sides and raked at an angle that allows the air to flow uninterruptedly off the bonnet, before making its way over a long roof (hence TWR using a Volvo estate rather than a saloon for BTCC racing, however unlikely it may have seemed to the casual onlooker). Cars

The beauty of good aerodynamics can be readily illustrated by the Porsche 356. With a 1.1-litre engine rated at 40bhp, it was capable of 140km/h (87mph). The vaguely contemporary but boxy 1.1-litre Austin A40 Farina, weighing almost exactly the same and having 8bhp more, had a top speed of 124km/h (77mph). In other words, the more easily a car slips through the air, the less power – and therefore fuel – will be needed to reach a certain pace. Porsche

The Ford Sierra of 1982 vintage really set the tone for modern aerodynamic thinking. Ford

While the Tatra concern can probably lay claim to the use of advanced aerodynamics on road cars before most (the Czech firm even employing Paul Jaray of Zeppelin fame as a consultant), in terms of groundbreaking mainstream saloons that adopted aerodynamic bodywork early on, one inevitably points to the Chrysler Airflow – a project headed by Carl Breer. The 1934 Airflow duly inspired a lot of makers across the pond in Europe – from Peugeot to Panhard & Levassor, and even conservative Volvo. On the other side of the world, the fledgling Toyota concern selected the Airflow as the inspiration for its first car, the Type AA.

After World War II, it was the Europeans who led the way, with cars like the VW Beetle (and Porsche 356 from the same family of engineers), and later, masterpieces such

The smooth underbody of a Porsche 964; the practice is no longer restricted to sports cars. The component parts underneath the first Lexus LS400 were refined and refined until drag and noise were reduced to an absolute minimum. Porsche

A Mercedes W211 E-Class model in the wind tunnel. Detail work got the Cd figure down to 0.26, which is excellent for a family saloon. Daimler AG

with a traditional boot should have the tail up high to try and disturb the air as little as possible.

These are the fundamental elements of streamlining, but today we see far more attention to minute details, with things like lighting units that become part of the body shape, tighter panel gaps, flush glazing and door handles, windscreen wipers that drop out of the airflow, sculptured door mirrors, revised cooling systems, underbody panels, tiny spoilers to redirect air around the tyres, and plain wheel designs (or wheelcovers), although alloy wheels with open spokes are better for brake cooling on high-performance machines. There are also manufacturers designing their cars to ride lower as speeds increase above a certain amount, as, according to Mercedes-Benz, lowering the ride height at speed can result in a 3 per cent improvement in drag.

One should remember, however, that the coefficient of drag is only part of the story. Frontal area is just as impor-

Unveiled at the 2011 Qatar Motor Show, Volkswagen's XL1 diesel-hybrid concept has a remarkable Cd of 0.19. This, combined with an exceptionally low weight of just 795kg (1,753lb) – thanks to the extensive use of alloy and carbon-fibre for the bodywork – gives us a view of what we should expect in the near future. Volkswagen

tant, and if we multiply the car's Cd by its frontal area, we get an index of total drag – the so-called drag area (or CdA) – which gives a far better indication of aerodynamic performance.

A Hummer H2 has a Cd figure of 0.57, and a CdA of $2.46m^2$. Compare this to Cd 0.26 and a drag area of $0.58m^2$ for a Toyota Prius (XW20), and one starts to see the difference. Add in the additional weight factor (a gap of 1,583kg/2,547lb in this case) in view of what we've discussed earlier in the chapter, and it's not hard to see why the 'Green' brigade is anti-SUV and anti-minivan. It does seem rather ironic that the countries currently most vocal in demanding better fuel efficiency and lower emissions, America and Japan, sell these vehicles in such huge volumes.

TYRE TECHNOLOGY

Says one old Grand Prix racer to another, looking at a modern F1 machine: 'I remember when the drivers were fat and the tyres were thin!' The same thing has happened with road cars, with tyre widths increasing at a rapid rate in the name of fashion, and not just on sporting models, either. If one takes the base Ford Escort as a fair example of an average family saloon, and compares it with today's equivalent, the Mondeo, one finds that the standard tyre width has increased by 46 per cent.

There's no doubt that wider rubber looks good, and generally enhances handling. So what is the problem, one may ask? Well, the wider the tyre, the greater the aerodynamic drag. Wider tyres also call for more noise insulation to keep NVH in check, which means more weight. For the sake of fashion, then, and minute differences in academic handling, figures that only really make a difference in magazine road tests (normal road users will hardly ever get near to approaching limits, and hard drivers can always change tyres if they want to), we find ourselves with needlessly wide tyres that make themselves heard over every surface irregularity.

Width also has a bearing on rolling resistance (also known as rolling drag, or rolling friction). According to the US Department of Energy, rolling resistance can account for around 4 per cent of fuel consumption in town driving, rising to an average of 7 per cent at highway speeds. This becomes all the more ironic when one thinks of all the hard work done to cut Cd figures through innovative ideas, not to mention the work on powertrains to make them more fuel-efficient. Specifying a narrower tyre width would reduce drag and rolling resistance at a stroke, thus improving economy and reducing emissions!

Unable to go the locomotive route (steel wheels running on steel tracks, the latter usually coming with a rounded top surface to further cut rolling drag), new technology is being introduced all the time to reduce rolling resistance without loss of performance. As an example, Dunlop promotes the Enasave range, with one type of tyre – the Enasave 97 – doing its bit for the environment by employing ENR (evolutional natural rubber) which is 97 per cent free of petroleum products, in addition to featuring tread patterns aimed at reducing rolling resistance (thus cutting CO_2 emissions during the manufacturing and disposal stages, and improving fuel economy whilst in use), while a second series saves energy through low rolling-resistance technology.

Yokohama uses solar power at some of its factories, and has its own eco-friendly tyre – the dB line, with reduced petroleum product content, and now the BluEarth range. Indeed, most of the makers are now starting to offer 'Green'

We grow up with wide alloy wheels shod with fat tyres being the ultimate symbol of glamour. But most of the time we just don't need all that rubber on the road, and narrower tyres save fuel. B. Long

The Fulda EcoControl tyre.
Fulda

As the current Michelin advertising campaign quite correctly says: 'The Right Tire Changes Everything.'
Michelin

unheard of. After scrapping, tyres are usually shredded or placed directly in landfill sites with no benefit to the world, although a few recycling projects are in hand – making floor coverings for playgrounds and running tracks, for instance, and a process known as pyrolysis that can generate fuel. With some further development, pyrolysis could provide the answer to a long-term headache, as it also allows steel bracing to be retrieved, and uses more than half of the tyre's weight effectively. A number of industries have also started using tyres instead of coal for fuel, employing tyre-derived fuel (TDF) in ever-increasing volumes – so all is not lost, it seems.

Finally, we can all do something as simple as using the throttle with a lighter touch (on and off) to reduce our carbon footprint. Correct tyre inflation also has a huge bearing on fuel economy: if tyre pressures are low, rolling resistance increases, so something as simple as regular checks to make sure the tyres are running with the right pressures can save fuel, as well as improve the vehicle's safety levels at the same time.

alternatives after years of stressing handling benefits in the sales blurb. As we said way back in the Introduction to this book, 'Green' sells in today's marketplace.

It should be noted that the tyres used on Henry Ford's 1941 'Hemp Car' were actually made from goldenrod plants to a formula invented by Ford's friend, Thomas Edison. Edison had been working on the idea from the early 1900s, but interest died off just before World War I, when synthetic rubber became all the rage. However, with modern science, maybe the thought of making tyres from plants should be reconsidered – we'd have less reliance on petrochemicals, and recycling or disposal would surely be far more straightforward.

Notwithstanding the efforts of manufacturers to help the environment, tyre disposal remains a serious problem. Retreading (or remould) services can extend a tyre's useful life, but this option is not as common as it was when the author was a child, and in some countries it is virtually

LIGHTER COMPONENTS

As discussed in the earlier sections, more body weight equals the need for more powerful engines to maintain

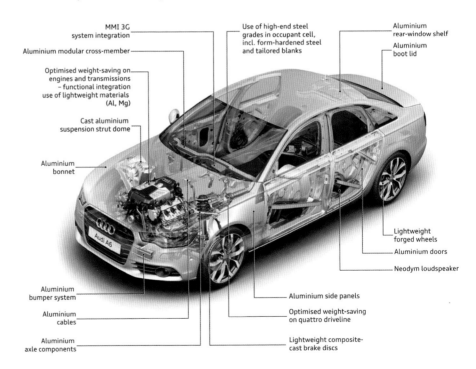

The Audi A6, introduced in 2011, uses all the know-how gained from earlier aluminium body production, as well as a host of other lightweight technology in order to save fuel, and therefore reduce emissions. Audi

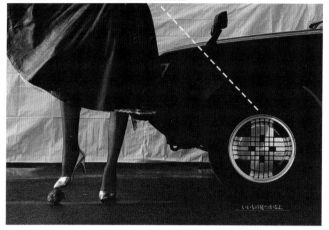

視線を自由に遊ばせてごらん。

MELBER ALLOY WHEELS DESIGNED by GIUGIARO

Advertising for Melber alloys, designed by Giugiaro.
Easyriders

performance levels. This calls for bigger brakes and heavier suspension parts, which in turn calls for yet more power to cancel things out. It's a vicious circle, which can either be tackled by a complete redesign, taking a new generation of vehicles back to basics (a costly and brave move), by reducing standard equipment levels (something that would almost certainly backfire in today's marketplace), or by the reduction of weight in components.

Alloy wheels are probably one of the most common routes in weight reduction. Aluminium alloys are the norm, with forging and casting techniques also making a difference in the final weight, while magnesium alloys are an exotic option. Although not a weight saver, from an ecology point of view, it's interesting to note that Toyota started a move a few years ago to reduce its use of lead, and specified different metals for wheel-balance weights.

For several years now, Mitsubishi Denki has been concentrating on making its starter motors and alternators lighter. And at Toyoda Gosei (a parts supplier that originated from the R&D arm of Toyota), too, more and more effort is directed towards weight reduction on smaller automotive components, gradually replacing metals with resins and polymers, and making good use of LED technology, which allows lower energy use and longer service life in lighting units. Even rubber seals are optimized to give exactly the required amount of sealing and cushioning effect, cutting out excess weight and material usage.

The Mitsuba Corporation is following the same lighter, smaller route with a lot of its electric motors 'to contribute to the realization of a low-carbon society by creating new technologies'. Certain things in the product listing, such as electric cooling fans and power-steering systems, saving a drain on engine power – thus saving fuel – are now com-

We Admit, There Are Still A Few Cars With Parts We Can't Replace.

You'd think with everything from alternators to emission systems to batteries, we'd have something to fit every car in the world. The fact is we do have quality parts for over 95% of all the cars and trucks on the road. Still, we've somehow managed to overlook the best-selling "car" in America. But then, considering that ACDelco already does offer over 65,000 reliable parts, getting our engineers to come up with a part to fit that should be childs play. For more info, contact 1-800-ACDelco or http://www.acdelco.com

ACDelco
It's like buying time.

Component makers play a large role in overall weight reduction. With an average of 15,000 parts per vehicle, saving a few grams on each soon adds up. AC Delco

Porsche's lightweight PCCB braking system. Porsche

The spacesaver spare is an excellent way of saving weight. B. Long

monplace (electric air-conditioning compressors are making inroads, too), but the company has recently developed a shutter grille actuator that controls the size of the opening in the front grille, balancing and optimizing aerodynamics with the necessary level of air needed for cooling and intake purposes. Something similar was introduced by Porsche for the 928, but this new version, controlled by the engine ECU, should make the technology available to a far wider audience.

The European and American component-makers are also committed to saving weight wherever possible. Ironically, some of the biggest savings are found in high-performance machines, such as the ceramic brake discs for the Porsche 911 range and a few other sports cars. The Porsche ceramic composite brake (PCCB) option, whilst fiercely expensive, offered a 50 per cent weight saving compared to steel discs. Full carbon discs promise even lighter weight, but their characteristics make them less suitable for road car use.

At the other end of the scale, we have companies such as Schaeffler working on lightweight differentials, a third smaller and lighter than the norm, as well as active electric differentials for EVs that provide and distribute motive power to an axle set through a single unit.

One thing that could be considered by makers as a far cheaper way of saving weight is the fitting of a slightly smaller fuel tank. We all have an image of how heavy a litre bottle of water is. Well, multiply that up until it amounts to 10 per cent of your fuel tank capacity, and before you know it, you have several kilos. A smaller tank would mean more fuel stops, but most people wouldn't even notice the difference over a month. It's a move that would reduce weight, thereby improving fuel consumption, with the added bonus that it would free up extra luggage space.

When it comes to the majority of road users, beyond throwing out all the unnecessary junk one finds in the boot and door pockets, making parts stay longer in service is more realistic than reducing weight. A stainless-steel exhaust system is a good investment, for instance, if one plans on keeping a vehicle for any length of time. It's not any lighter than an OE exhaust, but it does last longer and uses very little more in the way of energy to create, so is therefore an ecologically sound move.

A stand at the 2011 Tokyo Show, pointing out the formula for success in keeping emissions in check via the right components: low friction, downsizing, and weight reduction. Manufacturers are following the same route with vehicle design, with Mazda's Skyactiv programme providing a perfect example. B. Long

CHAPTER EIGHT

WHAT THE FUTURE HOLDS

Gazing into a crystal ball usually gives a very foggy image, and little else – certainly nothing of any use that we can rely on and start planning our future around. To give this chapter some meaning – whilst temporarily turning a blind eye to a lot of things, such as power generation techniques and the wide, often inexcusable disparity in industrial emissions regulations from country to country – it's perhaps easier to separate what's truly possible in the near future, and what would be nice to see happening in the long term.

WHAT CAN BE DONE NOW

On the petrol engine front, one wonders how much more can be done without having to pass on excessive cost to the customer. And at the end of the day, this is an important factor to remember – not everyone is in a position to pay for superior technology, even if they have good intentions with regard to saving the planet.

However, one has to admit that things such as higher compression ratios will be necessary to promote cleaner burning, which may be easier to accomplish if the petrochemical companies helped develop new fuels for the purpose. Mazda's Skyactiv powertrain is already making a 14.0:1 c/r

on a gasoline engine a reality, and other companies are sure to adopt a similar approach now we seem to have reached a limit on leaner mixtures.

Inspired engineering concepts such as the Volkswagen TSI engine and the promising Scuderi split-cycle unit point to the future, linked with new transmissions that make the most of power-bands, and more efficient exhaust systems that last longer and make greater use of readily available, preferably recycled materials.

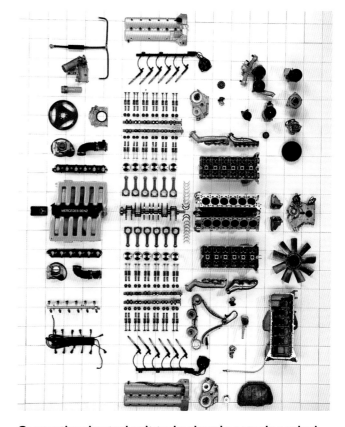

Conventional petrol unit technology has surely peaked. This Mercedes-Benz V12 from the early 1990s shows what goes into an engine, but other than lighter components and micro-hybrid add-ons, it's hard to see where any huge improvements can be made in the basic engineering. Daimler AG

Sony showing the 'Road To Zero' – an eco-friendly product development from start to finish, including power sources for manufacturing. Sony

Cheaper but more frequent testing is going to be a key factor in keeping cars 'Greener' for longer. Today's extended service intervals are a mixed blessing in many respects, and more needs to be done to encourage servicing of vehicles once they leave the care of approved dealerships. Ruben de Rijcke/Creative Commons

As well as lowering our oil dependence bit by bit as an obvious way of reducing our carbon footprint, more stringent but affordable testing, carried out on an annual, or even half-yearly basis, is possibly an answer, too, thus encouraging regular maintenance, and making sure that emission levels are acceptable.

In Britain, despite annual vehicle condition testing, a 1991 article in a leading automotive magazine proclaimed that with new carbon monoxide emissions checks coming into force, 263 out of 528 cars tested would fail the latest MoT test. This was a fascinating statistic – but it was also declared that over 85 per cent of the vehicles which failed the initial inspection could be serviced and/or tuned to give the required level of exhaust emissions. In other words, this points to the chance of almost half of the cars on British roads being out of tune, which tends to make a mockery of manufacturers' fuel economy and emissions figures published in the brochures!

Add in a snippet of information from Duckhams released in the same year, that British motorists were responsible for dumping around 40,000 tons of used oil into the ground and/ or water system, and one can see why environmentalists are up in arms. No matter how much the engineers strive to clean up exhaust emissions and solve other technological problems, once a vehicle is sold, all their good work is undone in minutes if a car falls into the wrong hands. Owning

an automobile requires more responsibility than simply filling it with fuel and washing it every now and again.

Looking elsewhere, the Japanese Shaken calls for testing every two or three years, which gives older cars the potential to be out of tune for many months unless they're serviced regularly. But with the high cost of the strict test, many choose to shy away from garages until the Shaken is due – false economy, but understandable for those on a tight budget, who often put money to one side to lessen the shock of the bi-annual bill on cars over three years old.

America has an even worse scenario, going from one extreme to the other, with no fewer than thirteen states allowing cars to stay on the road without any safety or emissions checks whatsoever. Even those states with some sort of test often enforce no more than a simple visual inspection on emissions equipment (no exhaust gas values are required) on cars of a certain age, with many places exempting vehicles over fifteen years old. California has a well-deserved reputation for trying to clean up the air, but testing is biannual, and not necessary at all on pre-1976 models; and New York's regulations have the potential to make it even easier for real polluters to stay on the road.

Compared to gasoline engines, diesel technology is still fairly new in regular saloons, for only recently has it been accepted as a mainstream form of motive power in passenger cars in historical terms. Only three decades ago, a diesel variant was still considered a rather quirky option for commercial purposes or those of a frugal bent who despised the high cost of petrol. It was a noisy, smelly experience, and refuelling was usually accompanied by a long session at a washbasin trying to get rid of a slimy residue that seemed to hold fast to one's hands for days.

Diesel technology had tended to be developed with trucks and buses in mind for many years, with more emphasis on improving power and torque figures than refinement. I can well remember an old Mercedes 200D (W115 series) owned by a colleague, which was agricultural enough to put me off diesel forever, despite regular servicing – but I can also remember the leaps and bounds in NVH control displayed in the Peugeot 306 owned by a friend about ten years later. More recent experience of the current Mercedes-Benz range has almost managed to convert me. But the key point is that progress is visible, whereas top class petrol-engined machines of the pre-war era can display the same level of refinement as the cars of today, despite the latter having had eighty years or so in which to take advantage of new technology.

If engineers put the same amount of effort into making the diesel engine burn cleaner as the marketing types did into increasing its general appeal, who knows what's possible? However, in the short term we can probably expect little more than cleaner fuels and better exhaust cleaning systems than pure mechanical improvements. After all, you don't fix what isn't broken, and right now, diesel is king as far as Europe's PR agencies are concerned.

The hybrid vehicle will probably have a greater impact on our lives than pure EVs for some time to come, although battery technology is sure to make progress in leaps and bounds, bringing the sight of roads filled with electric vehi-cles ever closer to reality. The main problem with EVs at the moment is not so much poor range (studies conducted all over Europe conclude our average mileage requirements can generally be met by even the feeblest of electric vehicles), but the fact that we need to clean up national grid power-generation first, and that might not happen for decades.

Meanwhile, other than in California where the General Motors EV1 project got things rolling, there is a distinct lack of infrastructure for EV users at the moment, probably

SELLING 'GREEN' TO MAKE GREENBACKS

A few years ago, a number of countries introduced scrappage schemes to encourage sales of more fuel-efficient vehicles. The timing just so happened to coincide with a global recession, triggered by the Lehman Shock of 2008, but – not wishing to sound cynical – we have to assume it couldn't possibly have been set in motion earlier, and the move was simply introduced to help the planet, rather than shift more vehicles in one of the darkest eras in the history of car sales (at least in established markets) since the Great Depression.

In all fairness, with automobile sales booming, China probably didn't have to announce such a scheme to increase showroom activity, but it did anyway (implemented in June 2009), which points to a more noble cause – getting heavy polluters off the road, and replacing them with more efficient vehicles. In addition, Canada announced its 'Vehicle Efficiency Incentive' and 'Retire Your Ride' schemes long before the financial crisis, kicking things off in the spring of 2007; Italy and Norway were other countries to offer a scrappage scheme early on.

Some countries were fairly blunt on their motives, with Britain saying it was to stimulate the car business after the Lehman Shock and the credit crisis that followed, and indeed, half of the trade-in incentive was put forward by the motor industry itself, with the other half from the government.

Most countries, however, packaged the bait in some sort of 'Green' wrapping – America, Japan, France, Germany, Austria, Ireland and a few others included – with special deals being given to those buying hybrids or LEV models. Ironically, it was later discovered that a significant number of cars hadn't been scrapped at all in some places, and had mysteriously found their way to poorer countries. Parts could also be sold on in certain schemes, which would naturally enable older machines to keep running for longer.

America's CARS incentive, aimed at 'reducing fuel consumption', found that the most common trade-in was the heavy Ford Explorer 4×4, with the best-selling car in the scheme being the compact Toyota Corolla. The CARS programme helped shift around 680,000 vehicles (a figure that was most welcome after the huge bailouts granted to US automakers) and is reckoned to have saved around 30 million gallons of petrol a year, as well as cut carbon dioxide emissions by about 380,000 tonnes – a drop in the ocean in the overall scheme of things Stateside, but something, as long as we ignore the energy used to produce the vehicles!

In reality, it was much like the William V. Roth proposal of the early 1990s, when the Senator put forward a scheme to give makers a credit against their CAFE rating whenever one of their cars was scrapped – a way of perking up business with a shallow environmental twist. A congress report stated that around 60,000 jobs were created (plus a fair few saved, of course, usefully reducing UAW pressure) and almost \$8 billion added to the US GDP figure – but one had to read a long way through before coming to the bit that read 'annual savings from the CARS programme represent roughly 0.02 per cent of both [fuel] consumption and [CO_2] emissions'.

On the other side of the Pacific, Japan even extended incentives to buy eco-friendly electrical goods, which was a great success, and the author can vouch for the added efficiency of modern air-conditioning units upon checking earlier bills for electricity against those after the new units were installed. But on the car side, whilst starting off with the best intentions, it soon became a trade war. America, in particular, complained that the scheme favoured certain Japanese cars, which, by strange coincidence, happened to be fuel-efficient – but apparently that doesn't matter. Hillary Clinton cried foul, threatening to take things to the WTO, and claiming it was a masked form of protectionism. The Japanese government caved in to this political pressure within minutes, and ultimately gave rebates to people trading in their frugal, lightweight Honda Civics for a Ford Escape SUV, or an even more unlikely Hummer H3. This was a shining example of how much the environment really counts when the chips are down.

Toyota Prius models lined up at a **US POE** in 2011. The hybrid is definitely here to stay, with **PHEVs** further extending the breed's 'Green' credentials, assuming utility companies do what is expected of them in the future. Long-term maintenance costs, such as replacing batteries and complicated electrical control units, handled by specialist mechanics, are a worry, though, and will probably prematurely retire a lot of vehicles.
Toyota

camera manufacturers did with data cards for digital cameras, we could see an age when slot-in batteries became the norm, changed at the service stations where we currently buy our regular fuels, and priced to include rental. Buyers of new cars would be required to pay a deposit only, as the battery packs would belong to either a chain of service stations, or a maker's association of some sort, either on the car side or the energy supplier one. It's hardly a new concept – an exchange battery service for EVs had first been proposed almost 120 years ago, in 1896.

The idea of exchangeable batteries isn't a new one – witness this **LE306 Mercedes** of 1972 vintage. The concept was continued for the **307E**, as battery life was only worth 48km (30 miles) at that time. Now batteries last longer and are lighter and far more compact, so a slot-in design shouldn't present a real problem. Daimler AG

An EV charging station set up in Saitama, next to Tokyo, in 2010. Honda Soltec made the solar power generation system, with the voltage supplied by the sun going through a power conditioner and a distribution board to give single-phase 100V and 200V AC supplies, as well as a three-phase line to supply the fast charger on the right in this picture. Honda has just established a solar-powered hydrogen generation station close to it. Honda

because there are still only a few electric cars on the road. But on saying that, high-voltage charging points in public places could be a mixed blessing, with the question of safety, vandalism and unauthorized use raising concerns in certain quarters. Granted, this isn't so much of a problem in countries like Japan, where some 7-Eleven convenience stores have them outside, but a lot of effort would have to be made to avoid abuse in certain parts of Europe and America.

However, rather than clutter streets with charging posts, which only adds cost and wastes a lot of energy in the set-up stages, if everyone could agree on a world standard, as

Smaller batteries are being recycled more and more, but a stronger network is needed for EV batteries. Some get used as storage batteries by energy utilities and households after their useful life as a car battery comes to an end (Nissan and Sumitomo Corporation launched a scheme to promote this in Japan, for example, which could help lower battery prices in the long run), but the stage after that needs looking into with more depth.
Call2recycle

As another alternative, Nissan has backed a Ukrainian idea for a floor-mounted contactless charging system, which is less open to abuse due to its car-only application, using a receiver on the underside of the vehicle and magnetic induction for transmission. Delphi is working on something similar. But again, for this idea to work effectively, all manufacturers would have to adopt the same system, or buyers would have to opt to stay loyal to the same marque forever.

If we are to embrace EVs in a big way, as some countries are pushing for, making it the number one machine in the household instead of a good second car, we need better battery disposal and recycling facilities (being put in hand in the States thanks to a Department of Energy grant to help companies such as Toxco of California), as well as an increase in the number of battery-reconditioning firms to keep running costs in check.

The number one requirement, however, as mentioned earlier, is the need for Greener and more sustainable methods of generating electricity. These need to be adopted quickly, and there's no excuse for not doing so, as the technology exists. For instance, Kyocera built an entire parking lot covered by suspended solar panel arrays as an experiment supported by the California Public Utilities Commission, and the idea has since spread to covered walkways and private carports. As carports are very common in Japan, why not replace the regular roofing materials with solar panels? Japan is, after all, known as the Land of the Rising Sun, yet its energy is wasted on a daily basis. Australia also needs to start thinking ahead, moving away from its reliance on coal for power generation.

A 1940 issue of *Modern Mechanix* showed a car with Scalextric-type pick-ups to transmit electricity to the two electric motors used to power the vehicle. The interesting thing, though, was the thought of using solar cells lining the roadside to provide the electricity, fed through inlaid copper tracks. Storage batteries, charged whilst driving, allowed the car to go to areas off the energized super-highways.

This may have been the inspiration for Swedish architect, Mans Tham, who has put forward the idea of coating highways with heavy-duty solar panels in places with space restrictions, calculating that a 24km (15-mile) stretch of the Santa Monica Freeway in LA covered with a solar panel array would provide enough energy to power the entire community of Venice, California.

If we're to make this truly shine 'Green' or 'Blue' (as some people prefer), we definitely need to clean up our act on energy generation. B. Long

WHERE WE STAND WITH CURRENT TECHNOLOGY

The figures in the following table were taken from the US Department of Energy website, and cover the automatic 2012 Model Year versions of each vehicle mentioned. Only one entry is missing, and that is the upstream greenhouse gas emissions figure for the Leaf, which was still being calculated. It will be fascinating to see what the final figure is, taking coal-fired electricity generation into account. The Leaf's EPA gas mileage figure is an equivalent, by the way, based on one US gallon of petrol being 33.7kWh of electricity, as is that of the plug-in Chevy Volt – petrol power only is rated at 35/40 in this case.

	Ford Fiesta	Hyundai Sonata	Honda CR-V	GMC Canyon
Motive power type	Petrol 1.6L	Petrol 2.4L	Petrol 2.4L	Petrol 2.9L
EPA mpg (city/highway)	29/40	24/35	22/30	18/25
Barrels of oil (driving)	10.0/year	11.8/year	13.2/year	15.7/year
Barrels of oil (electricity)	Zero	Zero	Zero	Zero
Tailpipe CO_2 emissions	269g/m	317g/m	355g/m	423g/m
Upstream GHG emissions	66g/m	78g/m	88g/m	104g/m
California smog score	6/10	9/10	6/10	6/10
Price (from)	$15,500	$20,000	$23,500	$17,500

	VW Jetta	Toyota Prius	Chevrolet Volt	Nissan Leaf
Motive power type	Diesel 2.0L	Petrol 1.8 HEV	Petrol 1.4 EREV	Pure EV
EPA mpg (city/highway)	29/39	51/48	95/93	106/92
Barrels of oil (driving)	11.6/year	6.6/year	8.9/year	Zero
Barrels of oil (electricity)	Zero	Zero	0.2/year	0.2/year
Tailpipe CO_2 emissions	308g/m	178g/m	240g/m	Zero
Upstream GHG emissions	82g/m	44g/m	59g/m	-
California smog score	6/10	9/10	10/10	10/10
Price (from)	$20,000	$23,000	$39,000	$35,000

The number of barrels of oil used is based on the average annual US mileage, multiplied by the EPA fuel economy figure. Electricity generation uses a certain amount of oil, too, but an awful lot more coal, which hasn't been allowed for in these calculations.

In the future, fuel cell and hydrogen cars will certainly become more commonplace, but high costs will keep FC vehicles in the 'rare novelty' category for a while yet. With the most innovative of companies struggling – the German firms being hit by the impact of EU bailouts, and Japanese ones hurting because of crazy exchange rates eating into profits – it sometimes makes you wonder if the fuel cell car will ever appear.

Employing low-weight, longer-lasting materials is an easy way forward for all manufacturers, as is the adoption of new thinking on tyre technology. With recycling matters being pushed harder, material selection can be used now to reduce carbon dioxide emissions with immediate effect, and in the long term at a vehicle's end-of-life.

In conclusion, one thing is irrefutable: no one piece of technology covered in this book will provide a fast, final answer to reducing our carbon footprint. A recent study conducted by the National Academy of Sciences in America proves this beyond doubt. It will take a combination of many small improvements, brave decisions

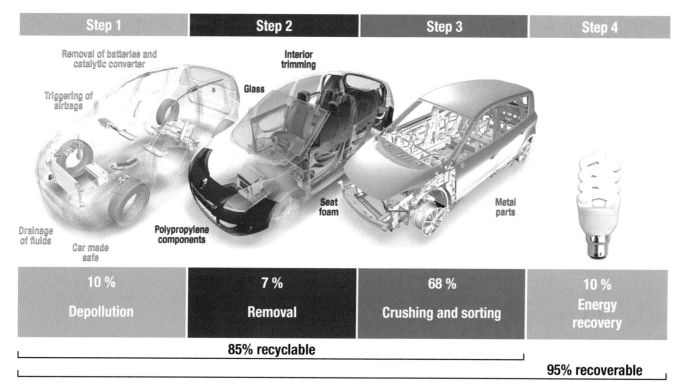

Step 1	Step 2	Step 3	Step 4

Removal of batteries and catalytic converter

Triggering of airbags

Interior trimming

Glass

Drainage of fluids

Car made safe

Polypropylene components

Seat foam

Metal parts

10 %	7 %	68 %	10 %
Depollution	**Removal**	**Crushing and sorting**	**Energy recovery**

85% recyclable

95% recoverable

ABOVE: **Renault's take on car recycling.** Renault

RIGHT: **One rarely thinks about the ecological impact of shipping cars from a factory to PDI centres, but in January 2012, Nissan pressed** *Nichioh Maru* **into service for the first time – a coastal car carrier using a low-friction hull coating, the latest diesel engine technology below decks, and solar panels to power the LED lighting. It should save 1,400 tonnes of fuel a year, cutting CO_2 emissions by 4,200 tonnes annually.** Nissan

from marketing men (who seem to work on a simple formula of 'cheap sells' with little other thought on alternative selling points), and a change in our own buying and driving habits.

Furthermore, engineers will need the cooperation of governments to provide the fuels that can make best use of the latest technology, and to push for cleaner energy generation from electricity supply companies. Working hand in hand with government departments is equally important in setting stable regulations on safety, freeing up valuable R&D time and funds, and establishing attainable goals on future emission levels – the latter taking on a far more rounded approach that uses weighting on all types of exhaust pollutants and fuel/energy production to provide a better balance on limits compared to the one-sided targets banded about in the rallying speeches of today.

THE KYOTO PROTOCOL

The Kyoto Protocol was a United Nations protocol signed in 1997, destined to go into force in 2005 with the noble aim of reducing GHG emissions to slow the global warming process. Unfortunately, America, one of the worst polluters of them all, looked the other way, and continues to do so, citing cost concerns, while others shipped manufacturing abroad to so-called 'developing countries' which are not dealt with so harshly within the terms of the agreement. At the same time, emissions trading was established, which does nothing to reduce the overall levels of pollution at source, just shifts responsibility for those who can afford it.

As far as the car industry is concerned, one really needs to question the tax break syndrome, with companies moving from place to place to pick up the best incentives (it only wastes energy and rarely creates any truly new jobs), and in particular, the farming out of manufacturing to countries with less-than-spectacular environmental records – outsourcing to nations that are unregulated (or partially regulated at best) on emissions, or produce power for the national grid by predominantly burning fossil fuels.

Ultimately, how long can China be considered a 'developing country' when it is known as 'the world's factory' and loans money to the most powerful of industrialized nations? From 2011, China became what is known as a 'newly industrialized country' (or NIC), which still gives it a lot of freedom on emissions compared to so-called 'developed' nations. India's wealth, too, is growing at a staggering rate, but it still wants to hang on to the NIC tag for its own, purely political reasons.

In a roundabout way, this brings us on to something we've already seen in cities such as Coventry and Detroit. A loss of jobs in the traditional car industry strongholds results in lower spending in other areas, leading to other businesses closing. This only encourages car manufacturers to build machines as cheaply as possible, because that's all the average customer can afford – but going down the cheap and cheerful route, and building cars that are ecologically sound, are rarely one and the same thing.

At least in December 2011, despite America continuing to sit on the fence and Canada withdrawing its support for the treaty, the main aim of the Kyoto Protocol came that much closer to serving its purpose, as it was agreed after protracted talks that legally binding rules will come into play in 2020. As Professor Michael Jacobs of Grantham Research Institute noted after the meeting ended: 'It has re-established the principle that climate change should be tackled through international law, not national voluntarism.'

A stunning array of solar panels on the roof of Toyota's Tsutsumi factory, where the Prius is built. Toyota has just won the Green Manufacturing Award for its European operations, an honour presented by the World Trade Group. Toyota

Local taxation also needs to be looked at. As an example, the author can well remember importing a certain brand of oil from South Africa – same oil, different packaging – but it was cheaper to buy it from thousands of miles away than it was from Wales, just down the road. Knowing what we know now about cargo ship emissions, politicians who are serious about 'Green' issues need to start looking at the big picture, and sooner rather than later.

LOOKING AHEAD

Starting with traditional technology, one has to take for granted that the petrol engine will still be around (assuming the oil reserve calculations are reasonably accurate!) in another fifty years. As a dyed-in-the-wool car enthusiast who has enjoyed the cream of the straight-six, flat-six, V6, V8 and V12 examples of the breed for several decades, nothing would make me happier than to see this form of motive power continue. Perhaps fuel companies will have a greater bearing on progress here, as the engineers seem to be getting close to the limit of technological input.

Given the popularity of the diesel engine, not just in European showrooms, but in the corridors of power around the world, one can lay odds that this will also survive unchallenged into the middle of the current century. With luck, the petrochemical industry will find a way to embrace and unlock the potential of bio-diesel, and the car manufacturers will have started to realize that on-paper performance is not all that important, because there are precious few chances to enjoy it anyway. This translates to the adoption of smaller and smaller capacity engines, perhaps linked to forced induction for greater efficiency, ensuring a further reduction in emissions when allied to new, cleaner-burning fuels.

But with space programmes being cut, the EU and US saddled with debt (the current Bank of England governor,

Although this will become an increasingly familiar sight, one can bank on traditional internal combustion engines still being around for decades. Honda

HIDDEN AGENDAS

Lobby groups have been around since the dawn of motoring, with the interests of British railway operators and horse owners in the carriage trade seeing to it that the motor car was restricted to walking speed until November 1896, for instance. Being an impractical form of transport, the automobile industry couldn't grow, protecting a certain element of society from competition.

Today's lobby groups have more money and more communication tools at their disposal than ever before, and these are probably the biggest threat to progress in achieving a true zero-carbon car industry – one that has an extremely low impact on the environment from the manufacturing process all the way through to a vehicle's end-of-life stage.

We've seen the way tobacco lobby groups have managed to keep things moving against all manner of obstacles, while the petroleum companies have far more money at their disposal. In fact, of the world's fifteen richest companies (ranked by revenue), nine are directly related to the oil and gas industry, while another made its name through trading in crude oil!

More than any other group, the oil giants stand to benefit the most if things stay exactly as they are. Some are making active efforts to develop bio-fuels, but there's no sense of urgency to move with the times in many of the firms, as they've already invested too much time and money in the extraction and refining of fossil fuels – it's simply a case of staying up to date with a few alternatives so that if the unthinkable does happen, and a country calls for an entirely new transport policy that's kind to the planet, they won't be left behind in the transition.

It's also fascinating to watch the reactions to the 4.2ltr/100km (56mpg) by 2025 proposal put forward by President Obama. Because the US manufacturers are quite happy to let things roll on, measuring change in fractions of a percentage point, they are saying that going for efficiency will cost as many as 220,000 American jobs. They are even twisting an Energy Information Administration report as an excuse, noting that a 14 per cent drop in sales would result. The makers zoomed in on one paragraph, which states:

> When manufacturers bring an advanced vehicle or technology to market, consumers must be willing to buy it. There is a high level of uncertainty about consumer willingness to pay significantly higher prices for fuel-efficient vehicles. In recent history, consumers have tended to value upgrades in performance, vehicle size, and other attributes at the expense of fuel economy.

The key point here is that extra cost kills sales, not frugality. Consumers will buy high-tech models if they offer a clear benefit without having to pay a vast premium – the success of the Toyota Prius should confirm that. Indeed, the buoyant sales of Japanese cars in general since the 1970s and the VW Beetle before that proves the point once and for all that consumers do have an interest in economical machines if they are offered them at the right price.

But if American buyers really do judge value on size and keep getting drip-fed with gizmo-loaded gas-guzzlers priced to sell and suitable for one country only on the one hand, and US makers keep augmenting smaller profits by putting their hands out for bailouts, tax credits for keeping factories open and research grants that virtually always come up inconclusive, promptly being abandoned the minute the cash stops flowing on the other, nothing will change any time soon.

Wouldn't producing cars that compete on a global scale, able to sell in countries where fuel prices are more expensive, make more sense than trying desperately to hold on to a falling share of a single market? But therein lies the key to the problem: why compete when you don't have to? The sooner the 'too big to fail' mentality comes to an end, the better – in all walks of life.

Mervyn King, recently said the current financial crisis could be the worst the UK has ever seen), and nations such as Japan – previously leaders in new technology – struggling to keep out of recession, will the progress slow down, as the automotive sector moves away from its traditional roots and into a new era of electronics and material usage?

One thing we can say with a fair degree of certainty, given the poor public transport network in countries such as Britain and America, is that cars will still be around in some form or another for the foreseeable future. Research has shown that in virtually every country in Europe, car ownership has risen steadily since 1970, doubling in the last thirty-five years in some places, tripling in others. With this in mind, rather than new technology, better roads will probably be the biggest factor in saving fuel and cleaning up automotive-related emissions with traditional ICE units.

At the last Tokyo Motor Show, stands bristled with amazing ideas of model cities with the car fully integrated into homes and businesses, and completely new infrastructures to cope with modern automotive thinking. But one only has

limits that only serve to bunch up traffic. Sort them out first, and motoring will automatically become cleaner – the burden shouldn't be placed solely in the hands of the car makers. Like Europe, financial woes will restrict the development of advanced transportation ideas, but replacing the millions of needless, poorly synchronized traffic lights with roundabouts would be a cheap and effective start, for instance. Easier still, as very little investment is needed, change national holidays into local level holidays – tailbacks of 30km (20 miles) or more are common on most of the Japanese expressways during the start and end of national holiday periods. How many years and billions in funding would it take an engineering team to counter one day of emissions at this level?

America is also too set in the old ways. One only needs to think of the traffic jams on the LA highways in a morning, with one lane that hardly anybody uses – the lack of people in the 'Pool' (car sharing) lane means that no one is willing to

The RAC Foundation is reckoning on a 43 per cent increase in Britain's traffic by 2035. There are many areas where roads can't effectively cope with today's volumes, let alone a jump like that.
Joseph Plotz/Creative Commons

to look around in Japan and live here for more than a couple of years to realize this is a far-off dream, and nothing more than a dream. No one has the nerve to call for radical change, but that is exactly what it would take. And how can a country struggling to rebuild after the 2011 earthquake possibly fund an entirely new road system, with new houses, offices and public buildings? It's never going to happen, so more realistic plans are needed, and needed fast.

Japan makes a huge effort in some eco-friendly respects, such as recycling, but its roads are a disaster – overcrowded, too narrow in most places, and posted with ridiculous speed

Different era, but the message is the same – one person to a car is wasteful. Being in a traffic jam with a clear 'Pool' lane available only serves to double the waste. NARA

クルマとくらしをつなぐ矢崎

私たち矢崎は電力ケーブルから家庭用のケーブル、
そしてクルマのなかのワイヤーハーネスを生産しています。
EVやPHVの普及で、発電所や家庭のソーラー発電などから
クルマまで、電気が一直線につながりました。
矢崎が開発した電気の制御技術は、
これからの社会に必要な電気エネルギーの効率的で
安全な利用を促進します。
矢崎は太陽熱やガスなどの熱エネルギーの利用でも
多くの技術を開発してきました。
電気エネルギーと熱エネルギーの
それぞれの特色を生かして有効に活用すれば、
無駄のないエネルギー社会が実現できます。
矢崎はクルマとくらしを電気や熱でつなぎ、
スマートエネルギー社会を提案していきます。

YAZAKI - Linking vehicles with daily life

The YAZAKI Group is engaged in production of a wide range of cables,
from power cables to home-use cables, as well as
wire harnesses for vehicular use.
With the spread of EV and PHV, electricity is now linked directly
from power stations and solar power generation
in the home through to vehicles.
We will continue to promote the electric control technologies we have
developed for various scenarios as a means of ensuring the efficient
and safe use of electric energy that is needed by society.
The YAZAKI Group has also developed many technologies
for the use of heat energy, including solar and gas.
By utilizing the characteristics of electrical and heat energy effectively
we can realize a society in which no energy is wasted.
The YAZAKI Group proposes a vision for a smart energy society,
linking vehicles and daily life with electricity and heat.

太陽熱温水器「ゆ
Natural Circu
Solar Water Heate

Ai

電力のネットワーク
Power networks

熱のネットワーク
Thermal networks

通 信
Communications

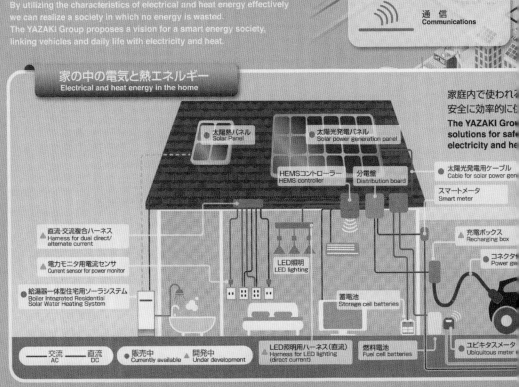

家の中の電気と熱エネルギー
Electrical and heat energy in the home

家庭内で使われ
安全に効率的に
The YAZAKI Gro
solutions for saf
electricity and he

太陽熱パネル
Solar Panel

太陽光発電パネル
Solar power generation panel

HEMSコントローラー
HEMS controller

分電盤
Distribution board

太陽光発電用ケーブル
Cable for solar power gen

スマートメータ
Smart meter

直流・交流複合ハーネス
Harness for dual direct/
alternate current

電力モニタ用電流センサ
Current sensor for power monitor

給湯器一体型住宅用ソーラシステム
Boiler Integrated Residential
Solar Water Heating System

LED照明
LED lighting

蓄電池
Storage cell batteries

充電ボックス
Recharging box

コネクタ
Power ge

交流 AC　直流 DC　●販売中 Currently available　▲開発中 Under development

LED照明用ハーネス(直流)
Harness for LED lighting
(direct current)

燃料電池
Fuel cell batteries

ユビキタスメータ
Ubiquitous meter

Cities of the future, with integrated charging systems using clean energy for cars, homes and businesses. All well and good, but retrofitting is an expensive proposition, meaning only new buildings are likely to benefit from this level of thinking. It could be decades before we see anything like this on a grand scale.

Yazaki

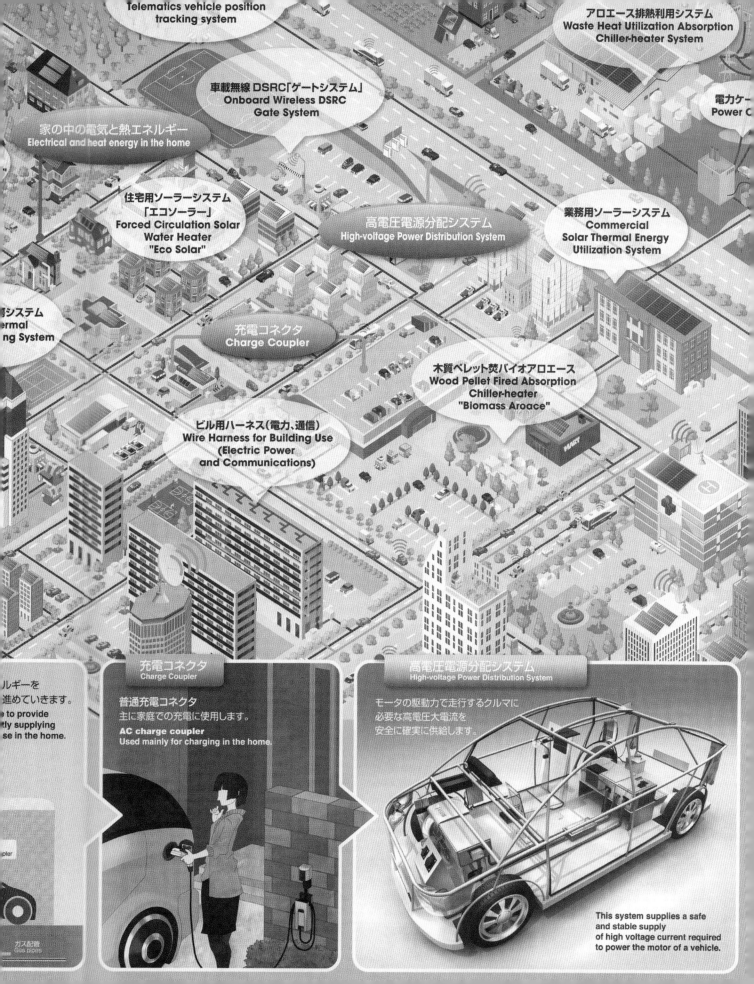

While the weight-saving techniques are to be applauded, and the Tata Nano will doubtless get a few dirty two-stroke bikes off the road, too (although many will pop up again elsewhere, run by those even less well equipped to keep the machine in a proper state of tune), doubtless India's congestion problems – like those seen here in the city of Gwalior – will only get worse until real investment can be pumped into overhauling the road system. Something needs to be done fast, as each day 1,000 new cars are added to the roads of Delhi alone – a shocking figure.
Yann/Creative Commons

Typical congestion in Japan, with poor right-turn filters and too many traffic lights simply adding to the problem of too many vehicles on roads not built for heavy traffic. Kinori

change their habits of a lifetime, even when the benefits are there for all to see. It probably also explains why no one is willing to invest in a good public transport system, despite a huge population in the area. Yet California has taken the lead in many environmental issues, which probably points to even less chance of things happening as one moves eastwards.

One also has to consider the small towns with hundreds of miles of wilderness between them in bigger countries such as America. While estimates show that 60 per cent of the world's population will be living in cities by 2030, one urban solution will certainly not provide an answer for the more isolated communities, be they in the States, or places such as Australia, Russia and most of China.

Finally, while Japan's love affair with the car may be all but over, new booms are starting in places such as China and India. Given the population figures we're dealing with here, this leads to the question of the impact an Asian car boom will have on global warming, and will the efforts of makers go anywhere near to balancing the effect?

Perhaps China and India could actually show the way forwards, as so much of the infrastructure is new, or better still, in the planning stage. The funds are there, too, but a reduction in profits goes against the grain, and it's doubtful whether anyone has the vision to think about air quality as a valuable asset. If scant regard is given to it now, in the midst of a booming economy and a desire to showcase industrial and technological might to the world, what chance is there of it taking priority when the economy starts slowing down, as it appears to be?

Having concluded that cars will never go away, and with numbers more likely to increase than decrease, whilst roads will probably stay much the same as they are now, it would seem we are reliant on Third Generation bio-fuels and the hope that solar power can be harnessed effectively, PV panels – or something better – being hooked up to batteries that can give the required performance for longer periods, yet be light, and clean to make and recycle.

After all is said and done, the big question we should be asking ourselves is not so much relating to whether we have to do something to clean up our act, but timescale. Do we wait until fossil fuels run out to make a move, or until the air we breathe contains more GHGs and toxic gases than fresh air? It is to be hoped that action will be taken long before these scenarios have a chance to prevail.

RIGHT: **We know how to address the problem of reducing our carbon footprint. Now all we need to do is apply the things we know.** Ford

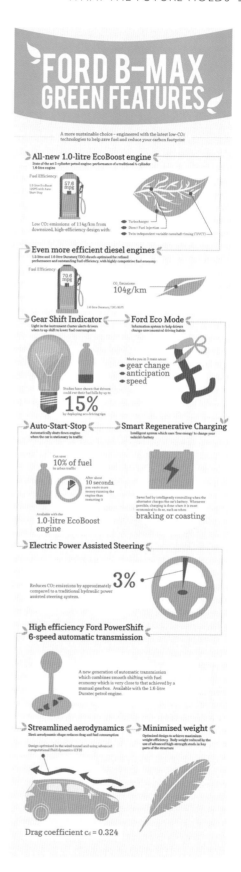

ZERO CARBON ABBREVIATIONS

4WD   Four-wheel drive (layout)

AAEM   Alkali anion exchange membranes (technology)

AAMA   American Automobile Manufacturers Association (organization)

AC   Alternating current (electricity)

AC   Air conditioning (component)

ACEA   European Automobile Manufacturers' Association (organization)

ACEEE   American Council for Energy Efficient Economy (organization)

ACIS   Acoustic control induction system (system)

AFC   Alkaline fuel cell (technology)

AFM   Active fuel management (system)

AGT   Advanced gas turbine engine (component)

APC   Accelerometer pilot control (system)

APU   Auxiliary power unit (component)

ARIS   Advanced reagent injector system (system)

AT   Automatic transmission, with prefix indicating speeds (component)

AT-PZEV   Advanced technology partial zero emissions vehicle (classification)

BAS   Belt alternator starter (component)

BDC   Bottom-dead centre (technology)

BEV   Battery electric vehicle (also BV) (classification)

BIW   Body-in-white (industry term)

BTL   Biomass to liquid technology (process)

BV   Battery vehicle (also BEV) (classification)

CAA   US Clean Air Act (mandate)

CAFE   Corporate Average Fuel Average (measurement, mandate)

CARB   California Air Resources Board (organization)

CCS   Combined combustion system (system)

Cd   Coefficient of drag (measurement)

CDE CO_2 equivalent rating (measurement)

CEV   City electric vehicle (also NEV or LSV) (classification)

CFCs   Chlorofluorocarbons (gas)

CFRP   Carbon-fibre reinforced plastic (material)

CGI   Compacted graphite iron (material)

CHP   Cooling, heating and power (industry term)

CI   Compression ignition (technology)

CIS   Continuous injection system (technology)

CN   Cetane number (measurement)

CNG   Compressed natural gas (fuel)

CO   Carbon monoxide (gas)

c/r   Compression ratio (measurement)

CRD   Common-rail diesel (system)

CTL   Coal to liquid technology (process)

CVCC   Compound vortex controlled combustion (system)

CVT   Continuously variable transmission (component)

DBFC   Direct borohydride fuel cell (technology)

DC   Direct current (electricity)

DCT   Dual clutch transmission (component)

DEF   Diesel exhaust fluid (technology)

DEFC   Direct-ethanol fuel cell (technology)

DI   Direct injection (technology)

DME   Dimethylether (fuel)

DMFC   Direct-methanol fuel cell (technology)

DOC   Diesel oxidation catalyst (component)

DoE   US Department of Energy (organization)

dohc   Double overhead camshaft (component)

DPF   Diesel particulate filter (component)

DSG   Direct shift gearbox (technology)

EAA   European Aluminium Association (organization)

ECU   Electronic control unit (component)

EDC   Electronic diesel control (component)

EFI   Electronic-controlled fuel-injection (also FI) (component)

EGR   Exhaust gas recirculation (component, process)

EI   Electronic ignition (technology)

EMS   Energy management system drivetrain (system)

EMT   Electromechanical transmission (component)

EPA   US Environmental Protection Agency (organization)

EREV   Extended-range electric vehicle (also REEV) (classification)

EV   Electric vehicle (classification)

EVAP   Evaporative emissions control system (component, mandate)

eVCT   Electric variable cam timing (system)

EVT   Electric variable transmission (component)

FAME   Fatty-acid methyl ester (fuel)

FC   Fuel cell (technology)

FCEV   Fuel cell electric vehicle (also FCV) (classification)

FCV   Fuel cell vehicle (also FCEV) (classification)

FCVT   Freedom, car and vehicle technologies (mandate)

FF   Front engine, front-wheel drive (layout)

FFV   Flexible fuel (or flex-fuel) vehicle (classification)

FI   Fuel-injection (also EFI) (component)

FR   Front engine, rear-wheel drive (layout)

FRP   Fibreglass (also GRP) (material)

FSI   Fuel stratified injection (system)

GCI   Gasoline compression ignition (system)

GDI   Gasoline direct injection (system)

GHGs   Greenhouse gases (gas)

GRP   Fibreglass (also FRP) (material)

GTL   Gas to liquid technology (process)

GWP   Global warming potential (measurement)

HCs   Hydrocarbons (fuel, gas, et cetera)

HCCI   Homogeneous charge compression ignition (technology)

HCFCs   Hydrochlorofluorocarbons (gas)

HC-SCR   Hydrocarbon-SCR catalyst (component)

HDI   High-pressure direct injection (technology)

HDPE   High-density polyethylene (material)

HEHV   Human-electric hybrid vehicle (classification)

HEV   Hybrid electric vehicle (also HV) (classification)

HFCs   Hydrofluorocarbons (gas)

HHO   Fuel cell (technology)

HPEV   High-performance electric vehicle (classification)

HSD   Hybrid synergy drive (system)

HSLA   High-strength low-alloy steel (material)

HV   Hybrid vehicle (also HEV) (classification)

HVAC   Heating, ventilation and air conditioning (component)

ICE   Internal combustion engine (technology)

IDI   Indirect injection (technology)

IDM   Injector driver module (system)

IMA   Integrated motor assist (system)

IMFC   Indirect methanol fuel cell (technology)

IMG   Integrated motor generator (system)

IWM   In-wheel motor (component)

KERS   Kinetic energy recovery system (technology)

K-ion   Potassium-ion battery (technology)

KS   Knock sensor (component)

LDPE   Low-density polyethylene (material)

LED   Light-emitting diode (technology)

LEV   Low-emission vehicle (classification, mandate)

LEZ   Low-emission zone (mandate)

Li-ion/LIB Lithium-ion battery (technology)

LiPo/LMP Lithium metal polymer battery (technology)

LiS Lithium-sulphur battery (technology)

LiTi Lithium-titanate battery (technology)

LNC Lean NOx catalyst (component)

LNG Liquid natural gas (fuel)

LNT Lean NOx trap (component)

LPG Liquid petroleum gas (fuel)

LPi Liquid phase injection (system)

LSR Land speed record (measurement)

LSV Low-speed vehicle (also NEV or CEV) (classification)

LTC Low temperature combustion (technology)

MD Modulated displacement (system)

MECA Manufacturers of Emission Controls Association (organization)

MGU Motor generator unit (component)

MK Modulated kinetics (system)

MMT Methylcyclopentadienyl manganese tricarbonyl (additive)

MPFI Multi-point fuel injection (also MPI) (technology)

MPI Multi-point injection (also MPFI) (technology)

MR Mid-engine, rear-wheel drive (layout)

MT Manual transmission, with prefix indicating speeds (component)

MTG Methanol to gasoline technology (process)

NA Normally-aspirated (technology)

NAC NOx absorber catalyst (component)

NaS Sodium-sulphur battery (technology)

NEV Neighbourhood electric vehicle (also CEV or LSV) (classification)

NHTSA US National Highway Traffic Safety Administration (organization)

NiCd/NiCad Nickel-cadmium battery (technology).

NiFe Nickel-iron battery (technology)

NiMH Nickel metal hydride battery (technology)

NLEV National low-emission vehicle (classification, mandate)

NOx Combination of oxides of nitrogen (gas)

NSC NOx storage catalyst (component)

NVH Noise, vibration and harshness (industry term)

OBD Onboard diagnostics (component)

OE Original equipment (industry term)

OEM Original equipment manufacturer (industry term)

ohv Overhead valves (technology)

OPEC Organization of the Petroleum Exporting Countries (organization)

PAFC Phosphoric acid fuel cell (technology)

PAS Power-assisted steering (component)

PCCI Pre-mixed charge compression ignition (technology)

PC-SOFC Proton-conducting solid oxide fuel cell (technology)

PCU Power control unit (component)

PCV Positive crankcase ventilation (technology)

PDI Petrol direct injection (technology)

PEMFC Polymer electrolyte membrane fuel cell (technology)

PEMFC Proton-exchange membrane fuel cell (technology)

PET/PETE Polyethylene terephthalate (material)

PFCs Perfluorocarbons (gas)

PHEV Plug-in hybrid electric vehicle (also PHV) (classification)

PHV Plug-in hybrid vehicle (also PHEV) (classification)

PM Particulate matter (emission type)

PMfLFC Precious metal-free liquid-feed fuel cell (technology)

PNGV Partnership for a New Generation of Vehicles (mandate)

POE Port-of-entry (industry term)

PP Polypropylene (material)

PPCI Partially-pre-mixed charge compression ignition (technology)

PPO Pure plant oil (fuel)

PS Polystyrene (material)

PSD Power split device (component)

PV Photovoltiac (or solar) cell (technology)

PVC Polyvinyl chloride (also V) (material)

PZEV Partial zero emissions vehicle (classification)

PZT Lead zirconate titanate ceramics (material)

RE Rotary engine (technology)

REEV Range-extended electric vehicle (also EREV) (classification)

RMFC Reformed methanol fuel cell (technology)

RON Research octane number (measurement)

RR Rear engine, rear-wheel drive (layout)

RTM Resin transfer moulding (process)

SAE Society of Automotive Engineers (organization)

SCR Selective catalytic reduction (technology, process)

SI Spark ignition (technology)

SMC Sheet-moulded composite (material)

SNCR Selective non-catalytic reduction (technology)

SOFC Solid oxide fuel cell (technology)

sohc Single overhead camshaft (component)

SOx Combination of oxides of sulphur (gas)

SRM Switched reluctance motor (component)

SULEV Super ultra-low emissions vehicle (classification)

SUV Sport utility vehicle (classification)

sv Side valves (technology)

SVO Straight vegetable oil (fuel)

TD Turbo-diesel (technology)

TDC Top-dead centre (technology)

TDF Tyre-derived fuel (fuel)

TDI Turbocharged direct injection (system)

TEL Tetra-ethyl lead (additive)

THS Toyota hybrid system (system)

TLEV Transitional low-emission vehicle (classification, mandate)

TML Tetra-methyl lead (additive)

toe Tonne of oil equivalent (measurement)

TSI Turbocharged stratified injection (system)

TST Two-stage turbocharger (component)

TZEV Transitional zero emissions vehicle (classification)

UAW United Auto Workers (organization)

UHTS/UHSS Ultra-high tensile steel (material).

ULEV Ultra-low emissions vehicle (classification)

ULSD Ultra-low sulphur diesel (fuel)

USABC United States Advanced Battery Consortium (organization)

V Polyvinyl chloride (also PVC) (material)

VCM Variable cylinder management (technology)

VGT Variable geometry turbo (also VNT, VTG and VVT) (component)

VIIs Viscosity index improvers (technology)

VLIM/VLM Variable length intake manifold (technology)

VNT Variable nozzle turbo (also VGT, VTG and VVT) (component)

VOCs Volatile organic compounds (gas, etc)

VTEC Variable valve timing and lift electronic control (system)

VTG Variable turbine geometry turbo (also VGT, VNT and VVT) (component)

VVT Variable valve timing (technology)

VVT Variable vane turbine (also VGT, VNT and VTG) (component)

V2H Vehicle to home technology (process)

WTO World Trade Organization (organization)

WVO Waste vegetable oil (fuel)

ZEV Zero emission vehicle (classification, mandate)

ZnBr Zinc-bromine battery (technology)

INDEX

7–Eleven 190
Aachen, Univ. of 173
AAMA 118–119
ACEA 29, 76
ACEEE 101
AD 96
ADAC 85
Advertising Age 131
Aerorider 97
AeroVironment 159
AESC 133
Agni 163
Aisin 97, 101
Aisin Takaoka Co. 170
Aixam 97
Akasol 97
Alfa Romeo 23, 26, 50, 63, 66
Allis-Chalmers 160
Altair Nanotechnologies 133, 144
AMC 116
AMG 85, 143
Anderson Carriage Co. 114
Anderson, Robert 113
Anheuser-Busch 50
Anslinger, Harry J. 39
Antro 159
Aptera 177–178
Aral 163
Argonne National Laboratory 42
Arthurs, Dave 116
Asahi Kasei 133
Associated Octel 61
Aston Martin 128
Atkinson, James 49, 91–92, 97, 100–101
Atlanta Checker Cab Co. 148
Audi 20, 22–23, 27, 34–37, 44, 69, 80, 83, 85, 88–89,
    97–98, 104, 109–111, 134–135, 144, 163, 171–172,
    178, 184
Austin 19, 52, 181
Auto Union 166, 173, 176, 180
Autocar 136
Auto-Mixte 73
AVL Powertrain Eng. 136
Azure Dynamics 139

Backus 80
Bacon, Dr Francis 160
Bajulaz 80
Baker 114
Ballard 160, 162–163
Ballard, Dr Geoffrey 162
BASF 84, 132
Battronic Truck Co. 116
Bedford 116
Beijing Olympics 164
Bell, Frank 154
Bendix 55
Bentley 50
Benz 49
Benz, Bertha 49
Benz, Carl 17, 48–49
Bergius, Friedrich 41
Berlin Show 19
Billings, Roger E. 152

Bladon 156
Bloomfield, Michael 74
BMC 20, 52, 122, 166
BMW (including New Mini) 16, 22, 35, 37, 43, 57–58,
    63, 66, 75, 78–80, 82, 84–85, 98–100, 103–104,
    120, 130–132, 135–136, 140, 143, 152–153, 162–163,
    166, 173, 175, 178–179
Bochum University 158
Boeing 115
Bolloré 127, 129, 141
Bonneville 37, 155
Borg & Beck 53
Bosch 19, 22–23, 26, 31, 52, 54, 57, 62–63, 67, 82,
    103, 111, 116, 132
Bothfeld, Robert 74
BP 41, 69, 72, 158, 163
Brabus 82
Breer, Carl 181
Briggs & Stratton 88
Bristol 181
British Grand Prix 97
British Motor Show 128
BRM 155
Broadspeed 122
Brookhaven National Laboratory 161
Brown, Yull 154
Brussels, Univ. of 39
BTCC 37, 181
Bugatti 50–51
Buick 116
Busch, Adolphus 50
Buschow, Kurt 132
Bush, George W. 41, 104, 119, 150
BYD 101, 141

Cadillac 20, 50, 98–99, 131, 159
California Fuel Cell Partnership 119
California, Univ. of 9
Caltech 116
Cambridge University 160
CARB 54, 74, 89, 107, 117, 119, 123, 127
Card, Andrew H. 119
Castrol 65
Caterpillar 35
CAV 55
Cedar, Dr Gerbrand 133
Chavanne, Charles G. 39
Chevrolet 57, 59, 69, 74–75, 87, 97, 99, 119, 127, 129,
    133, 135, 138, 140, 143, 148, 155, 163, 170, 175–176,
    179, 192
Chevron 40, 132, 160
Chrysler 26, 55–56, 59, 69, 85, 98–99, 108, 117, 120,
    131, 155, 162, 177, 179, 181
CITA 113–114
Citroën 19, 21, 52, 83, 85, 96, 111–112, 121, 141, 144,
    148, 176, 179, 181
City 97
Clean Diesel Technology 42
Clean-Tech 127
Clinton, Bill 25, 119, 172
Clinton, Hillary 189
Clooney, George 127
Cobasys 132
Coca-Cola 109

Cocconi, Alan 118
CODA 141
Columbia 114
Commuter Cars 127
Continental 31, 41–42, 75, 85
Corbin 126–127
Cord 50
Coskata 70
Coventry University 163
Cugnot 149
Cummins 36
Cummins, Clessie 19, 23, 36
Cutty Sark 170

Daewoo 148
DAF 20
Daihatsu 59, 81, 88, 94, 98, 117, 120, 122, 148, 162,
    164, 178
Daimler (GB) 50, 64, 73, 176
Daimler, Gottlieb 17, 48
Dakar Rally 37
Date, Tasku 56
Davenport, Thomas 114
Davy, Humphry 160
De Chasseloup-Laubat, Gaston 114
De Rivaz, Isaac 151
De Vries, Jim 173
Dearman, Peter 156–157
Delage 50
Delahaye 50
Delco (AC Delco) 50
DeLorean 170–171
Delphi 31, 42–43, 45, 67, 191
Delta Motorsport 141
Denso (Nippondenso) 23, 31, 68, 86, 100
Detroit Electric 114
Detroit Show 26, 98, 100–101, 104, 107–109, 112,
    122, 127–131, 135–136, 138, 152, 162, 172
Diesel, Rudolf 17–18, 38
Doble 149
Dodge 99, 120, 177, 179
Dohle, Dr Ulrich 31
Duckhams 188
Duesenberg 36, 50
Dunlop 183
DuPont 39, 73, 178
Duryea 50
Dynasty 141

EAA 173
Eaton Corp. 42, 109
Eberhard, Martin 127
ECD 118
EDF 129
Edison, Thomas 114, 132, 184
EDrive Systems 127
Elcar 116
Electric Lightning 141
Electrocity 141
Emancipation Run 48
Energetx Composites 177
Energine Corp. 158
Energy Information Administration 196
EnergyCS 127

Enfield 116
Enginion AG 156
Englehard Corp. 31
EPA 28, 40, 51, 53–54, 60–61, 74, 105, 116, 128, 192
Ethyl Corp. 60–61
Evans, Dave 36
Evelio 141
Exxon (–Mobil) 68, 72, 132, 160

FedEx 109
Ferrari 53, 166
FEV 82
Fiat 19, 23, 26, 52, 57, 66, 69, 76, 85–86, 122, 148, 155, 163, 166
Fischer, Franz 41
Fisker 97, 108, 125, 128–129, 142, 144
Fisker, Henrik 128
Flybrid Systems 75
Ford 20, 26, 30–31, 39, 43, 47, 50, 53, 55–56, 67–70, 81–82, 85, 95–97, 101, 108–109, 114–116, 122–123, 125–126, 128, 130, 132, 139, 146, 148, 150, 153, 155, 160, 162–163, 167–168, 172–173, 175–177, 179, 181, 183, 189, 192
Ford, Bill 95
Ford, Clara 114
Ford, Henry 39, 50, 70, 114, 175, 180, 184
Frankfurt Show 52, 67, 75, 77, 81, 89, 93, 97–98, 103, 120, 130, 134–135, 142–143, 153, 171–172, 180
Fuchs 180
Fuerst, John 42
Fulda 183
Fulmen 113

Garcea, Giampaolo 66
Garia 135
Garrard & Blumfield 114
GAZ 152–153
Gelb, Dr George H. 88
GEM 97
General Electric (GE, GEC) 42, 117, 160, 162
General Motors (GM, GMC) 20, 51, 55–56, 58, 63–64, 67, 69–70, 74–75, 77–78, 80, 84–85, 87–88, 92, 95–96, 98–100, 108–109, 116–119, 121, 126–129, 131–132, 138–139, 143, 148, 155, 159–160, 162–163, 169, 177, 189, 192
Geneva Show 35–36, 44, 72, 101, 104, 109, 112, 123, 127, 129–130, 135–136, 143, 145, 172, 176
Geo 120
Ghosn, Carlos 129
Gioia, Nancy 139
Giugiaro 185
Globe-Union 88, 117
Gore, Al 11, 129
Grand Prix 36
Grantham Research Institute 194
Grove, William 160
GS Yuasa 132
GTA 179
Guangzhou 138
Gulf 55

Haagen-Smit, Dr J.A. 54
Hanawa, Ikuo 142
Hanomag 19
Hanover Fair 172
Harrods 144
Hearst, William 39
Helfet, Keith 129
Henderson, Fritz 109
Henney Motor Co. 116
Hill, Graham 155
Hino 23, 42, 141
Hispano-Suiza 50
Hockenheim 116
Holden 139, 148
Honda 35, 46, 56, 59–60, 66–67, 69, 73–75, 77, 82, 85, 92, 96–97, 101, 105, 107, 122–123, 133, 137–138, 143, 157–160, 162–163, 172, 174–175, 189–190, 192
Honda, Soichiro 56

Horch 50
Howmet 155
HSE 28
Hughes Aircraft Co. 159
Hummer 119, 182, 189
HyperSolar 151
Hyundai 30, 44, 84–85, 101, 112, 145, 147–148, 162, 192
Hywet 163

IAV GmbH 156
ICI 55
IHI Corp. 31, 68
Ihrig, Harry K. 160
Illustrated World 149
Imbert, Georges 150
Indian Academy of Sciences 148
Indianapolis 36, 155
IndianOil 148
Inomoto, Yoshihiro 92
Iogen 70
Isotta-Fraschini 50
Isuzu 19, 21–22, 38, 56, 108
Iwate 148

Jacobs, Michael 194
Jaguar 52–53, 58–59, 63–64, 76, 103, 136, 172
James, Dilip 79
Japan Electric Vehicle Assoc. 117
Jaray, Paul 181
JCB 37
Jeantaud 114
Jenatzy, Camille 114
Johanson, Greg 159
Johnson, Boris 126
Johnson-Matthey 55
Joule Unlimited 40
Jungner, Waldemar 114, 132

K'Airmobiles 158
Kainz, Peter 135
Kamcorp 123
Keio University 126
Kettering, Charles 50
Kia 69, 96, 101, 143
King, Mervyn 196
King, Spen 154
Knight, Charles 50
Koehler, Bernhard 128
Korean Advanced Institute of Science & Technology 125
Krieger 73
Kung, Harold 133
Kurtis, Frank 36
Kyocera 21–22, 155, 191
Kyoto Protocol 76, 90, 154, 194

Lada 163
Lamborghini 53
Lanchester 50
Lancia 43, 179
Lawson, Harry 114
Le Mans 37, 155, 173
Le Mans 36
Legre, Guy 157
Lenoir, Etienne 154
Levassor, Emile 64
Lincoln 22, 101
Little, Dr Kitty 29
Lloyd, Alan C. 119
Locomobile 149
Lohner 115, 128
Los Angeles Show 101, 118, 122, 138, 158
Lotus 97, 130, 136, 155, 176
Lucas 55, 57, 116, 131
LuK 83
Lutz, Bob 127, 144

Magna International 139

Magneti Marelli 26, 57
Mahindra (& Mahindra) 97, 120, 141
Mahle 85
MAN AG 18
MARG Diesel Coalition 28
Martek Biosciences Corp. 41
Martinelli, Paolo 85
Maserati 53
Matsuhashi, Shigeru 92
May, Michael 58
Maybach, Wilhelm 17, 48
Mazda 28, 46–47, 59, 67, 74–76, 78, 80, 85–86, 96–97, 105, 116–117, 119, 126, 136, 148, 152–154, 162, 168–170, 173–175, 177, 186–187
McCabe, Mike 148
McLaren 179
MDI 157–158
MECA 61
Melber 185
Mellon, Andrew 39
Mercedes-Benz (Daimler-Benz, Daimler AG) 6, 19–21, 23, 26, 32–35, 37–38, 43–44, 48, 50, 53, 60, 64, 69, 72–73, 75, 77, 80, 85, 96, 98–100, 112, 115, 119–120, 128, 131–132, 134, 142–143, 149, 152, 160, 162–164, 166, 169, 171, 173, 177, 179, 182, 187–188, 190
Mercury 97, 101, 109
Merkel, Angela 136
Meyer, Stanley 154
MG 53
Mia 141
Michelin 113, 184
Microcab Industries 163
Micro-Vett 97
Midgley, Thomas 51
Miki Press 59
Miller, Ralph H. 49, 76, 80, 86
MIT 133
MITI 155
Mitsuba Corp. 185
Mitsubishi 44, 67, 69, 81, 85, 92, 96, 103, 107, 117, 120, 122, 127, 133, 137, 141–142, 155, 163, 168, 173, 185
Mitsubishi Fuso 141
Mitsui Chemical 72
Modern Mechanix 158, 190
Montlhéry 36
Morris 11
Morrison, William 114
Mother Earth News 116
Motor Trend 101
Motorola 131–132
MotorSport 36
Motul 65
Murray, Gordon 179
Musashi Institute of Technology 152
Musk, Elon 127
Muskie, Edmund 54
Myers Motors 126, 139, 141
Myers, Dana 127

Nardo 37
NASA 115, 150, 160–162
Nasser, Jacques 122
National Academy of Sciences 55, 192
Navistar 30, 35
NEC 133
New York Show 95, 114, 142
NHTSA 138, 167
NIOSH 28
Nismo 142
Nissan (Datsun, Infiniti) 34–35, 38, 44–45, 53, 59, 66–67, 69, 72, 82–84, 89, 95–96, 100–102, 116–117, 120, 122, 133, 137, 142–143, 145, 155–156, 162, 176, 191–193
Noel Penny Turbines 155
North American Solar Challenge 159
Northwestern Univ. 133
Nürburgring 37

Oak Ridge National Laboratory 125
Obama, Barack 41, 125, 163, 196
Oi, Toshihiro 94
Okuda, Hiroshi 87
Oldsmobile 20, 50, 64
OPEC 15
Opel 50, 53, 85, 116, 138–139, 148, 162–163, 179
Optimal Energy 129–130, 141
Orbital Autogas Systems 148, 158
Otto, Nikolaus 17–18, 49–50, 108
Overly, Lowell 175
Ovonic 118, 132
Ovshinsky, Stan 118, 132
Owen 115
Owens-Corning 175

Panasonic 42, 91, 95, 138
Panhard & Levassor 48, 181
Paris Salon 35, 73, 110–111, 115, 120, 129, 156
Paxton 155
Pearce, Harry 109
Pellandine, Peter 156
Penny, Noel 155
Pepsico 109
Peugeot 19–21, 23, 36–37, 48, 50, 69, 96, 111–112, 114, 121, 128, 134, 141, 148, 181, 188
Phoenix Motorcars 144
Piech, Ferdinand 36
Pieper 73
Pieper, Henri 73
Pike's Peak 142
Pininfarina 129, 135
Pivco Industries 123
Planté, Gaston 114
Plug In America 126
Plymouth 177
Pope (–Waverley) 113–114
Popular Mechanics 18, 175
Porsche 12, 28, 58, 60, 62, 66–68, 76, 81–82, 84, 96, 102–104, 106, 115, 128, 135, 166, 169–170, 176, 180–182, 186
Porsche, Ferdinand 115
Postal-Vinay 113
Powerplus 61
Pratt & Whitney 160
Primus 72
Prince 117
Prince Gas 148
Protean Electric 128
Proton 136
PSA Group 21, 30–31, 44, 69, 85, 104, 121, 162

Qatar Show 182
Quantum Technologies 128
Quasiturbine 158

RAC 48, 197
Rasul, Firoz 160
Red Line 61
Reithofer, Norbert 136
Renaissance Cars 120
Renault 31, 44–45, 69, 85, 120, 122, 129–130, 142, 148, 155, 162, 166, 193
Reva 120
Ricardo 70, 156–157
Ricardo, Harry 19, 21, 51
Riley, Matthew 76
Rinolfi, Dr Rinaldo 26
Rochdale 176
Rockefeller, John D. 70
Rolls-Royce 50
Rosen, Charlie 116
Roth, William V. 189
Rover (Land Rover) 19, 63, 112, 148, 154–156, 173

Saab 58, 69, 76, 98, 148, 156, 181
SAE 63, 65, 88

SAE World Congress 82, 156
Sanyo 97, 110
Sarich, Ralph 158
Saturn 75, 98, 119, 177
Scandinavian Electric Car Rally 122
Schaeffler 84, 128, 186
Schlichten, George 38
Schnitzer Motorsport 37
Schrempp. Jurgen 160
Scottish Aviation 116
Scuderi 79–80, 187
Scuderi, Carmelo 80
SEAT 37, 110, 142
Sebring-Vanguard 116
Shell 40, 60
Shimizu, Hiroshi 126, 142
Siemens VDO 31, 67, 119, 142
SIM-Drive 142
Sinclair 97
SinterCast 30
Skoda 120, 148, 156
Smart 82, 101, 143
Smith Electric 131
Smith, Roger 118
Solar Electrical Vehicles 159
SolarWorld 158
Solectria Corp. 120
Sony 133, 187
Southwest Research Institute 80
SR Drives 156
SsangYong 144
SSC 97
Stanadyne 55
Standard Motor Co. 19, 52
Standard Oil 70
Stanford Univ. 134
Stanley 149
Steinway, William 50
Stephenson, Robert 6
Stevens 129
Stevens, Brooks 88
Stewart, Jackie 155
Stirling, Robert 116
Stork, Erik 116
Stout 175
STP 61, 155
Subaru 35–36, 67, 72, 81, 89, 92, 101, 127, 133, 142, 174
Suminoe 165
Sumitomo 170, 191
SunDiesel 33, 41
Suzuki 59, 76, 81, 89, 92, 117, 132, 143, 148, 163

Tachikawa Aircraft Co. 117
Talbot 21, 50
TAMA 117
Tarpenning, Marc 127
Tata 142, 148, 157, 200
Tatra 181
Tazzari 139, 141
Tenneco Automotive 42
TEPCO 127
Tesco 16
Tesla 97, 125–127, 130–131, 138, 143–145, 178
Texaco 118, 132
Texas Propane Fleets 147
TH!NK 122–123, 126–127, 129, 135, 153, 162–163
Tham, Mans 191
Thyssen 170
Ticona 177
Tokai University 159
Tokyo Roki 45
Tokyo Show 44, 46, 89–92, 94, 98, 101–104, 107, 117, 120, 122, 126–127, 137, 140–141, 143–144, 147, 152–154, 163–165, 179, 186, 196
Tongji University 164

Toray 178–179
Torazza, Giovanni 66
Toshiba 133
Toxco 191
Toyoda Gosei 185
Toyoda, Akio 138
Toyoda, Eiji 90
Toyota (Lexus) 21, 35, 46, 53, 56, 60, 66–67, 69–70, 74, 76, 84–85, 87, 89–97, 99–102, 104–107, 117, 119–120, 122–123, 125–126, 132, 138, 140–143, 148, 155–156, 159, 162–164, 167, 174, 177–178, 181–182, 185, 189–190, 192, 194, 196
Trevithick & Vivian 149
Tropsch, Hans 41
Trotman, Alex 160
TRW Systems 88, 91
Tudor 73
Tudor, Henri 114
Twike 97
TWR 181

UAW 189
Union Carbide 160
United Nations 150, 194
UOP 55
UPS 109
USABC 117
USAF 150
USPS 116, 131

Valeo 44
Valmet 128, 135, 156
Van Doorne 82
Varta 116
Vauxhall 128, 139
Vedovelli & Priestley 115
Velozeta 80
Venturi 97, 123, 159
Verne, Jules 154
VIA Motors 144
Volkswagen (VW) 19–20, 23, 26–27, 30, 34, 37, 41–45, 52, 59–60, 69–70, 76–77, 80–81, 83, 85, 88, 103–104, 109–110, 113, 117, 119, 136, 143, 148, 156, 162–164, 166–167, 169, 174, 178, 181–182, 187, 192, 196
Volvo 20, 69, 75, 85, 107, 112, 120, 128, 142, 148, 150, 156, 169, 175, 181
Von Opel, Georg 116

Wagoner, Rick 119
Wankel, Dr Felix 77, 134, 136
Westfield 142
Wheego 141
Whittingham, M. Stanley 132
Whittle, Frank 154
WHO 51
Willcom 132
Willems, Johannes 132
Winterkorn, Dr Martin 113
Woods 87, 114
World Solar Challenge 159
World's Fair 38, 115
Wouk, Victor 116
WTCC 37
WTO 189
Wynn's 61

Yokohama 142, 183
Yoshino, Akira 133

Zachos, James 9
Zagato 129
ZENN 97
Zeppelin 181
Zero Pollution Motors 157
ZF 82, 84–85